POWER IN THE PULPIT

POWER
IN THE PULPIT

How America's Most Effective
Black Preachers Prepare
Their Sermons

CLEOPHUS J. LARUE

Editor

Westminster John Knox Press
LOUISVILLE • LONDON

Book design by Sharon Adams
Cover design by Design Point Inc.

First edition
Published by Westminster John Knox Press
Louisville, Kentucky

This book is printed on acid-free paper that meets the American National Standards Institute Z39.48 standard. ∞

PRINTED IN THE UNITED STATES OF AMERICA

    09 10 11 — 10 9 8 7

Library of Congress Cataloging-in-Publication Data

Power in the pulpit : how America's most effective Black preachers prepare their sermons / Cleophus J. LaRue, editor.
     p. cm.
   Includes bibliographical references.
   ISBN-13: 978-0-664-22481-3 (alk. paper)
   ISBN-10: 0-664-22481-4 (alk. paper)
   1. African American preaching. 2. Sermons, American–African American authors.
 I. LaRue, Cleophus James, date–

 BV4241.5.P68 2002
 251'.0089'96073—dc21   2002016864

In loving memory

of

Manuel L. Scott Sr.

(1926–2001)

This book is dedicated to the late Reverend Manuel L. Scott Sr., a prince of the pulpit and one of the most gifted preachers of the twentieth century. Scott, born in a small Texas town, was a Baptist pastor in California and Texas who rose to international prominence as an eloquent and effusive proclaimer of the gospel. Always humble in his public demeanor and private manner, he was indeed a lover of humanity and a friend to preachers. He was a unique coiner of phrases who unashamedly demonstrated his unspeakable joy while preaching the good news of Jesus Christ. Scott was a "royal peculiar" who brought dignity and grace to the office of pastor and held high the standards of the black preaching enterprise.

Acknowledgments

No work is complete without a word of thanks to those whose assistance made the coming together of this volume possible. My editor Stephanie Egnotovich made this a better book through her helpful advice. Research assistants Sharon S. Stewart and Rhonda B. Lemezis helped with organizing, editing materials, and corresponding with busy preachers. Jonathan R. Staples and Adetokunbo Adelekan were helpful in tying up loose ends of this project. Above all, many thanks to the preachers in this volume who took time from their hectic schedules to set down in writing what they do in a most effective manner in pulpits across America. I thank them all.

CONTENTS

Introduction

Black preaching is regarded in many quarters as one of the strongest preaching traditions developed on American soil. Though hard to define because of the many dynamics that come to play in this oral/aural word event, it is not now, nor has it ever been, univocal in form, substance, or mode of presentation. Characteristics purporting to shape its parameters abound, and yet none completely capture its depth and essence. Many things are happening in the black preaching moment, but exactly how, when, and where they come together, and to what effect and why, is most difficult to establish with consistency. The difficulty in grasping what is at the heart of black preaching is equally voiced by those who are considered to have achieved some mastery and adeptness in the field.

Even while we acknowledge its non-monolithic status, it is also true that the common threads of the oral tradition, black lived experience, and a shared history of subjugation undergird and sustain this tradition. Something in the black historical journey, something at once wistful and plaintive, finds expression in the black worship experience and flows freely in the black preaching event. It is most difficult to define for it is not something blacks deliberately add to their preaching; it is simply a part of who they are as a people of faith and what they are becoming in response to their lived situation in America.

Long recognized for its emotive power, rhetorical flair, and its uncanny ability to communicate the Holy to the least in society, the black preaching moment continues to be a much anticipated event in the black worship experience. The black church with its unquenchable thirst for the preached word has never forgotten what others are apparently struggling, even now, to remember: the church lives in her preaching—always has and always will. It is

1

the church's preaching that defines its message and mission. It is what is preached that determines what is important.[1]

Educational, denominational, geographical, and gender backgrounds notwithstanding, those in the black religious experience who have been most effective in the creation and delivery of the sermon have been those most adept at wedding the sad lyrics of black humanity to the invigorating and transformative melody of the gospel of Jesus Christ. In black churches preaching continues to be a high calling to that sacred desk—the Christian pulpit.

While it is hard to state with accuracy the exact date of the black preachers' beginning in America, the historical development of their roles and responsibilities can shed some light on the manner in which preachers came to such a place of prominence and esteem in black religious life. Historians Milton Sernett, Mechal Sobel, and Eugene Genovese in their historical works on the slave preachers give us some sense of who they were and how their leadership roles developed over time. Sernett's arrangement listed *ministers, exhorters, self-appointed preachers*, and *cult leaders*.[2]

Ministers were described as those who were principally active in the period when evangelical Protestantism was still seeking to win the South, and had yet to retreat from its earlier antislavery position. Preachers on the order of Harry Hosier, Henry Evans, and Lott Carey are listed in this group. They accompanied white clergy on preaching tours, preached to mixed audiences, and on the whole were well received by Southern Christians in the early days of evangelical revivalism. *Exhorters* were usually unordained and therefore unable to exercise all of the privileges of the ministerial office. They could not exercise their franchise in associational meetings, nor could they choose their own text on which to preach. They more often than not served as assistants to the white minister or "boss preachers" on the plantation.

The *self-appointed preacher* felt no compulsion to conform to the expectations of white society. God, they felt, had called them and no one but God could revoke that call. Self-appointed preachers, according to Sernett, were a continual threat to the police order of the South. Nat Turner would be the best example of this third kind of preacher. No church authorized him to preach. He felt that his call to deliver his people from slavery had come directly from God. He put together a message of religion and resistance that struck a responsive chord in his fellow slaves.

---

1. James M. Childs Jr., *Preaching Justice: The Ethical Vocation of Word and Sacrament Ministry* (Harrisburg, Trinity Press International, 2000), x.

2. Milton C. Sernett, *Black Religion and American Evangelicalism: White Protestants, Plantation Missions, and the Flowering of Negro Christianity, 1785–1865* (Metuchen, N. J.: Scarecrow Press, 1975), 95.

Sernett's last classification of religious leaders among the slaves is the *cult leader*. The voodoo cult was practiced especially in those areas where the slaves were most concentrated or most influenced by recent arrivals from the West Indies. While missionaries and Christian churches frowned upon these individuals, their influence was widespread and their abilities greatly feared by many slaves. Gullah Jack, who conspired with Denmark Vesey in his slave insurrection plot of 1822, was a native-born Angolan who brought to America practices he had known in Africa.[3]

While Sobel's classifications refer primarily to Baptists and thus have more to do with ecclesiastical designations as opposed to the manner in which slaves viewed themselves, they can still be helpful in providing some insight into the development of the black preacher on American soil. According to Sobel, the formal church organization recognized *floor, licensed,* and *ordained preachers.* In order to be an official preacher, a person needed a license from a church, which could be given for a limited time and specific area, or for a far more extensive outreach.[4] For such work, black preachers were licensed all over the South.

Moreover, if called by a church to be its presiding elder or minister, a preacher, upon examination by a board of ordained preachers, could be ordained in that church, a status he then gained for life. At least 106 black Baptist preachers were ordained prior to the Civil War.[5] Owing to the fact that the floor preacher was a category officially recognized by the formal church, preachers in such categories were probably new initiates into the ministry who hoped one day to be licensed and/or ordained by a church.

Included in the category of preachers not recognized by the formal church were *holders of papers, chairbackers,* and *exhorters. Privilege papers* were legal documents drawn up by a slave owner giving his slave preacher the privilege to preach and marry, and also to baptize anyone who made a profession of faith.[6] A *chairbacker* was a preacher whose pulpit was a common chair in a slave cabin. The *exhorter,* who in many instances had broader appeal than either the chairbacker or the holder of privilege papers, was a lay preacher who had not been licensed and had not been called by any congregation. Though never allowed

---

3. Ibid., 95–100.

4. Mechal Sobel, *Trabelin' On: The Slave Journey to an Afro-Baptist Faith* (Princeton, N.J.: Princeton University Press, 1980), 159–160.

5. Ibid. The earliest known ordination of a black took place in 1788 when Andrew Bryan of Savannah, Georgia, was ordained by white Abraham Marshall. White Baptists generally held that slaves should not be ordained, but whenever the question was formally raised they decided that free blacks had every right to ordination.

6. Ibid. Sobel lists this particular category in a footnote to her chapter on "The New Afro-Baptist Sacred Cosmos." See footnote 31 on p. 278.

in the pulpit, black exhorters were reputed to be very emotional, often even warmer than licensed preachers, and they were known to have moved many to accept salvation.[7]

Genovese's categories for the early black preachers include basically the same subdivisions as those listed by Sernett and Sobel—*conjurer, exhorter, plantation, regular,* and *denominational preachers.* Genovese does point out, however, that in the cities, slaves and free blacks heard black denominational ministers who were at least as well trained as their white counterparts, and innumerable class leaders or assistants or prayer leaders, who ostensibly assisted a white minister but who, more often than not, did most of the effective preaching to the blacks.[8] Early on the slaves heard their own black preachers, if not regularly, at least frequently enough to make a difference in their lives and to establish the black preacher as a central figure in black religious life. While one can be relatively certain that such designations were not strictly observed by the people of that day, the different categories give us some sense of the origin and development of the modern-day black preacher.[9]

As important a figure as the black preacher has been historically, preachers alone can in no way take credit for the continued strength of this tradition. Without question, the vibrancy and vitality of the entire black worship experience has in large part helped to shape, fashion, and uphold black preaching through the last four hundred years of black existence in America. Move the black preacher out of the vocal, participatory groundswell of a typical black church service and what you will hear more often than not is one struggling to find his or her way, or at least acknowledging that the preaching moment was made more difficult because of the absence of a full-fledged black worshiping community.

Unless one has broad exposure to cross-cultural preaching, often it is the case that the black preacher has become so accustomed to the immediate reaction and vocal encouragement of black worship that one's rhythm, cadence, voice, and celebratory close are all negatively impacted when the preacher is

---

7. Ibid., 160.

8. Eugene D. Genovese, *Roll, Jordan, Roll: The World the Slaves Made* (New York: Vintage Books, 1976), 255–79.

9. "Watchman" was another category found in some of the literature. His duties included advising on spiritual matters, opening and leading prayer meetings, counseling mourners, helping sinners seeking conversion, and generally setting a Christian example for the slaves. While many were exhorters and preachers on the plantation, after emancipation they became regular preachers. See Nancy Bullock Woolridge, "The Slave Preacher—Portrait of a Leader," *The Journal of Negro Education* 14 (winter 1945): 29; and Albert Raboteau, *Slave Religion: The "Invisible Institution" in the Antebellum South* (New York: Oxford University Press, 1978), 238.

removed from that setting. There can be no black preaching in the truest sense of the tradition without a black worshiping community.

The preachers who grace this present volume with their sermon-preparation methods and their model sermons were shaped, nurtured, and matured in the traditional black worship experience. They are indeed worthy witnesses to black life and to life as it is to be lived in the presence of the triune God. As only a true witness can, they rise from among the people to whom they preach that they might give effective voice and an eyewitness account to the "life situations" of those from whence they have come.[10] They go to the text on behalf of the people to watch and see what the text will say. They carry to the text the burdens and blessings, hopes and heartbreaks, joys and sorrows of a people who have known life in its extremes. They go faithfully week in and week out in search of an answer to the age-old question: Is there any word from the Lord and is it true?[11]

But they are also expert witnesses from the other side, for only those who have spent time in the presence of the Holy can mount the pulpit Sunday in and Sunday out and testify "effectively" as to those things they have seen and heard from the God who is made known to us in the revelation of Jesus Christ. There is yet in black churches an air of expectancy on Sunday mornings regarding the preached word. However, even with its awe-inspired expectations, participatory proclamation, and celebratory flair, the black church continues to demand of its preachers what the Greeks of old demanded of the disciples—"We would see Jesus."

Considered to be among the most effective preachers on the scene today, the preachers in this volume come from different parts of the country and different denominations. Some are pastors, some are teachers, and some are both. From church to chapel they bring their own special gifts to the preaching moment and are heard by thousands in churches, schools, conferences, and conventions throughout America. The writers were encouraged to pursue their own unique method of preparation. They were asked to reflect on and bring to conscious formation the methodological process they engage in each week. They were not privy to one another's work and were given the freedom to pursue their own particular take on the process. Though distinctive in their own right, there are at least eleven characteristics in their methodologies that many of the writers share with one another:

1. *A skillful articulation of the living voice*—In black preaching, the sermon from beginning to end is viewed as an oral/aural exercise. It is to be spoken

---

10. Thomas G. Long, *The Witness of Preaching* (Louisville, Ky.: Westminster/John Knox Press, 1989), 42–47.

11. Karl Barth, *The Word of God and the Word of Man* (Gloucester, Mass.: Peter Smith Publisher, 1978), 107–12.

and heard. The sermon manuscript is never regarded as an end in itself. What is written is but an "arrested performance" lying dormant on the page that can only be brought to life through the skillful articulation and mastery of the preacher's *viva vox* (living voice).[12]

People who come from cultures with a high oral residue consider the spoken word to have great power. All oral utterance that comes from inside living organisms is "dynamic."[13] Many black preachers rely on the power of the living voice to bring to full expression what they hope to accomplish in the preaching event. Ultimately, their ability to evoke, empower, challenge, and change comes not through that which they have written, but through their spoken word—articulated sound. An awareness of the oral nature of the finished product is a key element in the composition of the sermon.

2. *A sense of divine encounter*—Each preacher speaks in some manner of being encountered by God at the outset of the initial stages of sermon development. For some it involves a sitting silent before God, while for others it is a "tarrying" for the Spirit. Something comes from without and buoys the spirit and sparks the creativity of the preacher as he or she embarks upon the sermon creation process. All attribute this creative spark to something beyond their own subconscious mindset. They refuse to advance the preparation process until they have some sense that a power from beyond them is at work in and through them. Without this inbreaking activity, any number felt that the sermon would focus too much on process and not enough on purpose.

3. *The importance of wrestling with the text*—To a person, the writers speak of a serious, personal engagement with the text. While certainly referencing the commentaries before the end of the process, they all discourage a quick end run to the commentaries. In the minds of most, an overreliance on commentaries and the scholarship of others hinders the development of the creative process in the preacher. One writer speaks of walking up and down the street on which the Scripture lives in order to get one's own feel for the text. An ongoing invitation to the listening congregation to enter into the world of the text is a defining feature of traditional black preaching.

4. *The significance of the waiting congregation*—The people for whom the sermon is being prepared are never far from the thoughts of the preachers at the time of preparation. In fact, many speak of their need to maintain a constant focus on those who will hear the message. In a strange way, the preachers seem to anticipate the anticipation of the waiting congregation. Thus, every effort is

---

12. Charles Bartow, *God's Human Speech: A Practical Theology of Proclamation* (Grand Rapids: William B. Eerdmans Publishing Co., 1997), 64.

13. Walter J. Ong, *Orality and Literacy: The Technologizing of the Word* (London: Taylor and Francis Group, 1982), 38.

made to say *for* them and *to* them what they (the congregation) would say if they had the chance. Participatory proclamation not only impacts the rhythm and cadence of their delivery, it also affects the interaction of Scripture and context.

5. *An astute awareness of the culture*—There was a time in black religious life when some people believed that the truly "spiritual" preachers shut themselves away from the world and descended from the mountaintop of their studies on Sunday morning to deliver a word from on high. Today's preachers warn against such aloofness and detachment from the world. The preachers in this volume are in tune and in touch with the world around them. They sharpen their powers of observation by constantly seeking to name God's presence in every aspect of human existence. They encourage preachers to be mindful of the happenings in their social, political, educational, and economic surroundings. Many argue, in fact, that such an awareness actually strengthens one's preaching. The best of black preaching seriously engages the whole of God's created order in its beauty and splendor, its disorder and unruliness.

6. *The importance of a manuscript*—While many of the writers do not carry a manuscript into the pulpit, they were in agreement that to preach without a manuscript does not mean to preach unprepared. A manuscript should be written even though one does not intend to preach from it in the pulpit. Writing the sermon out helps to bring focus and clarity to the sermon, prevents one from rambling, and firms up language written for the ear. A tightly worded manuscript, where each phrase has been carefully considered, helps the preacher to paint the mental picture more effectively.

Moreover, a manuscript allows the preacher to get comfortable with the flow and contours of the sermon and thus serves to strengthen the rhythm and cadence of the oral delivery. To have the language of the sermon set down in writing and subsequently clearly set down in one's mind sharpens the oratorical thrust and limits unintended pauses and dead air in the preaching event.

However, those in this volume who do choose to use a manuscript in the pulpit do so with great effect because the oral nature of the event is never far from their minds even when reading from a prepared text. In black preaching the style of delivery determines, in large part, the success of the oral performer.[14] Verbal essays that sound like a lecture in the pulpit are a no-no in many black churches.[15] The oral delivery must be dynamic and invigorating.

---

14. Albert J. Raboteau, *A Fire in the Bones: Reflections on African American Religious History* (Boston: Beacon Press, 1995), 142.

15. Henry Mitchell argues that any preaching which is devoid of life and beholden to a homiletical model based on argument can be characterized as white preaching, even when it's done by black preachers in predominantly black churches. See Mitchell's essay in Richard L. Eslinger, ed., *A New Hearing: Living Options in Homiletic Method* (Nashville: Abingdon Press, 1987), 39–40.

Spontaneity that allows for improvisation and digression even when using a manuscript is not only acceptable, in black preaching it's expected. Senior ministers from a generation past urged their younger cohorts to use double-spaced type when preparing their manuscripts in order to allow room for the Holy Spirit to add a line here and there.

7. *A fitting close to the sermon*—Many expressed the importance of closing the sermon in a proper manner. For some the sermon should always end in a joyful celebration, while for others the most important thing is that the sermon end in a manner that is logically consistent with the controlling thought. On some occasions the close should cause one to reflect on faith and life. At other times it should move one to repent and to think more deeply on the mercies of God. At other times the close should call us to some specific action in the larger world in service to others. Sometimes the close should simply issue forth in ceaseless praise to the wonders of a God who is for us. The closing of the sermon should not be a disjointed distraction or some tacked-on ornamental rhetorical flourish intended to whip the congregation into a fevered pitch; rather it should send the listeners away with a clear sense of what the preacher was attempting to convey throughout the entire message. The writers were in agreement that the preacher should be clear in his or her mind how the sermon would open, where it would go, and how it would fittingly end.

8. *The sermon as continuous creation*—Our writers also spoke of continuous reflection on the sermon. For most, the sermon is never a finished product. After the sermon had been prepared and readied for Sunday service, they tell of how ideas and new ways of thinking about it continue to come. Many say even while preaching the sermon, new thoughts and ideas come pouring out and thus become unexpected additions to the sermon. Some spoke of editing the sermon soon after it had been preached in order to take advantage of fresh insights that came to them during its delivery or immediately thereafter. For some, the unplanned additions turned out to be some of the more creative parts of the sermon.

9. *Hymnody* — Preachers use the poetics of hymnody to express what mere words simply cannot say. Many of the preachers in this book sprinkled their sermons with familiar hymns. Some closed their sermons citing the cherished phrases of a well-known song. The use of hymns reaffirmed, in a way, the vital importance of the "sung word" in black religion. A recitation of the familiar— such as a hymn or some other well-known spiritual or gospel tune—encourages the congregation to join in the celebratory moment being called forth by the preacher.

One of the best ways to move a congregation to embrace the message as a word fittingly spoken to them is through the lyrics of some well-worn, beloved hymn. It is as if the congregation is saying in its audible response to the hymn,

"Yes, preacher, this song helps us to drink from the fountain of the familiar. Our testimonies are wrapped up in the words of that hymn. We have been this way before and we know exactly where you are going. Yes, Lord."

10. *Discipline and perspective*—Great preaching requires great discipline and sustained study. The preachers in this volume exhibited a healthy amount of both. Some are morning people. They study in the calm and quiet of a brand-new day. Others are night hawks. Their powers of retention are keenest when burning the midnight oil. They study with great profit when their home is undisturbed, their world is quiet, and the only noise about them is the rush of their own creative process.

Still others study "on the fly." They grab a read here and there—between meetings at the church, or when they have a little downtime in the afternoon, or on the road during revivals, or during some unexpected free time made possible through a cancellation in their schedule. While their reading requires more of a hustle, the realization that their time is limited seems to help them absorb more on the fly. All recognized that they had to study in order to remain fresh, vibrant, interesting, creative, and faithful.

The most effective preachers also bring a sense of proportion to their work. Preaching is not something they do every waking moment of their lives. While they take their vocation seriously, they also take their avocation seriously. When asked what they did when the preaching event was done, most said they rested. They took downtime seriously, and many engaged in some type of hobby that called them away from the rigors of sermon preparation.

11. *Preaching out of the overflow*—Each of the preachers in this volume gives evidence of preaching from an overflow of gathered materials. Most acknowledge that they will never be able to preach all they have studied and set aside in the week leading up to the sermon. One never has the feeling that they scrape the bottom of the barrel for something to say. William Stidger in *Preaching out of the Overflow* used an oil well metaphor to denote three types of preaching done by most preachers: dry holes, wells that have to be pumped, and wells that overflow.[16]

Those who preach out of the overflow preach from a wealth of materials, knowledge, disciplined insight, and experiences gained from a lifetime of diligent study and conscious reflection on God's presence in the world. Effective preachers preach from a full fountain. Or, to mix metaphors, they skim the cream from the top of their seasoned, disciplined study. When they are done with the preaching assignment, the waiting congregation is often left desiring more.

---

16. William L. Stidger, *Preaching out of the Overflow* (Nashville: Cokesbury Press, 1930), 13.

Such are the common characteristics that many of the preachers in this volume share in their sermon-preparation methods. Each pursues his or her own distinctive approach, but the paths whereby they reach the goal of the finished sermon are in a sense well-worn and familiar to all.

A book on African American sermon-preparation methods is long overdue simply because most blacks continue to learn to preach through imitation of the masters. The oral learning process of observation, participation, and subsequent mastery is the method many blacks continue to employ in their efforts to attain a higher level of proficiency in preaching. In their ground-breaking study *The Black Church in the African American Experience*, C. Eric Lincoln and Lawrence Mamiya estimated that approximately four-fifths of black ministers currently in the field were without formal training of any kind.[17]

The Association of Theological Schools's *Fact Book on Theological Education 2000–2001* listed just over seven thousand African American men and women in all of the degree programs associated with the ATS.[18] This is an unbelievably small number of students currently enrolled in ministerial training when one considers the thousands of churches in the two-hundred-plus denominations to which blacks belong in this country.[19] It is, however, a rather pointed reminder that most blacks continue to learn to preach by observing and then imitating the styles of preachers they have come to admire.

It is not in the formal setting of the divinity school or seminary that blacks first gain exposure to the crafting of the sermon. Most have had some experience in preaching before they reach the classroom. Rather it is on the "church circuit"—local and national gatherings, and television and tape ministries—that their favorite preachers teach them how to preach through the visible/audible enactment of the preached word.

Consequently, this project serves a threefold purpose: (1) it provides in-depth reflection on the sermon-preparation methods of some of America's most effective preachers; (2) it gives pastors and students a how-to manual directly from the hands of those who are most likely to influence their preaching; and (3) it makes available to the broader culture the distinctive sermon-crafting abilities of some of the most able and celebrated black preachers on the contemporary scene.

---

17. C. Eric Lincoln and Lawrence W. Mamiya, *The Black Church in the African American Experience* (Durham, N.C.: Duke University Press, 1990).

18. Louis Charles Willard, ed., *Fact Book on Theological Education, 2000–2001* (Pittsburgh: The Association of Theological Schools, 2000), 41.

19. Wardell M. Payne, ed., *Directory of African American Religious Bodies* (Washington, D.C.: Howard University Press, 1991), 21–147, 199–216.

Thomas Long notes that the preachers people seem most to admire often appear to have a certain innate flair and knack for preaching that seems more like a gift than a set of skills. They seem more born to the task than instructed in the craft. According to Long, while the church is blessed by the occasional preacher of exceptional ability, the church is nourished most by the kind of careful, responsible, and faithful preaching that falls within the range of most of us.[20] This volume is presented in hopes of broadening the preaching abilities of all preachers who take their craft seriously.

20. Long, *The Witness of Preaching*, 21.

Contributors

Charles G. Adams, pastor of Hartford Memorial Baptist Church in Detroit, Michigan

Charles E. Booth, pastor of Mt. Olivet Baptist Church in Columbus, Ohio

H. B. Charles Jr., pastor of Mt. Sinai Baptist Church in Los Angeles, California

Prathia L. Hall,[†] Martin Luther King Jr. Associate Professor of Ethics at Boston University School of Theology, in Boston, Massachusetts

Zan Holmes, pastor emeritus of St. Luke "Community" United Methodist Church and former adjunct professor of preaching at Perkins School of Theology at Southern Methodist University, Dallas, Texas

Carolyn Ann Knight, assistant professor of homiletics at the Interdenominational Theological Center in Atlanta, Georgia

Joe Samuel Ratliff, pastor of Brentwood Baptist Church in Houston, Texas

Cheryl Sanders, professor of Christian ethics at Howard University School of Divinity and pastor of Third Street Church of God in Washington, D.C.

J. Alfred Smith Sr., pastor of Allen Temple Baptist Church in Oakland, California, and professor of Christian ministry and preaching at the American Baptist Seminary of the West in Berkeley, California

Gardner C. Taylor, pastor emeritus of the Concord Baptist Church of Christ in Brooklyn, New York

William D. Watley, pastor of St. James African Methodist Episcopal Church in Newark, New Jersey

Ralph D. West, pastor of the Church Without Walls in Houston, Texas

[†] *deceased*

1

Preaching from the Heart and Mind

CHARLES G. ADAMS

Even to write about how I prepare to preach is a daunting responsibility. I can make no general rule for all to follow. These remarks can be no more than one preacher's way of preparing to preach. This is my testimony and/or confession. The first thing I try to do is to get in touch with Whose I am and Whom I preach, that I may be clear about who I am and why I do what I do. Jesus, quoting Trito-Isaiah said, "The Spirit of the Lord is upon me, because he has anointed me to bring good news to the poor. He has sent me to proclaim release to the captives and recovery of sight to the blind, to let the oppressed go free, to proclaim the year of the Lord's favor" (Isa. 61:1–3; Luke 4:18–19, NRSV).

Prayer is the beginning of my sermon as I speak to God and ask God to speak to me, that I may preach good news to the poor. I believe that every sermon is dictated, directed, and delivered by the Holy Spirit or it is not a sermon. I know that God called me to preach, but I now pray that God call me again to preach a specific sermon to a specific people. It is my deepest desire that the Holy Spirit will mandate, motivate, generate, and articulate good news to all people through my poor, lisping, stammering tongue.

Nothing brings me greater joy than to be God's delivery boy, carrying the proclamation of emancipation to slaves, the promise of healing to the sick, assurance of hope to the suffering, and consistent comfort for those who walk in grief. I rejoice to stand before depleted, disinherited refugees in East Africa and tell them, "All things are yours, whether Paul or Apollos or Cephas or the world or life or death or the present or the future—all belong to you, and you belong to Christ, and Christ belongs to God" (1 Cor. 3:21–23, NRSV). It makes me cry tears of eschatological joy to tell an entire race of people whom I believe were disfranchised by the Supreme Court in the presidential election of 2000 "We are more than conquerors through him who loved us" (Rom. 8:37, NRSV).

Leaning on the words of Phillips Brooks, I define the sermon as the truth of God delivered through the contingent, feeble, and vulnerable instrumentality of human personality. I am a comic and pathetic person. I who can only see and know in part am called to preach the vision, voice, and victory of the whole redeemed creation. I who am weak, weary, and worn must strongly declare to the weak, weary, and worn that we are recipients of the Spirit and power of God. I who am afflicted with blind spots must testify to the brilliance of the Light of the World. I who am broken on the "wheel of living" must preach the restorative, regenerative, renewing power of our Great Savior.

I who am captive and bound must proclaim liberty throughout the land. I who am an embarrassed sinner must from the hilltops declare to sinners that we have been saved by grace through faith (Eph. 2:8). I who am failing, falling, and losing all over the place must preach to others like me that "we are God's children now; what we will be has not yet been revealed. What we do know is this: When he is revealed we will be like him, for we will see him as he is" (1 John 3:2, NRSV).

Praying before writing is the only way I can come within hearing range of a conversation among the immortals concerning the saving work that God is doing in the world to bring the whole creation to redemption and completion. Only a miracle can save us. (See W. H. Auden in "Christmas Oratorio.") The substance of the gospel is that the miracle is here. I am called to preach what God is doing in the world to bring us all into the life and joy of God's new creation. With so vast and impossible a task before me, how can I begin any other way than by prayer and fasting?

My grand old uncle, the late Gordon Blaine Hancock, formerly pastor of Moore Street Baptist Church in Richmond, Virginia, and professor of sociology and economics at Virginia Union University, emphasized prayer as the primary source of the preacher's power. If I am to preach well, I must pray without ceasing. Only lively encounter with God can be the creative source of a new word from God.

In my tradition, a sermon must have a text from the Bible and a subject or title from the heart and mind of the preacher. Whether the text from Scripture precedes or succeeds the selection of the subject cannot be dogmatically declared. Sometimes it's one way, or the other way, or both simultaneously. Somehow, God brings all things together. The Creator never fails. In the work of God in the world, the one and the many, the subject and the text, pulpit and pew, preacher and people, church and society are brought together around the centrality of God, the Word made flesh and dwelling among us. The late D. E. King of Chicago inscribed a book he had written, "Charles, don't preach sermons, preach Christ!"

After much prayer, I will find the text from the Scriptures that preaches Christ. It is usually a great text, and not some very obscure or tangential, editorial comment. George A. Buttrick of Harvard used to tell his students, "Stick to the great texts of the Bible." If the sermon is not to be an exercise in playful curiosity or idle speculation, I must declare the great good news of creation, liberation, salvation, redemption, restoration, and new creation as God's way of dealing with our sin, sorrow, sickness, suffering, injustice, fragmentation, unkindness, hostility, and death. Such a sermon will require a great text well considered.

There are many new translations of the Bible. Each of them is worthy of commentary and study. I read my text, as best I can, in the original and in every translation that I can get my hands on. That is the bare beginning of the exegetical work that I must do later in order to prepare to preach. In reading the text at the start of my preparation, I do not consult the commentaries—it is too soon to read the comments of others concerning the text. If God is speaking to me, I do not want to drown out God's new word to me by the voices of others. I want to preserve the fragile element of my own unique sensitivity to God and creativity.

If I begin with the words and works of others concerning the basic text, I will suppress my own spontaneity, sensitivity, and creativity. The words and works of others are so excellent, so admirable, and so compelling that they must be deferred at the start of sermonic preparation, lest I become a mere puppet mouthing the words from the seemingly closed lips of some ingenious homiletic ventriloquist. The major problem with using the words of others is that one can destroy one's own unique gifts of personal perception, new perspective, and original expression.

Sometimes when I write what occurs to me at the start, I end up with a complete manuscript, but it is not the sermon—not yet. The next step must follow the first, and that is the prodigious consultation of as many commentaries on the text as are available. In order to do this I will comb my own personal library for commentaries on my chosen text. Then I will visit the nearest theological library and read everything on the shelves that teaches anything about my text. My aim is to know what the text said in the original so that I can hear what the text is saying in the present moment. This second step of commentary consultation requires an audience with scholars and specialists in biblical languages, history, and cultures. George A. Buttrick admonished us during this stage not to read sermons or homiletical commentaries. If we start with the sermons of others, we will be too much tempted to serve up the ripened fruit of their valuable labor than to do our own digging, plowing, planting, watering, and harvesting. I believe that I am called to produce a new harvest, and not to serve up canned food. There is thus no substitute for new research.

It is during this stage that I take notes on the text so that my sermon will not be built on poor scholarship, but steeled and structured by an empirical investigation of the facts that inform the biblical testimony. Much of this scholarly material is too terse and pedantic to be a part of the actual sermon. People do not come to church to hear a lecture, but to hear a sermon, a Word from the Lord that creates and sustains human life. Nevertheless, I think that I must be as informed as I can about the text that forms the perspective from which I will see the gospel, the people, and the world. Boykin Saunders of Virginia Union says, "Some preach the text; others preach the people who hear, feeding them a double dose of who they are and how they must think and feel; but others preach the gospel."

It is my aim to preach the gospel, good news to the poor, which is informed by the meaning of the text but is by no means identical with, or limited to, the empirical exegesis of the biblical record. Behind every sermon that I have time to prepare are notebooks full of exegetical notes that will never see the light of day. Just as there is more to the cathedral than the walls, windows, towers, and steeples, there is much more to any sermon than anyone can see or should see.

The third step of writing the sermon is to make notes from consultation with sermons by others on the text that I've been wrestling with for several days. I will, at this stage, read homiletical commentaries and sermonic anthologies that carry the words, works, and wisdom of other preachers on my text. I am particularly interested in their illustrations. If I refer to anything that I have read or heard from other preachers, I take care to give credit to whom credit is due. The people would much rather hear profound wisdom harvested and acknowledged from great gardens of effective sermons than hear something that may be quite original but totally meaningless, platitudinous, and inconsequential.

When we are honest enough to acknowledge our sources, we augment, not diminish, our stature in the eyes of the audience. The audience will give us credit for candor, honesty, and the example of openly appropriating the ideas of others for the good of the present audience. I feel I must acknowledge my sources as I strive to preach with sincerity, dignity, and integrity. If I pretend that I have thought what I never thought and created what I never created, I lose a powerful source of inner peace and public standing. Let me warn all my colleagues to be honest in acknowledging all your sources. It can only enhance our preaching to do so.

The fourth stage in writing is not to write. Just let the work of the other three steps be seasoned and marinated in contemplation at a distance from the pressure of having to produce anything at the moment. Go hear *Messiah* by Handel, *Elijah* by Mendelssohn, or the *Ninth Symphony* by Beethoven. Go watch a probing movie like *Finding Forrester* or *Music of the Heart* or *Shawshank Redemption*. Relax, chill, vacate, and let God form in you the mood, mind, and spirit of the Christ, whom you so deeply desire to proclaim.

The fifth step, then, is to return to my writing and attempt the first draft of the sermon. Many things will come up and fall neatly into place as if dictated from beyond. But there will also be the need for further searching, probing, reading, consultation, argumentation, and reconsideration. Consider the text again. Am I really faithful to it? I think about the people again. What do my words mean to them? Do they really need to hear what I think I need to say? Does it really matter? Have I done my very best? Absolutely not! I try to understand that no matter how good it may be, a first draft is only a first draft. There is a need to delete the unnecessary and expand upon the essential.

The sixth step is to relax again and venture to write the final draft that can never be final. The sermon will be revised and changed ad infinitum. It will never be completed, but the writing will temporarily cease after the production of a second writing.

The seventh step is intense prayer for power from God to deliver verbally the Word from God. Gordon Hancock said, "On your way to the pulpit, go to the closet, close the door, fall on your knees, and speak to your Heavenly Father in secret. Praise God's awesome excellence. Confess your ignorance and impotence. Thank God for the privilege and indulgence of divine confidence. Ask God to pour God's own self into you. Ask God, also, to open the hearts of the people that they may receive, believe, and achieve the challenge of the good news you will preach. Your information comes from the library, but your power and inspiration must come from the closet!"

The eighth step is to mount the stairs to approach the pulpit and face the people with the Word of God. It's not a show or a game. I do not stand to please the crowd or entertain the audience. I do not stand to exalt my work, or myself, but to proclaim God's name, God's love, and God's Son who is given to all for our hope and salvation. My aim is that none will miss the good news.

The ninth step is to come down and agonize over the fact that I didn't do it as well as I had hoped or desired. I said what I should have left unsaid. I failed to say what I should have said, and I beg for God's forgiveness and the transformation of my life that I may be more faithful and true to the agony, dignity, and profundity of my calling.

The tenth step is to revise the sermon after preaching it as I prepare to preach it again, sometime, somewhere and perhaps to the same people. Gardner Calvin Taylor, the world's greatest preacher, tells the story of a great Italian tenor who sang for the Metropolitan Opera in New York. He was not at his best on that particular Saturday afternoon when he received nine curtain calls to repeat his aria. They clapped him back nine times, and they wanted more, more, more. He said in exasperation, "How many times must I sing this aria?" Someone shouted, "Until you get it right!" I must preach my sermon again and again until I get it right and God gets me right.

Sermon: Faith Critiques Faith
Isaiah 58:6–9

CHARLES G. ADAMS

Is not this the fast that I choose:
to loose the bonds of injustice,
to undo the thongs of the yoke,
to let the oppressed go free,
and to break every yoke?
Is it not to share your bread with the hungry,
and bring the homeless poor into your house;
when you see the naked, to cover them,
and not to hide yourself from your own kin?
Then your light shall break forth like the dawn,
and your healing shall spring up quickly;
your vindicator shall go before you,
The glory of the LORD shall be your rear guard.
Then you shall call, and the LORD will answer;
You shall cry for help, and he will say, Here I am.

(NRSV)

These words written in 530 B.C. represent faith's critique of faith. The Third Isaiah is speaking to postexilic Israel. Things are not going well with the persons chosen to be a light to the nations. How could they be the light of the world? Their deficits were deep, their debts were great, their economy was shot, their society was shattered, their people were discouraged, and their religious institutions had lost their vitality.

Now mind you, they were doing all the right things. They were going through the motions of being pious. Though the restored temple was fifteen years from completion, they still understood themselves to be the people of God, and they were trying to behave like religious people should behave. They adhered to the rituals, they observed the Sabbath, they prayed, they fasted, they went by the book, but it was all empty and ineffectual. Things were not getting any better. God did not seem to be anywhere around.

They complained to a God who was distant, silent, and absent: "Why have we fasted and thou seest it not? Why have we humbled ourselves and thou takest no knowledge of it? Why do we pray and there is no answer?" God answered in effect, "Because you're doing all the right things for all the wrong reasons. You're observing the Sabbath, but your eyes are on the clock all the while, and your minds are far from me. You are praying, but only to further your own selfish ends. You are fasting, but only to go up in the polls and get favors from me. You want favors from me, but you want no part of me. You don't want me. You want no part of my will, no portion of my Spirit, no involvement in my social and political agenda."

That's how religion gets co-opted and commandeered for purposes that are against the Spirit of God. That is to say, for purposes that are diametrically opposed to God's social and political agenda in the world. What is the Spirit of the Lord interested in anyway? Jesus, quoting Third Isaiah, said, "The spirit of the Lord is upon me because the spirit has anointed me to preach good news to the poor. The spirit has sent me to proclaim release to the captives and recovery of sight to the blind. To set at liberty those who are oppressed, and to tell everybody now is the time to do it." The text spells out the political agenda of the Holy Ghost: "To loose the bonds of injustice, to undo the thongs of the yoke, to let the oppressed go free, and to break every yoke."

But too much religion and spiritual energy have been co-opted to tighten the bonds of justice, harden the yoke of poverty, to lock up and contain the oppressed, and to reinforce every prearrangement of unequal opportunity. And religion is not the only thing that gets co-opted; sometimes other things are co-opted against their true essence. Take justice in the courts, for example. How color-blind is our system of justice? If whites will not convict and punish white criminals in the first instance, not just after a riot in Los Angeles and a billion dollars' worth of property destroyed, and likewise if blacks will not convict and punish blacks, then the essence of justice shall have been corrupted, and the spirit of democracy shall have been compromised.

Sometimes, love can also be co-opted against itself and turned into the erotic solipsism and determinism of mechanical sex without serious commitment. Sometimes education and intelligence also can be co-opted for ends that are neither intelligent nor worthy. Two world wars, the Third Reich, and South Africa have taught us that the most intelligent can become the most barbaric.

The same Germany that gave the world J. S. Bach, Beethoven, Brahms, Immanuel Kant, and atomic energy also gave us Hitler, the Holocaust, and the tragic division of Germany and Europe. Right after World War I, Karl Barth, father of crisis theology, noted that just at the moment when the state thought it had succeeded in making men out of wild animals, it found it necessary for national security to make wild animals out of men.

Intelligence does not guarantee integrity. Education does not guarantee truth. Democracy does not guarantee justice, and religion cannot guarantee God. Sometimes religion becomes an enemy to God and an oppressor of humankind, and that can easily happen when religion takes as its center, source, and norm anything other than the spirit of the Lord. Now that is the mistake of conservative politicians and theologians who make "order" and "stability" their normative center and their ultimate concern.

This tendency to make social chaos the ultimate evil and social stability the ultimate good has caused Christians to submit uncritically to the tyrannical regimes of Nazism and fascism. This co-opting of religion to be a preserver of the prevailing order is echoed in the words of continental theologian Emil Brunner, who said: "The Christian must submit himself to a social order which is itself loveless. He must do this if he is not to evade the most urgent of all the demands of the love commandment, and that is the demand to protect the dike which saves human life from chaos."

To his credit, the early Reinhold Niebuhr rejected this conservative tendency in Eurocentric politics and Christian orthodoxy. Said Niebuhr of Brunner's statement, "This logic manages not only to express an excessive fear of chaos and to obviate any possibility of a Christian justification for social change by allowing only such change as will create a new order 'immediately and without interruption,' but it nearly dismisses the Christian ideal from any immediate relevance to political issues." The same type of logic and the same theory of government as a dike against chaos carried Friedrich Gogarten completely into the political philosophy of fascism. If fascism may be regarded as being informed by a frantic fear of the chaos that might result if an old social order broke down, we might come to the conclusion that fascism is really the unfortunate fruit of Christian pessimism.

Fascism is the bitter fruit of co-opted faith uncritiqued by living hope, uncleansed by perfect love, unchallenged by inexorable justice. The significance of Martin Luther King Jr. is that he never lost his messianic center; therefore he was able to participate in politics without being controlled by political considerations. He put his life on the line by opposing Lyndon Johnson's war in Vietnam. Mind you, Lyndon Johnson was the best friend the civil rights movement ever had. It was Lyndon Johnson who went to Howard University, identified with black folks, and intoned, "We shall overcome."

It was Johnson who signed the civil rights bills of 1964, 1965, and 1968. It was Johnson who issued the first and only executive order demanding affirmative action. Nevertheless, Martin Luther King Jr. would not allow himself to be co-opted, not even by our wonderful friend Lyndon Johnson. And we didn't understand that at the time, but today we praise God, not only because Martin Luther King was politically involved, but also because he was godly enough to maintain his theological integrity and his political independence. He was in the world and not for the world. The whole Board of the Southern Christian Leadership Council voted not to support King's stand against the war.

The White House closed its doors to Dr. King. Northern white liberals parted company with King. Highbrow intellectuals wondered aloud if Dr. King really had the expertise to speak on foreign affairs. Some prominent Jewish friends defected from the civil rights movement. Roy Wilkins of blessed memory and the NAACP denounced King's position. Carl Rowan chided Dr. King in his column. *The New York Times* condemned Dr. King. Many black pastors closed their pulpits to Dr. King. Funding sources for civil rights dried up, but Dr. King held on to his convictions. He was so focused and centered in a cosmic Christ that he would not permit political expediency to narrow the scope of his spiritual conscience, persistent love, or prophetic commitment.

Religion in the time of Third Isaiah, and in our own time, has not done as well. The church has been corrupted by the world. As Reinhold Niebuhr said, "We keep taking the miraculous wine of Cana and turning it back into the flat water of expedient compromise." That sounds like retreat, retroaction, and retrenchment. When religion gets aborted and corrupted wine turns back into water, the salt of the earth turns flat and the light of the world goes out. The early Reinhold Niebuhr and the Third Isaiah rightly recognized that when religious piety gets separated and isolated from lively encounter with God, it becomes dangerously delusive, politically opportunistic, oppressively barbaric, and totally deceptive.

This is exactly the problem I have with our modern-world cults that amount to "Bibliolatry"—the worship of the finite words of the Bible as separated from the spirit and social agenda of God. Whenever the Bible is interpreted and applied outside the spirit of the living Christ, the results are terrible, horrible, fascist, racist, and irresponsible. The Bible must be interpreted by the love and truth of the personality of Christ. Holy God must be present with human readers to make the finite words of the Bible bear the infinite truth of the eternal God. Put holy words into hellish hands and the results are disastrous, as in South Africa; Australia; Waco, Texas; and the rest of the Bible Belt of the United States.

That is what John Calvin meant when he spoke of the impossibility of understanding the Scriptures or even using the Scriptures correctly without the internal testimony of the Holy Spirit, and that involves buying into God's political reconstruction of the world as spelled out in Luke 4 and Isaiah 58. God does not imprison God in human language. God peeps up at us from behind the words and phrases of the Bible and says, "Here I am."

Ralph Ellison tells the story of a man copying what he thought was "Absolute Truth" in words on a piece of paper. Suddenly his pen broke through the paper, and he heard a voice speaking through the hole saying, "Here I am. You can't catch me on your paper. You can't imprison me in finite words. You cannot control me and contain me in your language, your church, your religion, nor your political party. None of these things can guarantee my presence. None of these things can be who I am."

Finite words and religious institutions are always plastic and subordinate to the finite minds and the pretensions of our own political perspectives. Satan's perennial scheme is to co-opt religion for demonic purposes. That is why Satan confronted Jesus in the wilderness—to oppose the living word with the written word. It is in the Bible lands of the world today that oppression abounds. Whenever anyone comes at me with a great, big Bible, I run for cover. Whole lot of Bibles in South Africa. Whole lot of churches there. But Nelson Mandela is free only after twenty-seven and a half years of unjust incarceration.

There is no real sharing of power in South Africa . . . not yet. Whole lot of Bibles in Hitler's Germany, but it was there that racism and xenophobia nearly destroyed Europe. Whole lot of Bibles in Reagan's and Bush's White House and the Supreme Court, but affirmative action's work of corrective justice is being dismantled every day. The Bible is being misused to suppress blacks, degrade women, oppress the poor, repress the Chinese, uproot Palestinians, murder Muslims, liquidate Sandinistas, devastate Africans, bust unions, and exploit workers.

Decades ago Shailer Matthews, then dean of the University of Chicago Divinity School, spoke at a Baptist convention. The fundamentalists were on the outside of the convention hall picketing with raised placards of protest because they did not want this "liberal heretic" to be heard in an orthodox Baptist convention. When the dean had finished his address, a stalwart fundamentalist stood up in the meeting, and with passion and aggression in his voice he shouted, "I want to ask you a question and I want a straight answer. I want a 'yes' or a 'no.' Do you or do you not believe that every single syllable of Scripture is the inspired word of God?" The dean responded calmly, "If the letter is greater than the Spirit, no, but if the Spirit is greater than the letter, yes."

Another anecdote has to do with Paul Tillich lecturing in Chicago on the night he was to have his fatal heart attack. After his thoughtful and provocative presentation, a young and restless student approached him, nervously clutching his Bible. He said, "Dr. Tillich, do you or do you not believe that this Bible is the holy word of God?" Tillich answered, "Yes, if it grasps you. No, if you grasp it."

Religion loses its vitality when it no longer radically searches and challenges the spirit of humankind. If in our practice of religion we are only confirmed in our accustomed ways of thinking and doing things, and if we are not deeply questioned, thoroughly searched, totally confronted, completely challenged, powerfully corrected, and spiritually changed by our religion, then we have used religion for our own purposes rather than permitting ourselves to be addressed and used of God. External pietistic conformity is a very clever device to save the society from change and to hide the soul from God. In the demonic diversions of religious orthodoxy and verbal inerrancy, the continuity of the Bible is denied, the voice of God is ignored, the vision of the kingdom is blurred, the agenda of the Holy Ghost is thwarted, and the challenge of Christ is rejected.

I was somewhat taken aback when Harvey Cox said to me that he could not celebrate the mandating of Martin Luther King Jr.' s birthday as a national holiday. He took all the air out of my celebrative glee when he reminded me that the holiday bill was passed by essentially the same Congress and signed by the same president that had refused to pass a new civil rights bill in the 1980s.

They mandated the Martin Luther King Jr. holiday bill, but they refused to demand the immediate release of Nelson Mandela. They refused to protect affirmative action. They devastated the U.S. Commission on Civil Rights. They cut off necessary support systems for the poor.

They snatched $15 billion from poor babies in order to reduce the tax liabilities of the wealthy. They polluted the air. They destroyed American jobs. They carried on an illegal war in Nicaragua. They despoiled the environment. They denuded public education, and these are the same people that made Martin Luther King Jr.'s birthday a paid federal holiday. Now why did Ronald Reagan sign that bill? Could it be that Mr. Reagan understood that the easiest way to get rid of Martin Luther King Jr. is to worship him, to honor him with a holiday that he never would have sought, to celebrate his birth and his death without committing ourselves to his vision and his love? It is easier to praise a dead hero than to recognize and follow a living prophet.

The best way to dismiss any challenge is to exalt and adore the empirical source through which the challenge has come. That is also the easiest way to dismiss the challenge, the offense, and the raw reality of the cross. Gild it with gold. Make it a precious piece of jewelry. Decorate the altar with it, wave it, or hang it around your neck as if Jesus calls us to wear the cross and not to bear the cross. We have cherished and worshiped the old rugged cross to such an extent that it does not challenge our cravings for comfort, safety, security, continuity, and order. It does not address our glorification of numbers and power, our delusions of grandeur, our selfish accumulation of material things. It does not redistribute economic opportunity. It does not cleanse the political

process nor transform the social order. We have lifted up Christ so high that
we think him to be irrelevant to our everyday workday decisions and dilem-
mas. Isn't that the cutest way to get rid of God? That's exactly the way to do it.

Straightjacket the living word into your own hard-line, atomistic, chopped-
up, out-of-context interpretation of the written word. Transmute the story into
a scheme. Fit and fix the Savior into a plan of salvation. Freeze the Christ into
a creed. Harden gospel into a structure. Embalm amazing grace into stiff
authority. Change love into law. Beat blessings into bureaucracies. Hammer
faith into conformity. Ossify freedom into procedure, liquefy liberty into license,
rationalize redemption into rhetoric, subvert Holy Spirit into religious habits,
preempt resurrection into regimentation, pickle Jesus into ecclesiastical uni-
formity, wrap Christ up in the sacerdotal shroud of orthodoxy, lay Jesus out
in a tomb of detached irrelevant ritual, keep Jesus out of the fight for freedom,
out of the struggle for justice, out of the march for peace, and expect God to
stay away from us.

Expect Jesus to stay in the tomb fixed and fitted and frozen where we have
put him. But it won't work. God will not stay away. Jesus will not remain dead.
Faith cannot remain captive to politics. The Holy Spirit will not be obedient
to our selfish economic interests. The voice of God will not be suppressed.
The light of love cannot be extinguished. The challenge of Christ will not go
away. Jesus will not lie still, will not keep quiet, will not stay put, will not be
held down in the grave, or tied to the temple, or chained to the church, or
captivated by the culture, or sealed in the system, or nailed to the nation, or
riveted to the race, or locked into a location, or domiciled in a denomination. I see an angel standing at the open door of an empty tomb, saying, "He
is not here. He is risen like he said." I hear a voice calling from beyond the
sacred page and the sacred place saying, "Here I am."

Take nothing less than that! Empowered ministry is not so much getting
something from God as having an enlivening, energizing, and transformative
encounter with God because you have made yourself available to God. It is
to accept the invitation of God to be in partnership with God where God is
at work in the world. It is hearing the voice and call of God and answering,
"Here I am with my full humanity, my total self. I am available to you. I'll go
where you send me."

"If you send me to liberate the oppressed in China, I'll go."
"If you send me to stand and bleed with dying students in Tiananmen
Square in Beijing, I'll go."
"If you send me to cure AIDS in Southern Africa, I'll go."
"If you send me to break the yoke of oppression in Australia, I'll go."
"If you send me to stop the killing and feed the hungry in Somalia, I'll go."
"If you send me to rebuild and develop Afghanistan, I'll go."

"If you send me to use my faith and my freedom to transform economic
systems here in America,
so there won't be any more hunger, homelessness,
no more ignorance,
no more poverty,
no more unemployment,
no more lack of health care,
no more AIDS,
no more injustice,
no more urban abandonment, misery, hopelessness, and blight—
I'll go."
"If you send me to deliver people from their addictions to
drugs, guns, and despair,
I'll go."
"If you want me to break the barriers of racism, sexism, homophobia,
classism, ageism,
in the church and in the world,
here I am, send me, use me, pour me out, and fill me up again.
I'll go."
Only then will religion be meaningful,
will worship be powerful,
and will prayer be effectual.
Only then will you be able to call
on God and hear God
answer you, "Here I am."
Why take anything less than that?
Why have a religion that has not been challenged and critiqued?
Why have a counterfeit religion when you can have the real thing?
Why have something that is worthless
when you can have something
that is powerful?
Why have a religion that is unquestioned
when you can have a religion that has been cleansed,
corrected
fortified
clarified
purified
rectified
sanctified
beautified
magnified

qualified
true religion
real religion
authentic religion
good religion?

There is an old black spiritual that asks the question "Is you got good religion?" Not just, "Is you got religion?" But is it good religion? There's a whole lot of dangerous, bad, sick religion in the world; bad religion can make you hard, cold, mean, and insensitive. Bad religion is worse than no religion. Krister Stendahl said that there's not an evil cause in the world that has not been sponsored by somebody's sick, perverted, bad, hateful religion. Bad religion spawned the medieval military crusades. Bad religion grabbed the enforcement of the state to destroy freedom of conscience. Bad religion set up the inquisitions to enforce religious conformity. Bad religion murdered the Anabaptists, burned Joan of Arc at the stake, executed John Huss and Hans Denck.

Bad religion killed William Tyndale for translating the Bible into the vernacular of the people. Bad religion took apartheid to South Africa; brought slavery to America; fostered segregation, bigotry, and exploitation; organized the Ku Klux Klan; generated the Nazi Party; created the moral majority; produced Jim Jones, Jimmy Baker, Jimmy Swaggart, Jerry Falwell, David Koresh, and Osama bin Laden.

Bad religion assassinated Mahatma Gandhi, murdered Anwar Sadat, slew Indira Gandhi, cut up Lebanon, destroyed Iran, devastated Iraq, oppressed the poor, toppled the Twin Towers in New York City, crucified Jesus, killed Martin Luther King Jr., bludgeoned Rodney King, murdered Malice Green, devastated Yugoslavia. That's why Grandma wanted to know, "Is you got good religion?"

Bad religion takes life.
Good religion gives life.
Bad religion destroys folk.
Good religion liberates folk.
Bad religion talks about national defense.
Good religion talks about national purpose.
Bad religion divides folks.
Good religion unifies folks.
Bad religion makes you hate folks.
Good religion makes you love everybody.
Bad religion segregates.
Good religion integrates.
Bad religion stays in the church.
Good religion breaks loose in the world.

Bad religion hangs around the altar.

Good religion walks down the Jericho Road.

Bad religion is shaped like a spurious pole, trying to reach up to God without reaching out to anybody. Good religion is shaped like a cross, the vertical beam reaching up to God for power, and the horizontal beam, reaching out and sharing love, power, peace, joy, hope, life, freedom, jobs, education, opportunity, all around. Is you got good religion?

When we get good religion, true religion, strong religion, inclusive religion, we will not be discouraged by anyone, defeated by anything, destroyed by any evil. Wherever you go, wherever you preach, wherever you pray, wherever you work,

problems will be solved,

prayers will be answered,

doors will be opened,

barriers will be shattered,

nations will be freed,

races will be reconciled,

churches will be saved,

burdens will be lifted,

yokes will be broken,

people will be liberated,

children will be educated,

churches will be empowered, and

religion will be responsible.

If you have a hard way to go, you will walk it by faith.

If you have a problem, you will work with it until you get through it.

If you have a misunderstanding, you will settle it.

If you have hatred or resentment, you will shake it off.

If you have a high mountain, you will move it by faith or climb

it by prayer.

If you have a battle, you will fight it.

If you have a handicap, you will rise above it.

If you have prejudice, you will overcome it.

If you have temptation, you will conquer it.

If you have evil, you will destroy it.

If you have a challenge, you will face it.

If you have trouble, you will take it.

If you have a cross, you will bear it.

If they talk about you, you will keep praying for them.

If they kill you, you will rise again!

"For this is the fast that God has chosen;

to loose the bonds of injustice,
to undo the thongs of the yoke,
to let the oppressed go free and
to break every yoke.
Then you shall call, and the Lord will answer.
You shall cry for help, and he will say, 'Here I am.'"

2

The Wedding of Biblical Truth with Social Justice

CHARLES E. BOOTH

It is not a difficult task to share that which one does on a weekly basis, and that is precisely what this attempt reflects. Serious and thoughtful preachers carefully and prayerfully approach their work with the intent to be exegetically accurate; clear in focus and perspective; and contemporary in the sense of application. Undergirding all of this is an honest presentation of the preacher's true self.

I have always contended that the best definition of preaching was suggested by Phillips Brooks, who said that preaching, succinctly put, is "truth through personality." Truth represents what is immutable or changeless while the human personality is always in a state of evolving, becoming, developing, and maturing. It is hoped that the preacher does have a sense of what biblical truth is and of what his or her true convictions are, as well as what have been and continue to be shifts and changes in his or her own evolution. All of this is important when the preacher begins to think through and construct the sermon.

Honesty compels the preacher to confess that with the passing of time there are changes in one's thought about issues and positions. Preachers must assess their convictions. They must determine their personal biases and prejudices. All of this must be flushed against the biblical text with which one wrestles so that the sermon will, one hopes, reflect truth as it is recorded in Scripture and not simply the propagation of personal prejudice or the echo of one's own wail. These are foundational issues and concerns that are always resident in my thinking as I prepare to craft the sermon to be heard in the community of faith.

When I attended seminary, I was mandated to take a course in biblical hermeneutics. Such a course in biblical interpretation has all but disappeared from the seminary itinerary. I consider such a course of study to be essential. Preachers must always be conscious and cognizant of what we believe because, as we stand before people and propagate the gospel, we must always seek to declare "what thus saith the Lord" and not "what thus saith me!" I am disturbed that a lot of today's popular preaching represents personal thought and opinion and not eternal truth. I must always, therefore, take into account what I think and believe, and measure that against the yardstick of that which has been held accountable across the ages as biblical or scriptural truth.

Whether the sermon is delivered with or without notes is inconsequential. What is important is that the sermon be thoughtful, organized, and passionate. Even though I preach without notes, I do write out the sermon in full manuscript so as to be as precise in my development as possible. My own experience has taught me that a good theological education and sound study habits will produce a thoughtful and creative sermon. I only consult the commentary when it is absolutely necessary. If I am specifically in need of particular facts about a biblical person, text, place, or event, I consult the commentary. If specificity is required beyond my ability to recall, I consult the commentary. Exegesis must always be precise and accurate.

Many years ago, I was told by that legendary pastor-preacher, J. Pius Barbour, never to consult the commentary immediately when preparing to preach because such habitual use allows the commentary to become a crutch, thus stifling one's own creative approach to the text. It was Barbour's belief that the same God who gave creative insight to those who wrote the commentaries can do the same for you. However, I do think it is a wise procedure, after one has carefully, prayerfully, and thoughtfully considered a text, to consult a "good" commentary to ensure that one is not far afield, but very much in the area of sound biblical interpretation.

Confession is good for the soul, or so we have been told. All biases and prejudices are not necessarily bad. Allow me to confess one of mine. I believe that the unique genius of African American preaching has been the ability to wed biblical truth with social justice. The Scriptures are riddled with such reality all the way from the deliverance of the Jews through the eighth-century prophets to Jesus of Nazareth and the apostles. Jesus firmly stated this point in his inaugural message in Nazareth when he quoted from the prophet Isaiah verbatim—"The Spirit of the Lord is upon me, because he hath anointed me to preach the gospel to the poor; he hath sent me to heal the broken-hearted, to preach deliverance to the captives, and recovering of sight to the blind, to set at liberty them that are bruised, to preach the acceptable year of the Lord" (Luke 4:18–19, KJV).

The passion, imagination, and articulatory skills of the African American preacher have historically been wed to the Scriptures as thrust and lift for our liberation. I am proud to admit that I do not hesitate to align myself with this rich tradition that so wondrously accents the African American pulpit. It is my belief that authentic gospel preaching must always seek to be contemporary, for the gospel is never antique. The admonition of Karl Barth yet rings true in that the preacher should always read the Bible with split vision—one eye on the Scriptures and the other on the newspaper. I have further discovered that one's embrace of history and literature is a sound investment when it comes to preaching, for what is history but "His" story.

I am now approaching my thirty-seventh year as a gospel preacher and my thirty-first year as a preaching pastor. It is an undeniable fact that there is a qualitative and categorical difference between one's itinerant experience as a preacher and one's pastoral proclamation. With the preparation of every sermon, I mentally picture several individuals in my congregation who represent different mindsets and perspectives. There is the believer who accepts the gospel message with little or no doubt. Then there is the incessantly inquisitive individual whose questions abound. Still there is the cynic or the skeptic who by nature or conditioning must be convinced of the truth being promulgated. There may well be those who do not believe.

Finally, there is the person who appears in the gathering who needs spiritual uplift and encouragement and the expectation is that the courier of the day will be able to provide that which will grant spiritual sustenance for the continuation of the existential journey. For me, the preacher has the awesome task of attempting to address this myriad of mindsets with the truth of the everlasting gospel of Jesus Christ through his or her maturing personality. One does not always succeed in such an undertaking, but a serious and valiant attempt should always be made.

I am deeply indebted to the late Samuel DeWitt Proctor, under whom I did my doctoral studies and with whom I taught as a doctoral mentor at the United Theological Seminary in Dayton, Ohio. It was he who gave me and countless others the homiletical handles by which we craft and develop the sermon. Proctor always contended that anyone who preached any semblance of an organized sermon did so dialectically. He saw, as do I, a wonderful homiletical device in the Hegelian dialectic of thesis, antithesis, and synthesis.

Georg Friedrich Hegel suggested that in the ebb and flow of human history there is a season of progress, which he defines as the *thesis*. This season of progress is always met by an opposing force or forces known as an *antithesis*. It is out of the struggle and conflict created by the thesis and antithesis that a synthesis or resolution of the struggle takes place. I believe, like Proctor, that the dialectic is a wholesome and wonderful approach to sermon construction. This particular method of sermon construction allows me the opportunity to do my exegetical work, use illustrations, drive home meaningful and salient points, and make contemporary applications.

Once text and subject have been prayerfully selected, I must be able to say in a proposition (one simple, declarative statement) what the theme or thrust of the sermon is. If the theme or thrust of the sermon is unclear to me, then, obviously, it will be unclear to my hearers. The proposition must be clearly fixed in my mind so that it remains the guiding focus of my entire sermonic effort. My hope and expectation is that once the sermon has been delivered, the hearer will be able to walk away with the proposition clearly apparent even though the proposition has not been stated. If this is not done, then I have failed at my task.

There must next be the establishment of the thesis and the antithesis. The thesis position is that which represents the good, the positive, and the constructive part of the text or narrative. The antithesis represents, of course, the mitigating forces that work against or in opposition to what is clearly the good and the godly. It matters not whether the preacher begins with a thesis or antithesis. What is critically important is that a clearly discernible tension or struggle be established between the thesis and the antithesis. It is out of this tension that the relevant question of the sermon emerges. The sermon has only one relevant question! If there is more than one question, then one has more than one sermon.

The sermon seeks to answer only one question. I am convinced that the sermon is tremendously enhanced by the preacher's ability to wrestle with an antithesis. The antithesis unfolds and presents the predicament and dilemma with which one wrestles. It is in the antithesis that most people live and struggle. The quest of the sermon then becomes the pilgrimage or odyssey out of which the individual emerges so that he or she can clearly see what it is that God is seeking to convey through that particular sermon. For me, the thesis and antithesis represent the introduction of the sermon, and the stating of the relevant question commences the body of the sermon, or what the dialectic calls the synthesis.

The synthesis of the sermon seeks to resolve the conflict, struggle, and tension created by the thesis and antithesis. It is the synthesis that answers the relevant question. I must always ask myself when dealing with the tension created by the thesis and antithesis: "While there are many possible questions I could raise, what is the most relevant question I can propose?" My answers to the relevant question (the body or synthesis of the sermon) must arise out of the stated biblical text or narrative.

If not stated in the biblical text or narrative, the answer(s) ought to be strongly inferred or implied. This not only keeps the sermon tight, but, more important, the sermon is kept in proper focus and does not haphazardly wander in the space of private and personal opinion. I further believe that there must be integrity in the sermon and that such integrity can only be achieved when one wrestles with and draws from the stated biblical text or narrative.

The conclusion or celebration of the sermon should always be an out-growth of the synthesis. It should be naturally derived and not "tacked on" to the sermon, having no attachment whatsoever to what has been developed. I still believe in the old sermonic adage "Good meat makes its own gravy."

My discovery across these years is that strong preaching is always biblical. While one may run out of topics or themes on which to preach, one will never run out of biblical texts. It is impossible to exhaust the Holy Scriptures!

Following is a sermon preached from the pulpit of the Mt. Olivet Baptist Church in Columbus, Ohio, where I have been privileged to serve as pastor since 1978. This sermon, titled "Three Responses to a Miracle," illustrates the use of the dialectical method in sermon preparation. While the proposition of the sermon is not necessarily stated verbally by the preacher in the proclamation of the sermon, it ought always be uppermost in his or her thinking and should be, by the sermon's conclusion, clearly apparent to the listener. For the purpose of this printed sermon, I have chosen to state the proposition so as to illustrate the approach.

Sermon: Three Responses to a Miracle
Acts 16:25–32

CHARLES E. BOOTH

Proposition: Miracles always require a response(s) from the believer.

INTRODUCTION

We live in a day and time when the vast majority of persons do not believe in miracles. I define a miracle as an extraordinary manifestation of the supernatural in a situation or occurrence. There are those who contend that miracles no longer take place as they did during the biblical era. We must understand that miracles occur every day of our lives. Even though we are able to attach scientific definition to such things as the rising of the sun, the setting of the same; the beating of the heart; the rotation of the planets; and the change of the seasons—still these occurrences are, in the mind of the believer, miraculous. One of the reasons people have a difficult time accepting the reality of miracles is because we are creatures and, thus, captives of logic, reason, and the rational.

Those of us who embrace and believe in the God of the Judeo-Christian experience believe that our God is the God of the miraculous. With great delight, we love to talk about God inserting himself in what seems to be an impossible predicament and delivering us from that ordeal. Is there not in the daily grind of our existential pilgrimage the tremendous need for the supernatural in terms of help, healing, and deliverance? The cynics, skeptics, and antagonists would declare that there is no such thing as a miracle when a phenomenon or occurrence cannot be defined logically.

However, those of us who authentically embrace the Christian faith know beyond the shadow of a doubt that God does avail and present himself in situations that appear impossible and that with a stroke of his omnipotence, God performs the miraculous. There must be consideration given to what occurs in the aftermath of a miracle. We are not allowed the luxury of silence once a miracle has transpired in our experience. How strange that when we are in the midst of a predicament or crisis, we cry out for God's help and assistance, and when aid comes, we suddenly turn mute and allow life to continue along its daily continuum. The Bible is replete with examples of miracles and their aftermath. Have you ever taken the time to read what happened after the children of Israel came through the Red Sea? They held a praise and worship service in which Miriam sang. After David slew Goliath? He took the head of Goliath to Saul, and from that moment, David never went back to Bethlehem to live. Instead, he lived in the palace of Saul and became fast friends with Jonathan. After Samson brought down the temple of Dagon? Even though it was a great victory for Samson, he, nevertheless, died with his enemies. After the Hebrew boys came out of the fiery furnace? A decree was signed that the God of the Hebrew boys be praised and each one of them was promoted in the Babylonian government. After Daniel came out of the lions' den? Daniel's enemies and their families were thrown into the lions' den and killed while Daniel prospered even the more.

In the text under consideration, Paul and Silas have arrived on the European continent and for the first time, the gospel is being preached there. They are in the city of Philippi and their evangelistic efforts have proven to be successful. Their first convert is a businesswoman, or entrepreneur, whose name is Lydia. She represents the middle or upper echelon of Philippian society. There is no furor over her conversion. However, when a young girl possessed of a spirit of divination is converted, Paul and Silas are immediately thrown into jail.

This young lady's conversion has tampered with the economics of men who have used her for their own selfish gain. Paul and Silas are seen as threats to an enterprise that had proven to be economically and financially successful. So determined are the Philippian magistrates to confine Paul and Silas that they are stripped, beaten, severely flogged, and thrown into the inner part of the jail. They are placed in solitary confinement. Their feet are fastened in stocks. What is noteworthy in this situation is that neither Paul nor Silas panic or throw a temper tantrum. They do not believe for one moment that their situation is hopeless or helpless. They fully believe in the power of God and his ability to do the miraculous and release them from their captivity. The text plainly states that these men of God wait until midnight to begin a prayer and praise service. Midnight—the darkest moment in the nocturne!

Midnight—when men and women rest from the labors of the day! Midnight—when fields drowse and wickedness prowls our streets! Midnight—when mythology declares that witches get on brooms and goblins make their appearance! Midnight—when people duck and dodge to do what they have not the courage to do in daylight!

It was at midnight that Paul and Silas prayed and sang hymns to God. Luke does not say with specificity what Paul and Silas prayed and sang. Our imaginations are left wide open at this point. Since both were God-fearing and devout Jews, one can safely assume that they could have chosen any one of the 150 Psalms in what we now call the Old Testament. They could have sung Psalm 1—"Blessed is the person that walketh not in the counsel of the ungodly, nor standeth in the way of sinners, nor sitteth in the seat of the scornful. But that person's delight is in the law of the LORD; and in his law doth he meditate day and night." They could have sung Psalm 23—"The LORD is my shepherd: I shall not want. . . . Thou prepareth a table before me in the presence of mine enemies. . . ." They could have sung Psalm 27—"The LORD is my light and my salvation: whom shall I fear? The LORD is the strength of my life; of whom shall I be afraid?" They could have sung Psalm 46—"God is our refuge and strength, a very present help in trouble" (KJV).

It is not important that we know precisely what they sang and prayed. What is utterly important is that while singing and praying, a miracle took place. There was an earthquake; the foundation of the prison was shaken; the prison doors flew open; and every prisoner's chains were dropped. Paul, Silas, and every prisoner in that Philippian jail were suddenly liberated. However, this is not the end of the story. The question must be raised—how did Paul and Silas respond to this miracle?

The first response to this miracle is a testimony, for Paul and Silas know that their deliverance is not of their own doing. Every miracle demands a testimony. All of us are uniquely private and personal people. We do not want people to know "our business." Sometimes we are embarrassed, ashamed, or just plain hurt when it comes to those personal issues that we desire to keep uniquely private. These issues may pertain to family, finances, health, employment, or other personal matters. However, once the miracle takes place, the deliverance cannot be private. The miracle must become public.

The miracle experienced by Paul and Silas in that Philippian jail was no longer their private domain. The jailer and all the other prisoners were privy to what happened. Once the miracle transpires, it cannot be contained. How can you contain an earthquake? How can you contain the shaking of the prison's foundation? Noise had to accompany the opening of the prison doors as well as the sudden loosening of the prisoners' chains. Once God delivers us, performs a miracle, helps, heals, delivers, or brings us out of a calamity, there should always be a public acknowledgment. Your calamity, crisis, illness, or predicament may be private, but the deliverance is always public. It must be acknowledged. This does not mean that one must define what his or her private issue was. One can declare deliverance and the miracle without stating specifically the issue.

Paul and Silas may have prayed and sung in their midnight situation, but only God could have provided the miracle of their deliverance. Therefore, God not only wants but deserves the credit. We as Christian believers should never be ashamed or embarrassed to make public our miracle, our healing, our deliverance, or our release! There are those who thought our situation impossible. Perhaps we even thought our situation impossible. However, God wants it made public what he has done and accomplished!

Do you remember what happened after the Gadarene demoniac, Legion, was delivered? It was his desire to go with Jesus, but Jesus told him, "Go home and tell everybody what good things the Lord hath done for you!" When the prodigal returned home from his sojourn in that far country, his father threw a party for him and made public that his son "who was lost is now found!" We must not be embarrassed to admit publicly that God, through the miracle of medicine and divine healing, has in fact cured illnesses, delivered persons from chemical and substance abuse, liberated people from low self-worth and esteem, put relationships back together again, and brought rebellious children back to their senses. Your public declaration of your private problem is your testimony!

II

The second response to this miracle is opportunity. The text clearly states that Paul and Silas do not isolate or insulate themselves once the miracle occurs. The jailer awakens from his slumber and assumes that his prisoners have escaped. When he wipes the cobwebs of slumber from his eyes and surveys the situation, he takes his sword from its sheath and proceeds to point it at his abdomen. The Philippian jailer remembered that according to Roman law, if a prisoner escaped during his watch the penalty was not a polite slap on the wrist, but one literally paid with his life. Therefore, the jailer is about to commit suicide when Paul stops him with the words, "Do thyself no harm! We are all here!"

Paul and Silas recognized that when God grants deliverance, help, or a miracle, this is one's opportunity to be a blessing to someone else. When the Philippian jailer was about to commit suicide, Paul did not say, "Go ahead and kill yourself! After all, you are the enemy! You are a part of the system that wrongly and unjustly imprisoned us!" Paul saw himself as an instrument of life and not death; an instrument of deliverance and not bondage; and an instrument of hope and not despair!

Whenever God performs the miraculous in our lives, we must recognize that this is the time to be a blessing to someone else. Every testimony gives birth and vent to an opportunity to do good. I vividly recall the story of Reuben "Hurricane" Carter as he tells of his life in his autobiography, *The Sixteenth Round*. All of us know that Mr. Carter was falsely accused of a crime that he did not commit and after two trials was unjustly sentenced to three life sentences. Most persons confined to penal institutions for crimes they did not commit become mean and bitter. This was not the case with this Paterson, New Jersey, native. He believed unendingly in his own innocence and the force of right—so much so that he clung tenaciously to the thought that somehow, someway he would be free.

This did not mean that he was without his moments of doubt and despair. Hurricane Carter wrote his autobiography under the cloak of secrecy and by the grace of God was able to get it published. As painful as his story was, Hurricane Carter knew his story was worth telling. Unbeknownst to him it would provide encouragement to a young African American boy from Brooklyn, New York, who would pick up Carter's autobiography from a table in a secondhand bookstore, read it, and be so inspired that he would hunger and thirst to read and learn.

One must remember that the young man inspired by Hurricane Carter had been lifted from his Brooklyn neighborhood and taken to Canada by three white Canadians who were willing to commit themselves to this young man's betterment. The Brooklyn school system declared this young man educationally deficient. His learning disability had prevented him from doing well in that school system; thus, he had been written off as another African American educational casualty. When this young man read Hurricane Carter's story, he determined that he would not only make something of himself, but commit himself to the liberation of the man who had become his hero.

One never knows what opportunities avail themselves when we position ourselves to be a blessing to someone else. Not only is Hurricane Carter free today and his story known to all, but the young man who picked up that autobiography is today an attorney-at-law. We do have a duty and obligation to be a blessing to others when God blesses us.

III

There is a third and final response to this miracle. It is the lesson of discovery. Paul and Silas discover in this experience that God is more than a theoretical assumption or theological speculation. Their discovery in that Philippian jail is that God is real. Paul has certainly encountered and discovered the resurrected Christ on the Damascus Road as Savior, but in that Philippian jail cell, Paul discovers Christ as Deliverer. All of us need such an encounter and experience as we move from knowing Christ theoretically to knowing Christ experientially.

All of us come to know God on three distinct levels. Our first encounter with God is a vicarious one. This experience suggests that we learn about God through someone else's experience. Mama said, "God is a wheel in the middle of a wheel," or Daddy said, "God will feed you when you are hungry." While these declarations represent reality, the reality is someone else's and not our own.

Second, we learn about God academically, that is, through study, reflection, and meditation. This is an intellectual approach to God. This we do through such channels as Sunday school, Bible studies, conventions, conferences, seminary, and so on. This is needed and necessary, but is not enough. Third, at some point our understanding of God must move beyond the vicarious and the academic to the practical and the real.

This is the experience of Paul and Silas in Philippi. Their discovery of God as Deliverer is uniquely their own. Many years ago, Dr. Martin Luther King Jr. related in his book *Stride Toward Freedom* that when his house was bombed during the Montgomery bus boycott, there was the possibility that his wife and his then one daughter, Yolanda, could have been killed. He remembered sitting at his kitchen table over a cup of coffee and experiencing the presence of God in a way he had never experienced before. That experience superseded every experience he had at Morehouse College, Crozier Theological Seminary, and Boston University. For him, that night at a kitchen table, God became more real than ever before.

Paul had learned about God at the feet of Gamaliel. Paul is considered a most studious and learned rabbi. But it is not until that midnight experience in that Philippian jail cell that Paul discovers just how real God is. God does not become real unless and until he becomes practical! Practical means he shows up and delivers us from crises, calamity, plight, circumstance, situation, predicament, and sickness. God is real when one is delivered from bondage, disease, frustration, guilt, abuse, misuse, anxiety, frustration, low self-worth, drugs, sexual promiscuity, negative attitude, pessimistic mindset, gossip, jealousy, envy, insecurity, lying, anger, and temper. When you know God has met you in and delivered you from your calamity, you can say with the hymnologist

> There are some things I may not know,
> there are some places I can't go,

But I am sure of this one thing,
That God is real for I can feel him deep within.

Some folk may doubt, some folk may scorn,
All can desert and leave me alone,
But as for me I'll take God's part,
For God is real and I can feel Him in my heart.

I cannot tell just how you felt
When Jesus took your sins away,
But since that day, yes, since that hour,
God has been real for I can feel His holy power.

Yes, God is real, real in my soul;
Yes, God is real for He has washed and made me whole;
His love for me is like pure gold,
Yes, God is real for I can feel Him in my soul."
(Elisha Hoffman, "There Are Some Things I May Not Know")

CONCLUSION

The marvel, beauty, and wonder of the Christian experience is that ultimately it is and should be utterly personal. All of us deeply treasure those meaningful and profound moments when we know that God has broken in on our circumstance in miraculous fashion. It matters not whether we are believed or disbelieved because we know the reality of our experience. No one can ever tamper or tinker with what is our experience. As fantastic and seemingly unbelievable as some of our experiences have been, we know beyond the shadow of a doubt that they are real. Paul and Silas could boast of their miraculous deliverance from the Philippian jail!

Dr. King could boast of his experience in his kitchen in Montgomery! Reuben "Hurricane" Carter can boast of his deliverance from the New Jersey penal system! I can boast of my own personal experiences of deliverance and how God has shown himself to be miraculous in my life, and so can you! We know who God is and what he can do. He is El Shaddai—the Lord God Almighty! He is Jehovah—the Lord! He is Jehovah Elyon—the Lord Most High! He is Jehovah Shammai—the Lord Ever Present! He is Jehovah Shalom—the Lord my Peace! He is Jehovah Jireh—the Lord who will provide!

Fanny J. Crosby did not allow her blindness to prevent her from expressing her feelings about the reality of God. All who believe in the Lord, Jesus Christ can sing with her:

Blessed assurance, Jesus is mine!
O what foretaste of glory divine!
Heir of salvation, purchase of God,
Born of His Spirit, washed in His blood.

This is my story, this is my song,
Praising my Savior all the day long,
This is my story, this is my song,
Praising my Savior, all the day long.

3

Explaining What the Text Means

H. B. CHARLES JR.

I am a student of expository preaching; that is, preaching that explains what the text means by what it says. I am convinced that the Bible is God's self-revelation. Therefore, to misinterpret the text is to misrepresent God. So the stakes are high. And the preacher must be extremely disciplined if he or she is to prepare at least fifty sermons a year without lying on the Scriptures, by which I mean, if he or she is to be faithful to what the text is actually saying. Second Timothy 2:15 puts it this way: "Be diligent to present yourself approved to God, a worker who does not need to be ashamed, rightly dividing the word of truth" (NKJV).

This is one of my life-verses. The basic questions I ask myself both before and after preaching are tied to it: Is God pleased with me? Am I ashamed of the work I put into this sermon? Did I handle the text correctly? For me, these are the bottom-line issues of preaching. Thus, in my preparation process I am simply trying to please God by doing the hard work of faithful and clear exposition. And during the typical workweek, I divide this process into two parts: inductive Bible study and Sunday sermon construction.

Of course, these two labors overlap. But I try to keep them distinct, as much as possible. This keeps me honest and prevents me from introducing myself to the text by saying, "Hi. How can I preach you?" I really do want to let the text speak to me before I try to speak about it. And when I let the text speak to me first, I stand on the Lord's Day with something to say. But when I don't, I stand merely having to say something because it's Sunday again.

So the first priority of my study week is to come to a proper understanding of the text. And if I get to the end of the week and I don't understand the text, I have two options: either preach something else or let someone else preach. I take the position of that commercial: "I preach no sermon before its time."

Until I understand the details, theme, and progression of the text, any attempt at preaching it would be nothing more than homiletical filibustering. So I dive into the text first, trusting that the same Spirit that led the ancients to write will lead me to an understanding of what was written. And I use the inductive principles of Bible study in seeking that understanding: observation (what does it say?), interpretation (what does it mean?), and application (how does it work?).

I begin my actual study with observations, but this assumes certain preconditions that I should mention. Because I preach in series (either entire books or sections), the text is usually already assigned when the week begins. I am already familiar with the vital statistics of the book (author, intended audience, theme, special characteristics, and so on). In fact, I usually have a file of material on the text that I have collected over an extended period of time leading up to the week I actually intend to preach it.

All of this working ahead is important for one who has to teach his congregation several times a week, not including the out-of-town speaking engagements. It is natural for me to think about just one sermon at a time. But because it seems that every other day is Saturday night, I can't afford to waste most of my study week on determining what I should study that week. So I work ahead. And this allows me to move directly from my devotional time to my research of the text. And my research begins with observations of the text.

There are several reasons why I begin with this time of "sanctified" brainstorming. First of all, this helps me to deal with the primary text first, rather than beginning my study by asking, "What does MacArthur, Wiersbe, or Barclay say on this text?" Likewise, beginning with observations helps me to put my cards on the table. We all bring baggage to the text. And I want to be up front about mine so that it won't get in the way of the truth. So I begin by using the principles of interpretation that I know. I diagram the text. I determine the words I need to learn. I make note of the sermons or writings of others that shape my thoughts about the text. I jot down the personal sermon ideas that I already have on the text.

I ask questions of the text. I even argue with it, when there is something I don't understand or with which I disagree. I do this until I have exhausted the process, no matter how long it takes. After all, you won't understand what a text means until you first understand what it says. Then I turn to secondary sources. I go through the text in as many translations as possible. This can be tedious, but I don't want to preach something that can be easily trumped by those in the congregation who have something other than the NKJV in their lap.

I then study the cross-references of the text. Indeed, Scripture is its own interpreter. So I read through all of the cross-references in the *Treasury of Scripture Knowledge* (Thomas Nelson). Then I do my word studies. In my observations and reading of the comparative translations, I have identified the words I need to learn. I am not a Greek or Hebrew scholar, but I know enough to use the tools effectively. Then I focus my study on the context and background of the text, remembering my professor's warning: "We often misinterpret the text because we read the oriental text with an occidental mindset."

So I use my tools to understand the historical, political, social, religious, and literary context of the passage. This is actually one of the more enjoyable parts of the study to me, for it is in understanding the context that the meaning of the passage most often becomes clear to me.

The last part of my research consists of reading commentaries. And let me testify that I am not ashamed of my friendship with commentaries. I know that there are those who say we shouldn't use them. But my position is that we should use them; just don't abuse them. And I believe it's arrogant to think that you cannot or should not draw from the wisdom of others, some who have spent their lives studying the book of the Bible you're working on. So I humbly submit myself to the wisdom of others. I read my favorite authors. I read those who are known for their work on a particular passage.

I read scholarly and popular commentaries. I even read people who I know up front I'm going to disagree with. In fact, I try to collect at least thirty commentaries on a book before I begin a study on it (which is another practical reason why I preach in series). Now, I don't recommend that for everyone. But I would recommend that you chase down as many ideas as possible in your search for one good idea. An old preacher put it to me this way: "There are no better minds, just better libraries."

And since I'm giving advice, let me also recommend that you record everything. No, your memory is not that good. Write it down. This way, you'll have ready access to the ideas you come up with in the research for this Sunday's sermon. And if you have done a good job in your research, you'll usually have a file of information to go back to for later sermons. Plus, if you record study notes and keep them, you'll never have to study that text from scratch again. You can just add material to it over the years. It'll be your own commentary on the passage.

Now, after I have completed my inductive study of the text, I move to sermon construction. Admittedly, throughout my research I have been recording quotes, illustrations, and references that may become actual sermon material. But I would just record it and then refocus on my actual research of the text. Now, however, my focus is on actually building a sermon. And the goal of this part of the process is to develop a sermon that is worthy of the truth revealed in the text. Unfortunately, many times I've messed up a good idea with a sloppy sermon. I refuse to go to the pulpit without an understanding of the text. But I have gone to the pulpit not ready to clearly present what I have understood.

I'm a pretty good extemporaneous preacher. And there have been times when God has honored this. But it doesn't matter how many people shout or come down the aisle or compliment you after the sermon; it doesn't make up for the empty feeling you have when you know that you did not give God your best. I've been there enough times to know that I don't want to live there. I want to get in the bed on Sunday night being able to say, "Lord, today's sermon may not have been the greatest. But you know that with what I had this week, I gave you my best." And so I strive to develop good sermons based on faithful exposition of the text.

Now, I do not swing for a "home run" every Sunday. I'm a pastor. And my pastoral concern for those entrusted to me leads me to take the long view of preaching. That is, I believe that God is able to change a life in an instant. However, as a shepherd, I must feed the entire flock as well as go after the one lost sheep. And the fact is that while a person's life can be radically transformed with one sermon, it doesn't happen that way with congregations. Pastoral ministry is a marathon, not a sprint. And so I don't expect the congregation to become healthy after Sunday's sermon.

Instead, I view Sunday as another link in the chain that binds us together in Christ. So I don't swing for the fence every Sunday. Most often, I just want to get on base. And if the message is faithful to the text and clear in its presentation, then I believe I've succeeded. They don't have to shout. They don't even have to agree. That's between them and the God who wrote the text. I just don't want to get in the way and cause them to miss the encounter with Christ that the text intends. And to this end, I work to develop what I call the "sermon skeleton." And then I put flesh on that "skeleton" by writing out a complete sermon manuscript.

"Sermon Skeleton" is what I label the sheet on which I record the purpose and structure of the sermon. It consists of the text, title, doctrinal theme, point (the sermon in a sentence), and outline. I believe these are essential things I need to know before I try to collect further material for the sermon. After all, what's the use of finding an introduction or illustration for a sermon if you don't even know what the point or outline of that sermon is going to be?

Call it what you will, but you need to establish your sermon objectives (what you intend to say) before you start collecting sermon material (how you want to say it). If I cannot write this out, I am not ready to preach this text. And once these fundamentals of the sermon are established, then the rest of my preparation time is spent constructing the sermon.

I am a manuscript preacher—sort of. I write out a word-for-word manuscript most weeks, but I typically do not carry anything but my Bible to the pulpit. Yet, I do not put a lot of effort into actually memorizing the manuscript. My writing process causes me to go over the same material over and over, until

I have kind of "absorbed" it in the process of writing it. As mentioned, I usually have a file on material on the text before the week I intend to preach it. And during the week I intend to preach the text, I spend a portion of every day on it.

On Wednesday through Friday I intentionally neglect everything but emergencies, for extended and uninterrupted study time (our church Bible study is on Tuesday night). I know this sounds miraculous to some pastors. But it really hasn't been a struggle over the years to get my congregation to honor this time. I am clear with them that I believe the pastor's primary task is to teach and defend sound doctrine. And I regularly inform and remind my church that sermons don't grow on trees. I even ask for prayers when I know I have a difficult text or busy week ahead.

God be praised, for it cannot be fairly said that I come to the pulpit on Sundays unprepared. The Lord has honored his word in the lives of his people. And so I am blessed with a congregation that gives me the time and resources I need to think, read, and pray. Of course, my study schedule is adjusted if my week includes travel. But with sacrifice, hard work, and the benefit of a laptop, it's usually not a crisis.

Plus, having an organized system of study that I've used over the years usually keeps the sense of panic at a minimum. I am confident that if I just go through the process, no matter how I feel, it will bear fruit. The observation process is like going through the text with a fine-tooth comb. And the translations, cross-references, word studies, and context and background research adds insight into the text, like moving from a little black-and-white TV to a color big screen.

The commentaries keep discussing the same context, words, and references, even though the conclusions may be different. So by the time I complete the sermon skeleton, I usually have the text in my system and a message on my heart. Now I must gather and organize the material that will go into the sermon.

I hate writing sermons. I love studying the Word of God. And I love the actual preaching event. But sermon construction is a frustrating process for me. First of all, there's the bondage of weekly preparation. Good ideas just don't come in seven-day cycles. And yet every week you're expected to be fresh, compelling, and better than last Sunday. And then there's the diversity of the congregation. I preach to some who taught me the Scriptures when I was a child and some who are hearing Bible exposition for the first time. I preach to some who have postgraduate degrees and some who are illiterate. I preach to some young adults who need to be equipped to defend their faith in a hostile work environment. And I preach to some seniors who showed up just to make sure the old landmarks are still there and to hear me whoop.

I preach to some . . . well, you get the picture. You name it, and it may be in the congregation on Sunday. And they all sit there with different expectations that you must meet with just one sermon. And take into account the fact that I have just one sermon for them this Sunday. But there are as many different needs as there are people in the congregation. They're sick. They're discouraged. They're heartbroken. They're having marriage trouble. Their bills are due. And the next text in your exposition of Philippians does not have anything to do with any of those subjects. Then, add to that the tradition in which I preach where some will judge your sermon based on how many shouted or came down the aisle.

And, if you preach this text in Philippians faithfully, it will directly confront some of your most loyal members. Really, I don't know why anyone would dare preach without having confidence in the sufficiency of God's Word to save, change, and guide people's lives. For even with that confidence, preaching is scary business. Your only hope is to hide in the text. And from the safety of the text, you preach, looking to God to penetrate hearts through the message. And so, believing that I have something to say about this text that matters, I strive to develop a well-prepared sermon. It's a process that spans from Friday morning to Sunday morning, with basically no sleep in between. But nothing overcomes the frustration of hard preparation like the joy of a good preparation.

In the Friday-to-Sunday-morning stretch, I work on my introduction. Ironically, this often takes me the longest to develop, though the introduction of the sermon itself will not be that long. The older and wiser I get, the less time I spend playing on the "porch." I want to get to the meat of the matter. I just want to use the introduction to state my point in a clear and interesting way. Then I rush to the text to explain, defend, and apply the point.

I also take great care in selecting the quotes and illustrations that will go into the message. I picked this up from my late father, who was my pastoral predecessor. He was a great storyteller. In fact, he would often end his sermons by saying, "If you miss my message, keep my story." And the church would surely keep the story. So much so, that to this day, it's hard for me to tell one of his stories. So I try to chase down an appropriate illustration of my own for every major point in the outline. And my favorite source is the Bible itself.

I am a young man; yet, I have personally witnessed the decline of biblical literacy of church people over the years of my ministry. The fact is that many of the people we preach to don't even know, much less remember, the basic stories of the Bible. So I quote a lot of Scripture in my sermons, word for word, chapter and verse. And I often creatively retell the stories of the Bible. It gives me a chance to teach Scripture and illustrate at the same time.

I also find illustrations and quotes from my normal course of reading. I try to read at least one book a week. And this yields a lot of good sermon material. So I mark up my books, guard them fiercely, and try to use the good material I find as soon as possible. I'm really not organized enough to use a filing system any more complex than that.

I try to stay open to those times when the Lord will give me a sermon idea through a potter's window, as he did with Jeremiah. But I don't actually go looking for those kinds of "potter's house" illustrations.

I am particularly nervous about using personal illustrations. I know there's a current emphasis on being transcendent and vulnerable in preaching. But we must be careful not to violate 2 Corinthians 4:5: "For we do not preach ourselves, but Christ Jesus the Lord" (NRSV). Pulpit ministry is ego-enhancing enough on its own. I don't want to exacerbate that by constantly pointing to myself in the sermon. And so I get most of my illustrations from books, even sermon-illustration books.

I laugh when I read homiletics professors who say that we shouldn't use illustration books. These are the same professors who tell the same well-worn stories every new semester to a fresh group of students. Pastors, on the other hand, have to teach the same group of people several times a week, year after year. And so a few good illustrations are worth the price of the book, as far as I'm concerned.

After I have collected enough material, I begin writing. I've been thinking about how to present this all along. But now I am going to put it on paper. I pace the empty sanctuary preaching the ideas to myself. This is not for practice as much as it is to hear how I will sound saying the words. What looks good on paper doesn't always work well in the heat of preaching. And so I preach the sermon to myself, jotting down notes on index cards. Then, I periodically stop and type out the shorthand notes word for word.

I continue this process until the manuscript is complete. And by the time I finish, I have, in effect, done three drafts of the sermon (one oral, one shorthand, and one word for word). And so by this time, the sermon is in my system. Most often, all that is needed is for me to remember the order in which I wrote it and the quotes or details of stories I intend to use. When I have finished, it's usually Sunday morning already. I typically can't sleep on Friday and Saturday nights, so it's no sacrifice for me to spend that time on my sermon. So I pray. I get dressed. And I go preach. And when the service is over, I eat. Then I usually sleep the afternoon off. After all, doesn't Saturday night come again right after Sunday morning?

Sermon: God Uses Weak People
2 Corinthians 4:7

H. B. CHARLES JR.

A certain little boy received a beautiful blue bicycle on his third birthday. It was brand new, complete with training wheels, protective padding, and streamers. He couldn't have asked for a better bike, and his family couldn't wait to see his reaction. But, much to their chagrin, he was not impressed with the present at all. When they pulled it out of the box, he looked at it for a moment, smiled, and then began playing with the cardboard box the bike had been packaged in! It took the family a few days to convince him that it was the *bike* that was the actual gift. How often do we do that? How often do we pick the package over the present? How often do we choose the wrappings over God's true gifts?[1]

God knows that we are prone to put the outer wrappings over the true gift, but he seeks to dissuade us from that tendency, especially when it comes to the indescribable gift of salvation through his Son, Jesus Christ. This is what he does: he gives this priceless gift, but he puts it in worthless packages. He puts treasure in trash. The apostle Paul puts it this way in 2 Corinthians 4:7 (NKJV):

> We have this treasure in earthen vessels, that the excellence of the power may be of God and not of us.

What a thought! God has a treasure he wants to share, but he places it in earthen vessels—jars of clay; cheap, common pottery; perishable containers; the ancient equivalent of cardboard boxes.

The central phrase of this awesome sentence is "We have this treasure." The emphatic term of this phrase is the word *this*. The text does not say that we have *a* treasure, but *this* treasure, that is, something specific and partic- ular. What is this treasure? Verse 6 affirms that it was God who caused light to leap out of darkness when he declared, "Let there be light." It goes on to say that this same God of creation, who made light leap out of darkness, is shining in our hearts, and he shines in our hearts in order to enlighten others with the knowledge of his glory, which is revealed in the person and work of Jesus Christ.

Let me insert a footnote here: this passage affirms the fact that true spirituality happens from the inside out. Don't miss that. Bible study, sacrificial giving, faithful service, moral living, and church attendance are not adequate reasons to automatically assume that a person is a Christian. No—Christianity is more than the activities of religion. True Christianity is about a relationship with God. It is about faith in God, love for God, and commitment to God, demonstrated through submission to the lordship of Jesus Christ. Now, don't get me wrong, the external aspects and exercises of Christianity are important, but none of them mean anything if one has a "darkened heart." Salvation happens when God shines in our hearts. We are saved when God shines in our hearts the light of the knowledge of his glory in the face of Jesus Christ. Or, as verse 6 puts it, the God who turned darkness into light in creation also turns darkness into light in regeneration.

First Peter 2:9 (NKJV) says:

> But you are a chosen generation, a royal priesthood, a holy nation, His own special people, that you may proclaim the praises of Him who called you out of darkness into His marvelous light.

Salvation, in essence, is God calling us into his marvelous light. But, on the other hand, in salvation, not only does God bring us into his light, but he also brings his light into us. And here's why: even though you have come into the light, others around you are still in darkness. There are people in your sphere of influence who are still in darkness. You have friends, relatives, classmates, coworkers, and neighbors who are still in the dark. So when God saves you, he brings you into his light and he shines his light in you, "to give the light of the knowledge of the glory of God in the face of Jesus Christ." However, the fact that the light of God's glory is shining in your heart does not make you inherently better than other people. The fact that you have the knowledge of God does not give you the right to look down on other people. The fact that you have seen the face of Jesus Christ does not give you permission to be judgmental, arrogant, and critical. That's why verse 7 goes on to say, "but we have this treasure in earthen vessels, that the excellence of the power may be of God and not of us." That is to say, God uses weak people. And he does it so that he will be the only one who gets the credit for what he does.

Have you ever said, "I am simply too weak for God to use me"? If so, I want to help you rethink that idea. First Corinthians 1:26–29 (NKJV) says:

> For you see your calling, brethren, that not many wise according to the flesh, not many mighty, not many noble, are called. But God has chosen the foolish things of the world to put to shame the wise, and God has chosen the weak things of the world to put to shame the things which are mighty; and the base things of the world and the things which are despised God has chosen, and the things which are not, to bring to nothing the things that are, that no flesh should glory in His presence.

The message of Christianity is magnificent, but the messengers are not. Therefore, the reason God is not using you greatly has nothing to do with the fact that you are weak. In fact, the problem may be that you are not weak enough. Think about that. Are you weak enough for God to use you? Are you weak enough to totally depend on the Lord for strength? Are you weak enough to stop believing in yourself? Are you weak enough to lean on others for help? Are you weak enough to stop using your pain, fear, background, limitations, and circumstances as excuses for not serving God?

Second Corinthians 12:7–10 is one of my favorite passages. Paul was given a "thorn in the flesh" in order to keep him from becoming proud, arrogant, and puffed up. He further describes this "thorn" as a hellish henchman roughing him up, which solidifies the idea that whatever he was going through was painful. So he carried this thorn in the flesh to God in prayer. In fact, he prayed repeatedly about it, pleading with God to take it away from him. But the Lord's first, full, and final answer was "No!" Instead, the Lord assured Paul that his grace was good enough and that his power works best in weak people. The passage ends with Paul's new decision to rejoice in his weakness, so that the power of Christ may rest on him. Here's why: through his painful situation, Paul discovered the paradoxical power of weakness: "When I am weak, then I am strong." And I submit to you, that when you learn to acknowledge and embrace your weaknesses, you will then discover the mystery of true spiritual power, growth, and usefulness. You will be able to enjoy the power of weakness, spoken of here in our text. So let us examine the reality, ramifications, and result of our weaknesses in relation to God's mighty work.

THE REALITY OF OUR WEAKNESSES

Matthew 16:16 records what we call "the Great Confession." Jesus asks his disciples, "Who do the people say the Son of Man is?" after which the disciples begin to give him a laundry list of popular opinion about him. But then Jesus asks, "What about you? Who do you say that I am?" to which Peter responds, "You are the Christ, the Son of the living God." This is the Great Confession of Christian ministry. In fact, in Matthew 16:18, Jesus declares that confession to be the foundation upon which he would build his church. But in Acts 14:15 there is another great confession upon which Christian ministry is built. In that passage, God uses Paul to bring healing to a crippled man in Lystra and when the natives see this miracle, they conclude that Paul and his partner Barnabas are gods. They even prepare to offer sacrifices to them. But when the apostles see this, they tear their clothes and rush into the crowd screaming for them to stop, saying, "Men, why are you doing this? We too are only men, human like you." Both Matthew 16:16 and Acts 14:15 record for us foundation confessions for Christian ministry. On one hand, if the Lord is going to use you, you must confess that Jesus is the Christ, the Son of the living God. But on the other hand, if God is going to use you, you must confess that you are only human. And that's the reality 2 Corinthians 4:7 is trying to get us to come to grips with.

The phrase *earthen vessels* speaks of our humanity. It affirms that we are only human. Get that: the fact that we are saved, called, anointed, empowered, and sanctified does not make us superhuman. And it definitely does not make us "little gods." We are mere human beings and the Word of God uses this phrase, earthen vessels, to describe our humanity in a way that will help us stay in touch with reality. Let's walk around this phrase.

Unworthy. To say that we are earthen vessels is to say that we are unworthy. Notice that the text does not describe us as expensive vases or masterpieces or even works of art. It describes us as cheap, common pottery. You have probably seen that sign that says, "I know I'm somebody, 'cause God don't make junk." Well, not according to this verse. To call us earthen vessels is to call us junk. And it describes us that way in order to contrast the utter pricelessness of the treasure and the total unworthiness of the vessel. God uses us in ministry the same way he adopts us into his family: by grace, through faith in Christ, which means that your unworthiness does not disqualify you from being used by God. In fact, the exact opposite is true: a sense of unworthiness is a sign of spiritual health. What disqualifies you is when you begin to think that God ought to use you; it is when you begin to feel that you have earned the right to be on God's program that you get into trouble. Mark it down: God uses weak people who know that they are simply trophies of his amazing grace.

Dispensable. To say that we are earthen vessels is to say that we are dispensable. It has been well said that, "Without God we can't do it. But without us God won't do it," but don't confuse that statement to mean that God *can't* do it without you. Mark it down: you cannot make it without God, but God *can* make it without you. We got here too late and are going to leave too early to have a monopoly on God's program, and that's why we are called earthen vessels. We are not rare, extraordinary, or irreplaceable instruments.

Therefore, whatever we do for the Lord should be done in a spirit of submission, humility, and gratitude. We should remember that it is a privilege to be on God's program, anywhere on God's program. God doesn't need us. We are dispensable. I love Warren Wiersbe's definition of ministry. He says, "Ministry happens when divine resources meet human needs through loving channels to the glory of God."[2] Yes, when you minister, it only means that you are being a loving channel of God's divine resources. Don't miss that: you are the channel, not the source. God is the source, and when we become unwilling, unloving, and unusable, God is able to plug into another channel to touch lives to his glory. God does not need us. We are dispensable.

Fragile. To say that we are earthen vessels is to say that we are fragile. We break easily. Whether it be physically, emotionally, or even spiritually, it doesn't take much for us to break. We are all broken people, that is, we all have inherent and/or inherited weaknesses. The good news is that many of us are getting to the place where we can acknowledge and accept our weaknesses. However, it is unfortunate that some of us have taken the fact of our brokenness to the extreme, using the fact of our brokenness to claim victim status. Consequently, in some places, the message of the gospel has been altered, making therapy its theme rather than redemption. This is a great shame! The fact that we are broken people does not make us victims. It actually gives us an opportunity to be evidence for the truth that God cares about, works through, and rules over our brokenness. God has to break us in order to use us! A candle must be sacrificed for it to give light. Coal must be burned to furnish heat. Grapes must be crushed to get wine. Wheat must be ground to produce flour. And we must be broken in order for God to use us.

Gordon MacDonald, in his book *Rebuilding Your Broken World,* tells of a childhood experience where he knocked over a lamp that was precious to his parents. When it hit the floor, the ceramic shaft of the lamp cracked on one side, but because he was alone in the room at the time, he was able to place it back on the table and turn the lamp so that the crack was not visible. It remained that way for days, and every morning he would wake up in fear that this was the day the crack would be discovered and he would face the wrath of his parents. He froze every time his mother or father went near the lamp.

He imagined their reaction in that fearful moment when the inevitable discovery would be made. Surely, it seemed to him, the longer the confrontation was delayed, the worse the consequences promised to be. Then it came: the day his mother dusted the lamp and found the crack. "Did you do this?" she asked. He could only answer yes and brace himself, telling her what had happened. But she never said a word. She took it to the kitchen, glued the pieces so that they once more fit tightly together, and within a few hours returned the lamp to the table. The crack was always there, but the lamp was rebuilt, and it served its purpose for years.[3]

Have you been living in fear, guilt, and defeat as you try to hide the broken pieces of your life? If so, I want to say to you: stop hiding and bring your broken life to God. He is ready, willing, and able to rebuild, renew, and restore you with the glue of his grace so that he can use you.

THE RAMIFICATIONS OF OUR WEAKNESSES

How then should we live in light of the fact that God uses weak people?

Sincerity. We should live with sincerity. Remember that in 2 Corinthians Paul is defending himself against an attack that has been launched against him by some would-be leaders in the church of Corinth. The specific issue that Paul seems to concern himself with in this chapter is the accusation of hypocrisy: in verse 2 Paul reminds the Corinthians that he did not handle God's Word shamefully or deceitfully, but he set forth the truth plainly, commending himself to every person's conscience in the sight of God; in verses 3 and 4, he admits that there were those who did not see, but this was only because Satan has blinded the minds of unbelievers; and in verse 5 he asserts his confidence that the truth will be manifested in and through his ministry. He was so sure that this would happen that he never preached himself, never built himself up. He preached Christ, and he felt free to spotlight Christ, not himself, because the God of creation had shone in his heart "to give the light of the knowledge of the glory of God in the face of Jesus Christ." Yes, this treasure was put in earthen vessels, but it is only so that God will get full credit. Paul is saying here that since God uses weak people who possess the sacred treasure of the gospel, he did not have to be deceptive, manipulative, or hypocritical in order to prove his spiritual authenticity or ministerial authority. He needed only to be sincerely open to God's will and God would shine in his heart, and the same is true of us. Thank God we don't have to run around pretending to be something we are not. God uses weak people. If we will only be humble and available, God will work through us, weaknesses and all.

Stewardship. We should live as stewards. The text says, "We *have* this treasure," that is, we possess it, but we don't own it. The treasure is ours by stewardship, not by ownership. The treasure belongs to God. I am merely a trustee of the treasure. This is a very significant thing for me to keep in mind. See, if I am the owner of a thing, then I can do whatever I want to do with it. But if I am just the steward or manager of that thing, then I am accountable to the owner of it, so I must guard the treasure with my life. I see in this text a call to holiness, godliness, purity, discipline, and sanctified living. It says to us that we must avoid living in any way that would cause the worth of the treasure to be diminished or devalued in the eyes of others. This word *earthen* (ostrakinos) in the phrase *earthen vessels* is used only twice in the Greek New Testament, here in 2 Corinthians and also in 2 Timothy. Second Timothy 2:20–21 (NKJV) says,

> But in a great house there are not only vessels of gold and silver, but also of wood and clay, some for honor and some for dishonor. Therefore if anyone cleanses himself from the latter, he will be a vessel for honor, sanctified and useful for the Master, prepared for every good work.

The term *vessel* (skeuos) in *earthen vessel* is also used only twice in the Greek New Testament, here and in 1 Thessalonians 4:4, which says, "Each of you should know how to possess his own vessel in sanctification and honor." Verse 5 of that same chapter goes on to tell us what that means: that we should not live in the passion of lust, like the Gentiles who do not know God. Here is the issue: How are you living? Are you a clean vessel? Can people see God through you? Take note that weakness and wickedness are not the same thing. To say you are weak is to say that you are fragile, limited, and human, but wickedness is when you use your weakness as an excuse to commit sin. God endorses our weaknesses, but not our wickedness. Our lifestyle must not bring down the property value of the gift. You cannot live a cheap life of the world and be a faithful steward of the treasure at the same time. Don't worry about the vessel. Guard the treasure with your heart. God will guard the vessel, if you guard the treasure. Or, as I like to put it, if you take care of God's business, God will take care of your business.

Self-worth. We should live with self-worth. Many, if not most, people in America are not happy with their lives, and unfortunately, the same is true of many people in the church. But this ought not be. The fact that God uses weak people, that he puts his priceless gift in worthless packages, means that you must always view yourself in terms of the treasure within you, rather than external things.

There is an ancient Eastern parable instructively titled, "The Wealth Is Nearer to You than You Think." It tells of a wealthy merchant who had undertaken a lengthy journey, carrying with him his most valuable jewels. Along the way, another traveler befriended him, making it look like a chance meeting but with the sole intent of laying his hands on those precious stones. At the end of each day when they arrived at a local inn, they would share the room for the night. As was customary, each received his mat and pillow, as well as a washbasin with a towel for his nightly wash-ups. The merchant, somewhat suspicious of his newfound friend's motives, devised a scheme to safeguard his valuables that would prove to leave his ill-intentioned companion completely befuddled. Before they turned in for the night, he would graciously offer the would-be thief the privilege of washing up first.

As soon as the thief would leave the room, the rich man would take his bag full of precious stones and hastily hide it—under the pillow of the thief! When the thief would return, the rich man would make his exit, taking his turn at cleaning up. Seizing his moment of opportunity, with almost predatory glee the rogue would plunge into the rich man's belongings, rummaging through his bag, even ransacking it, feverishly searching for the precious stones. His frenzied and fruitless attempts at every stop left him utterly frustrated, and eventually he would lay his sleepless head on his pillow, angry at his failure to locate the treasure. Finally, as it came time to part on their last day together, the rich man began his farewell pleasantries and, to the speechless astonishment of his companion, informed him that all along he had been aware of his true motives. Then came the agonizing revelation: "You poured all your energies into looking everywhere except under your own pillow. The wealth was nearer to you than you realized."[4]

Herein lies a difficult and painful, yet very important, lesson that God wants each of us to learn: it is bad stewardship and shameful ingratitude that cause us to become fixated with what we do not have, rather than appreciating all that we do have in Christ. We must remember that no gift God gives *to* us is greater than the gift that God has placed *within* us. We must remember that, as St. Augustine said, we are not loved because we are lovable, but we are lovable because we are already loved.

THE RESULT OF OUR WEAKNESSES

Paul ends this verse by telling us the spiritual results of God using weak people: "that the excellence of the power may be of God and not of us." Get that: God uses weak people because he wants everyone to see that the power is his, and his alone. This phrase teaches us three things about the sovereign power of God.

Transcendent power. First of all, it teaches us that God's power is transcendent. The term *excellence* translates the Greek word *huperbole*. It is the word from which we get our term *hyperbole*. It is made up of the preposition *huper,* which means "over or beyond," and the verb *ballo,* which means "to throw." They are put together to make the term huperbole, which means "to throw beyond." It denotes superiority, preeminence, and excessiveness. It says to us that God's power is over our head.

Inherent power. Likewise, this phrase teaches us that God's power is inherent. The word translated *power* here is the term *dunamis,* where we get our words *dynamite* and *dynamo*. It means "might," "strength," or "ability." Most important, it speaks of power that is not derived. It speaks of a person or thing that has ability in and of itself. This term is used here to speak of the inherent power of God, that is, God does not need anything or anyone to make him God. God is God all by himself. He is able to perform the desires of his will, whether you say "Amen" or not.

Consistent power. Third, this phrase teaches us that God's power is consistent. The phrase *may be* in the clause is in the present tense, which speaks of continual action. That is, the power is perpetually God's. Hallelujah. You and I have up-days and down-days—God doesn't. His power is eternally consistent. As James 1:17 says, he does not change like shifting shadows.

I submit to you that it is the greatest of sins for us to take credit for what God uses us to do. Isaiah 42:8 (NKJV) says, "I am the LORD, that is My name. And My glory I will not give to another, nor My praise to carved images." Our text gives us one of the ways that God ensures no else will get the glory and praise that rightfully belong to him: "But we have this treasure in earthen vessels, that the excellence of the power may be of God and not of us." You have here some bad news and good news. The bad news is that you are weak, fragile, and limited. But the good news is that God uses weak people, and if you just glory in your weaknesses, God will strengthen you, bless you, and use you. That's why Paul goes on to say in verses 8 and 9, "We are hard-pressed on every side, yet not crushed; we are perplexed, but not in despair; persecuted, but not forsaken; struck down, but not destroyed."

There was a little T-ball player named Bobby. It was his first T-ball game ever, and he was ready because his dad had taught him everything he needed to know—well, almost everything. Bobby walked up to the plate with a swagger that would make Ken Griffey Jr. jealous. And when he swung at the ball, he really let fly. One of his hits sailed into the outfield, sending the opposing team scrambling to retrieve it. Bobby was excited—in fact, he got so excited that he forgot to run. "Bobby! Run!" screamed his coach. The boy looked around, realized time was running out, and took off. In spite of the momentary lapse at home plate, this looked like a sure in-the-park home run.

As Bobby rounded second, his coach cupped his hands over his mouth and yelled, "Now, run home as fast as you can!" So Bobby ran home: after a slight hesitation, he made a sharp left, ran straight across the infield, over the pitcher's mound, and neatly slid home, totally bypassing third base. The other team cheered. Bobby's team groaned. The coach was a study in disbelief. He stood frozen in position with his hands pressed into his forehead. Then, realizing that his player had simply taken him literally at his word, he walked over to home plate to console the bewildered boy.[5] Run home: that may be bad T-ball, but it's great Christianity.

I must tell Jesus all of my trials,
I cannot bear these burdens alone
In my distress he kindly will help me
He ever loves and cares for his own
I must tell Jesus! I must tell Jesus!
I cannot bear my burdens alone.
I must tell Jesus! I must tell Jesus!
Jesus can help me, Jesus alone.

NOTES

1. Adapted from Joshua Harris, *I Kissed Dating Goodbye* (Sisters, Ore.: Mult-nomah, 1988).
2. Warren Wiersbe, *On Being a Servant of God* (Grand Rapids: Baker, 1999).
3. Adapted from Gordon MacDonald, *Rebuilding Your Broken World* (Nashville: Thomas Nelson, 1988).
4. Ravi Zacharias, "Being a Man of the World," in *A Life of Integrity,* ed. Howard Hendricks (Sisters, Ore.: Multnomah, 1997).
5. Adapted from Ron Mehl, *Meeting God at a Dead End* (Sisters, Ore.: Mult-nomah, 1998).

4

Encountering the Text

Sometimes I preach a sermon and think I am finished with it, but the sermon is not finished with me. In such instances I find myself returning to a biblical text over and over again. It is as if the text is saying, "I am not through with you yet." My sermon "Encounters with Jesus from Dying to Life" evolved in this way from Mark 5:21–43. What would ultimately become this sermon initially began as a way to solve an awkward problem in our church calendar.

It turned out that Women's Day and Father's Day were scheduled to fall on the same date, so somehow I had to find a way to speak to both women and fathers. There had been quite a bit of debate among the members of my congregation. Some thought that combining the two celebrations would embarrass the men. They argued that the women should pick another day, in order to give the men proper status. However, most expressed their trust in me to give a sermon that would please everyone.

Discussion heightened in the weeks leading up to that Sunday. People talked about it on their jobs and invited friends to the service. One of the brothers in our church bore the brunt of criticism from a coworker who did not believe in women pastors and saw the scheduling dilemma as proof of it. That a woman pastor would have Women's Day on Father's Day, so the critic contended, meant that she didn't care and that she didn't respect men at all. I certainly did not want to dishonor the men, so I sought to find a way to honor both groups. After saturation with prayer, I came to the verses in chapter five of Mark and saw in them a message for everybody. There was a sermon for women, many of whom were weighed down by the responsibilities of single parenting, low income, and low self-esteem.

There was a sermon for fathers, for here was the anxious father of a dying daughter. I knew that anyone, male or female, could sympathize with this father's story. Anyone could put himself or herself in his shoes and say, "My goodness, look at him, he's an important man and he came to Jesus first." Yet when I initially worked on this text, I simply wanted to deliver a sermon that was successful in speaking to the brothers and the sisters and the husbands and the wives at the same time. At the foundation of my methodology is a theology of partnership, so I wanted to reveal Jesus' response to the bleeding woman and Jairus as one of gender inclusiveness.

When the sermon was over, my congregation was delighted. The man with the hostile coworker was very happy. He expressed how much he wished that this naysayer had been present to see that "our pastor is not like that." He had even invited the coworker to church, although the man did not come. I heard my members repeating, "Our pastor has something to say for everybody." So that was my joy, and I put the sermon on the shelf of my mind, thinking that I was done with it. But sermons have a way of working on you.

I found myself returning to the text in Mark 5—this time developing in more graphic detail the condition of the woman with the issue of blood. From a methodological standpoint, I wanted to address meanings behind words—to talk about the obvious and the not so obvious. This concept of the obvious is important because what we see and take for granted always needs further explanation. It is necessary to pause, reflect upon, and discuss such things. For example, it is obvious that the woman in the text is suffering because she has been bleeding for many years. I decided not to gloss over this fact, but to spell it out so that my listeners would not misunderstand or minimize, in any way, the depth of her agony.

In so doing, I had to speak about matters that are not always considered appropriate to discuss in public, much less in church. I said in the sermon that as a child, I wondered about the issue of blood—and in the course of time I came to understand. I could speak from the experience of being a woman, and so I described the issue of blood by relating it to an incredibly long menstrual period, to the fear of bloodstained clothing, to the effort to hide a foul odor. These are details that are not mentioned in the text, but without them the full meaning of the woman's problem is not really obvious to people.

I knew that some persons might find my candor offensive. For example, my mother is very conservative about most things. She probably would have had serious questions about my talking in such great detail about women's personal matters. This is women's stuff, women's matters. But some of it actually came from her, because I asked her about what sanitary protection was like and what she had to do in her day. If my mother had to go through so much inconvenience, I wondered what in the world the first-century woman had to go through. I had no idea, but I just wanted people to think about some of these things that we have not thought about.

I thought that if I took time in describing the issue of blood to my listeners, then the obvious would become profound. I wanted people to see beyond the words of the text. And so I spoke as graphically as possible—breaking down the bleeding woman's condition into all its implications—so that her obvious anguish could become poignantly real and applicable to today's understandings. We learn from the women in our congregation and women in our lives how often they are taken for granted by the medical establishment. They are told that their problem is in their heads. They spend their money to get proper diagnosis and treatment, often finding out too late what their problem is. This is an outrageous social injustice. We do not know from the text all the details of the bleeding woman's infirmity, but what we do know helps to give insight into what women go through in our own time.

When I preached this sermon at the Women's Communion at the annual meeting of the Progressive National Baptist Convention, the president of the Kentucky women came up to me afterward with her hands in the air and tears in her eyes, proclaiming, "All these years I wondered about this issue of blood, and I wanted to understand. Now I understand the need for the woman preacher." That alone was justification for my ministry. That woman blessed my ministry by saying, "Now I understand."

There are things in the Bible that women can explain in ways that men cannot. And that should be all right. Women in the congregation listen attentively to men preachers give football illustrations and boxing analogies. Surely men can listen and learn about what their wives and daughters go through. Women came to me after the sermon and said, "My husband doesn't understand me, or what I'm going through. He thinks I'm just making it up, but here it is, you told it, you just told it." I knew what the women were saying to me. I had uttered forbidden language. Women weren't supposed to talk like that, but I had dared to be brazen enough to tell their story. It was just wonderful to hear women bless me for speaking the unspeakable. It is hoped that the story of the woman with the issue of blood leads to a better understanding of the social isolation resulting from such illness as HIV/AIDS. If we can relate in any way, sometimes it takes many suggestions and many illustrations before people will get the message, but we just have to keep trying. If we put one illustration out there and then another, maybe the next time somebody will understand.

I returned to the text yet another time and began to feel as though the sermon had taken on a life of its own. I was haunted by the idea that people just don't watch Jesus enough. They watch the rabbis and the rulers, all of these other people, but they don't watch Jesus. I wanted to show how watching Jesus makes a difference in our lives. As a social ethicist, I find this text to be very rich in issues related not only to faith but also to society. In Jesus' day as in our own, a man like Jairus enjoyed status in his community. His office in the synagogue gave him a position above other men, not to mention women.

What is Jesus doing? This is the critical question. I believe that if we would watch Jesus, we would learn a great deal about how to function in our society and in our churches. Preachers often quote Paul on such issues but with too little reference to Jesus. If we would follow the model of Jesus, we would have lessons galore about how we should conduct business in our organizations, in our congregations, and in our families.

When I prepare a sermon, I feel the need to linger in the text, in order to understand it. Mark 5:21–43 is a very popular text, and when you deal with a popular text you have to be careful because people assume that they know it. They have heard it read, they have read it themselves, and they have heard what somebody said it said. I believe that you can't just go with the first thing you think the text says or what somebody says the text says, but that you have to dig in and walk around in the text until it makes absolutely no sense. At the time when the text starts to make no sense at all, that is when you are on to something. Don't leave the text. Jesus is getting ready to show you something, if you will watch. You can't just peek or take a look and run with the text. You have to read closely.

So I began to watch Jesus and to ask questions: What is Jesus doing? Why is Jesus doing this? Jairus is a man, an important person. Since Jairus comes first, why does Jesus take him out of religious and social order to deal with an unnamed woman? In fact, it is quite improper for Jesus to deal with a bleeding woman. This is against societal rules. Nor does Jesus observe the rules that say he must cleanse himself after being touched by a bleeding woman. Why does Jesus knowingly and intentionally go against the rules? I wanted to show clearly what all this meant for women—that Jesus did not treat her the way society treated her. He honored her faith.

Yet I also wanted to capture the importance of the juxtaposition of the unnamed woman with Jairus, for he, too, is desperate. His daughter is dying and he came to Jesus first. What about him? What about his turn? Can you identify with him? I certainly can and on a very personal level. I buried a daughter, so I deeply feel his pain. It was essential to describe the urgency of time, and thus I describe him as stepping all over Jesus' toes and thinking, "Come on Jesus, hurry! Can you get to my house now?" The many questions constitute a key part of my exegetical work. Indeed, this interrogation is a two-way process. As the exegete I bring my questions to the text, and in turn, I am questioned by the text. This is what I mean when I say that I walk around in the text until it makes no sense.

At this point the text has begun to question me, challenging and pushing me to think in new ways. Interrogation is critical to my homiletical and hermeneutical methods, since it also allows me to ask questions for the people in the pews. I try to anticipate questions that they might have, in order for them to get hold of the text, get into it, and participate in it. It is very important to me that my listeners identify with everyone in the text. Asking questions helps to make this happen, since my listeners are seeking to know and understand the answers—to hear and learn what they did not know before.

I also ask questions in order to contrast individuals. In contrast to Jairus, the woman is unnamed. I wanted to make it plain that she is anonymous and untouchable, while he is a man of social standing. I wanted to contrast them because society does so. The woman is a social outcast. Indeed, the disciples often ask Jesus why he stops to talk to particular women—for example, the Samaritan woman at the well. Most of the time Jesus does not answer such questions with his lips, but rather with his actions. This is why we have to watch Jesus and see what he does.

My methodology also depends on narrative, which is the heart of my preaching. I tell stories—that of Jesus, Jairus, and the bleeding woman. As the narrator I make decisions as to what I emphasize and analyze. There are many themes that I could emphasize, but I want to highlight Jesus' discernment of being touched while in a crowd. In the sermon I portray people all around him—brushing against him, pushing, and touching him. Yet I wanted to make a real distinction between this form of touch and a very unique touch.

I was reminded of something that I borrowed from Samuel Proctor, who said, "Jesus didn't ask who bumped me. Jesus didn't ask who bruised me. He asked: 'Who touched my clothes?'" At that moment Proctor communicated to me the profoundness of the touch of faith. Sometimes as preachers, we don't remember where ideas come from, but I have preached a thought I heard from my father when I was a child. Some time later I remember where I heard the thought. Our preaching is informed by ideas that come out of the worshiping community and the secular community.

We bring our memories to our sermons. When I spoke of the woman touching Jesus courageously yet trembling, I remembered an experience I had when I was a Student Nonviolent Coordinating Committee (SNCC) worker in the 1960s. The image that came to me was my standing on the Sasser Road in Georgia in front of a white man who was firing bullets around my feet. I didn't know anything about courage operating in me. I just knew that I was numb, so I didn't move. That I didn't move was probably life saving; had I moved I would have made the man more nervous and given him the excuse that he needed to raise the gun point blank and fire. When I have thought about that experience over the years, I have thought about the old gospel song:

You're standing in the safety zone
Sometimes you have to stand alone,
But if you want to get to heaven, my friend
You've got to stand in the safety zone.

In wanting to convey how different the touch of faith felt from every other touch, I also wanted to tell the woman's story in such a way as to shift the focus onto Jesus, thus moving the narrative from the image of a suffering sister to the image of a sensitive Savior. Jesus has the capacity to hear and to be touched by our suffering. It is this realization that spurs the woman to act courageously. I describe her as trembling when she reaches out to Jesus, knowing that society proscribes her touching him. Something in her recognizes that Jesus is sensitive enough to understand. Probably the woman and Jesus are the only two people in the whole crowd who do understand the courage of her touch. Her touch becomes a form of communication.

Jesus responds, showing that he is not offended by her bleeding. He, too, would bleed as a social outcast. On the cross the blood of Jesus was shed for our eternal life. Jesus reversed death. The sensitivity of Jesus is very precious to me. Why else do we pray? We pray because we have a listening Savior, because we are convinced that the object, the one to whom we pray, is listening. He listens and he understands. This is the whole story of Calvary, that Christ has tasted death and overcome. He interrupts our deathward journey and offers us salvation.

Seeing Jesus as our focal point permits us to see not only that he turns things around but also how he does so. Radical reversals occur not only in Jesus' actions, but also in the narrative structure of the text itself. This is why it is necessary to reveal that Jesus healing the woman is not the text's conclusion. His affirmation and approbation of the bleeding woman are clearly evident in his words: "Daughter, your faith has made you well." But the story cannot end with these words, since we already know from the text that Jesus has yet another daughter to heal—the dying twelve-year-old daughter of Jairus. Although some preachers separate these two stories by disconnecting the text—picking up Jairus somewhere by himself—this text in Mark should not be disconnected. The woman's story is situated in the middle of Jairus's story for a reason.

At first glance, it might appear as if the Gospel writer got sidetracked, but the interruption speaks to how Jesus took the social structure out of order. Indeed, how better to represent this reordering than disturbing the progression of the narrative. The text itself appears out of order. I agree with Brevard S. Childs, who argues in *Introduction to the Old Testament as Scripture* (1979) that there is a reason for the arrangement of a text. In this particular case, it is fascinating how the telling of Jairus's critically important story gets interrupted.

When Jesus stops to address and heal the woman, he knows that Jairus is there alongside him. This is why I accentuated what I thought Jairus must have been thinking: "Hurry, Jesus, hurry." The interruption of the woman permits us to evaluate Jairus's behavior and to learn from him. This is one of the most crucial points of my sermon—that the "encounter between life and death" sets priorities. Indeed, Jesus sets things straight, since the situation of the suffering woman and dying child throw social protocol and religious ritual to the wind. To Jesus, Jairus's stature in the synagogue takes no precedent over the unnamed bleeding woman. Neither he nor Jesus say anything about social and religious conventions. Jairus is not concerned with matters of ritual cleansing; all that matters to him is saving the life of his girl child. What matters is his love for his daughter.

Thus only after responding to the bleeding woman who touched his clothes does Jesus continue on to the household of Jairus. Moreover, Jesus defies the mourners' assertions that it is now too late for the girl. Jesus speaks life into her lifeless body: "Girl, get up." She rises in obedience to the voice of Life. Twice Jesus has reversed death to life.

Today, just as in the past, life and death issues confront our communities. Our task is too great to be slowed down by traditions that prevent women from working as equals with men. Men are not always present to address and solve family and societal problems. When nations go to war, women do work that simply was not allowed before. In times of life and death situations, we throw tradition to the wind. In this story Jesus gives us all the authority to turn things around and save our communities. We have the authority via the example of Jesus. Watching Jesus shows us the appropriate way.

In discussing my methodology, I ultimately realize that the preached sermon and the written sermon are two different phenomena. The black traditions that I draw upon cannot be heard on the printed page. The pronunciation, intonation, rhythm, and sing-song modulations in my voice can only be captured by the voice, not by the mere choice of words. Yet my repetition of certain words and phrases gives greater power and effectiveness to voicing themes of suffering and celebration. This is important to facilitating a "listening" imagination. For example, I call attention to the length of time the bleeding woman suffered by prefacing the various descriptive statements about her condition with the phrase "twelve years."

In the repetition "twelve years" I draw upon resources of the black tradition—verbally, musically, harmonically—which is largely the way our people have expressed their suffering. They come to prayer meeting, and they cry out to God in their own personal and explicit ways, as did their slave foreparents in the spirituals.

We have such a wonderful heritage, and my hope is that we will not lose it. Through the power of the black voice we have maintained the richness of what we already have and what has been passed on to us, in the way our people have communicated. We carry on their voice. We bring the traditions along with us. The preacher I most hear in my own voice is my father, although his was a totally male voice. This has nothing to do with gender, but rather with the passion and pathos my father exhibited when he talked about suffering—the suffering of Jesus and of our people. The sound and style that I heard in my father now comes through me.

When I find a text such as Mark 5:21–43, I am doing more than reading it or reading into it. I am also hearing expressions of suffering. I want very much to use the resources of our tradition, so that the pathos of the suffering sister and frantic father would come out in me and come through me. I praise our black faith traditions, for we as a people have learned a great deal through suffering. Because we knew what we had come through from the days of slavery, we could sing "we shall overcome" in the 1960s. When we learn our past— what we have already come through—then we are empowered with respect to what we must go through to cure the social ills of the twenty-first century.

I end my sermon with words of celebration, applying black vocal expression to "Blessed Assurance" by the blind, white hymn writer Fanny Crosby. Some people might think that there is no methodology when a preacher begins to quote from a hymn, but celebration is an integral part, often the culminating part of a sermon. The celebration picks up themes in the text, the words of the hymn hearkening back to the specific verse in Mark that reads "the woman told Jesus the whole story."

I incorporate celebration into my sermon because it is good news to the people. If we as Christians say that we are carrying the good news of the gospel, then how can we not celebrate? Celebration does not mean that the preacher simply snatches something out of the wind. Good preaching entails thought about every part of the sermon, not just words that make the congregation jump. I sometimes tell my congregation to wait awhile—to listen carefully to the message—so that at the celebration moment of the sermon, we know what we have to be joyful about.

Sermon: Encounters with Jesus from Dying to Life
Mark 5:21–43

PRATHIA L. HALL

Have you ever noticed that when some Christian people look for patterns that instruct personal, family, and even congregational life, they seem to observe everybody in the New Testament except Jesus? They assign tremendous importance to the teachings of Paul, and this is fine. Brother Paul is one of my very best friends.

However, I am perplexed why some Christians cast only cursory glances at Jesus as a model and example for personal, family, and church relations. In so doing they overlook the truly transformative message found in his inter-action with male and female believers. Indeed, Jesus' praxis turned around social and religious norms of his day. Thus I believe that Jesus offers us pro-found wisdom and guidance in the way he conducted his ministry.

In Mark 5:21–43 Jesus provides significant lessons to us as he ministers to a suffering sister, a frantic father, and a dying daughter. The scene of Jesus amidst the crowd is fraught with tension. A synagogue ruler, Jairus, has pressed through the multitude of people to meet Jesus as he steps off the boat. He pleads with Jesus to come home with him and heal his dying daughter. Jesus accepts, and as they press through the ever-growing crowd of people, a woman seeks to lay her own plea on the heart of Jesus. Secretly, cautiously the woman weaves her way through the crowd. She is unnamed in the text.

We are not given the details of her family context. We do not know if she is a single woman or a member of a large family, or whether she lived as a mother or a sister or a cousin or other relative. We can assume only that she is profoundly isolated by her circumstances. Yet she is certainly our sister, because the blood of Jesus makes us all blood relatives. Jairus, on the other hand, is a public figure—a synagogue ruler. He is a father, a family man with a wife and at least one child—a twelve-year-old daughter who is dying. He is the first to meet Jesus in the passage. But let us take a closer look at this unnamed woman, this suffering sister.

While I do not wish to offend any sensibilities regarding appropriate pulpit subject matter, I do not wish us to minimize the suffering of this sister. I might also observe that in the church we often sow seeds that become a harvest of pain because we fail to speak plainly about life, about the facts of life, and certainly about the facts of women's lives. We relegate to backroom whispers, mythology, and mystery subjects that are so much better understood if only allowed the light of day. Having made that preliminary comment or disclaimer, I want to discuss plainly the suffering of the sister in our text.

The Bible tells us that she had been bleeding for twelve years. I remember rather graphically the old King James description of her ailment as "an issue of blood." As a child this was a great mystery to me. I wondered, what in the world was an "issue of blood"! In the fullness of time I came to understand something about her condition. Again, I don't want to offend anybody, but let me ask the sisters here: "Can any of you imagine a twelve-year period?" I don't think so. Indeed, if the monthly flow lasted twelve days, most of us would run quickly to a physician.

Imagine this poor woman's condition—365 days of checking for stains, worrying about overflow, and planning what she would wear based on what was happening in her body. Twelve years times twelve months—that is, 4,380 days of life dominated by bleeding. Twelve years during which time every day was that time of the month. We do not know the specific duration of each hemorrhage, but suffice it to say that the sister had no rest. Twelve months times twelve years of bloating. Twelve years times twelve months of cramps.

Twelve years times twelve months of light-headed weakness. Twelve years times twelve months of fabricating adequate sanitary protection first-century style. Twelve years times twelve months of raging hormones. Twelve years times twelve months of suffering. Now a note to the brothers: A male preacher could not have given you these details of her condition, and if he had you would probably look at him very strangely.

I have described the personal pain, daily discomfort, and utter inconvenience of the sister's suffering. There is yet another side. She had spent herself into poverty trying to get well. According to the text, she had endured tremendous frustration under several physicians. Can you imagine twelve years of doctors taking your money and telling you it's all in your head? I suspect the doctors might have told her after the first year that they could not help her. After she spends all that she has and is no better, they tell her that she is beyond medical help. In pain and in poverty, she has been grossly inconvenienced, and she is dying!

Her case is terminal. For twelve long years life has been draining from her body, drop by drop by drop. Perhaps she suffered from uterine cancer. We do not know. Her disease was like other devastating diseases, for example, breast cancer for women and prostate cancer for men. When that which has defined our sexual identity turns against us, our body becomes our own enemy. How long can a person linger, losing life daily in dripping blood? Deathly ill, drained of her strength, poor, and in pain, this is a suffering sister.

And what does the community do for her? Does it take her in and minister to her? Absolutely not. The community labels her ritually unclean. She is ostracized. Any man who is bumped or tapped by her is considered contaminated. He must remove himself from the community and subject himself to ritual washing before reentry. This woman whose body and soul are bleeding is utterly isolated by her religious community. But she heard about Jesus. She joined that multitude of persons with crippled limbs and crippled lives who heard about Jesus. She pushed through the crowd that pressed in upon him, compelled to seize the initiative and take her desperate need to Jesus.

This woman with the "issue of blood" knew the rabbinical codes all too well. She knew what the law required. She did not want to subject Jesus to the inconvenience of ritual cleansing. Nor did she want to call attention to herself, already bowed down by sickness, weakness, neediness, and pain. She reasoned to herself, "I will sneak up behind him, for if I can touch even his clothes, I will get well." Some view her statement of faith as a superstitious belief in magic clothes. But they have not walked in her sandals. Surreptitiously, she crept up behind him and touched his cloak.

In the very instant when she felt her bleeding stop, Jesus felt the touch of faith. He asked, "Who touched my clothes?" Now the disciples thought his question to be rather ridiculous. Perhaps they wondered if the heat had gotten to him, or if he was, as we sometimes say in the African American community, "a little touched in the head." With a sea of people pushing, pressing, bumping, and bruising, why would Jesus ask who touched him? Oh, if only I could explain the anatomy of a touch, but I cannot do it. Preachers often cannot do what they wish they could, but Jesus is very clear about what happened. I remember hearing the great preacher Samuel Proctor capture how Jesus must have responded to the disciples: "I did not ask who pushed me. I did not ask who pressed me. I did not ask who bumped me. I asked who touched my clothes!"

Jesus recognized the touch of faith. Although the curious as well as the needy were bumping into his body, the touch of faith felt very different. Faith transformed the moment from an incident into an event. In that very instant, there was a transfixing transfer from a suffering sister to a sensitive Savior— from the body of a bleeding woman to the source of Gilead's balm, from her weak and dying body to that body which soon would be broken, bloodied, and bruised for hers and our salvation.

No wonder Jesus related to women so differently. He was neither queasy nor offended by the fountain of her blood. After all, "there is a fountain filled with blood, drawn from Emmanuel's veins, and sinners plunged beneath that flood, lose all their guilty stains." Her fountain of seemingly endless, painful, foul-smelling flow dried up, because she touched his clothes. Her touch went straight to his own healing fountain. He felt the power flow from himself to the woman. "Who touched my clothes?"

Courageously, she trembled. Courage often trembles. It really isn't courage until you are sure 'nuf, no-doubt-about-it scared. She knelt down before him and told him the whole story. She told him the truth. "Lord, my life was so hard." She had begun to wonder in the words of the old spiritual, "'Lord, how come me here?' I wish I'd never been born. Twelve long years, Lord. Twelve long years of bleeding. Twelve long years of hiding. Twelve long years of doctors. Twelve long years of frustration. Twelve long years of disappointment. Twelve long years of wretchedness. Twelve long years of grief. Twelve long years of living death." And he who had already healed her, now presented to her much more than a healed body: "Daughter, your faith has made you well." Now that's affirmation. What greater gift can be given to one who has been negated continuously for twelve long years? Indeed the very fact that she was a woman meant that she belonged to a negated group. But watch Jesus closely. He affirms her faith, but he does not stop there.

He gives holistic healing—wellness of body, mind, and spirit. Yet he has even more for her. Jesus grants to her Shalom: "Go in peace, be cured, be healed, be well, be free. Let no one negate you, let no one abuse you, let no one demean you, let no one degrade you, let no one defraud you. I give you wellness and wholeness in your womanhood. I give you peace. You are restored to your community." I wonder what it was like to return to her community, clean, whole, well, and to be known as the woman whose faith had been affirmed by Jesus.

Sisters and brothers, the story does not end here. The conclusion of this story is not what she told Jesus, but what Jesus told her. Throughout these two thousand years we have been told what women can and cannot do based on what this or that person said. Rarely have those who set the rules consulted Jesus. When they have even bothered to glance in his direction, they argue that there can be no women pastors and priests because there were no women among the twelve disciples. Yet this argument is absurd; there were no Gentiles among the twelve either. By that reasoning, we would disqualify just about every male in the pulpit today. The real problem of these gatekeepers is that they have not watched Jesus closely enough. Let us not leave our sister and her story without closely watching Jesus. It was the very nature of Jesus to engage in profoundly consequential reversals. He turned stuff around. If it was upside down, he set it right side up. The very purpose of his sojourn on earth was to reverse the death process—to give us eternal life, if we would but believe in him.

Jesus reversed the course of death, but more than this is turned around in our text. Remember, the woman's story actually interrupts Mark's telling of Jairus's story. Jairus met Jesus before the woman. Not only did he get to Jesus first, but the very structure of the society required that he be served first. The woman interrupts Jesus while he is on his way to Jairus's home, to Jairus's dying daughter. At the most fundamental level, his maleness alone would have qualified him for priority status. More than this, he was an important man, a ruler of the synagogue. But keep your eyes on Jesus.

Jesus could have kept walking after the bleeding woman touched him. She was already healed, and surely Jesus could walk and heal at the same time. He could have healed her and still avoided delay. But will you just look at Jesus. He stops cold in his tracks and insists that his question be answered: "Who touched my clothes?" Jesus' actions rejected society's protocol. He gives immediate personal attention to the weakened, trembling, bleeding woman. And also remember, her bleeding makes her unclean in that society. Does Jesus offer one word of rebuke to her about having contaminated him? Does he move one step toward ritual purification? He does not say one mumbling word about any of that. No, he pauses to commend her faith and to grant her salvation and Shalom.

The order of service here is intentional and significant. Mark's account of it only heightens the tension in the text. From a stylistic perspective Mark could have chosen to present Jairus's story in full, returning only afterward to the woman's story. However, Mark chose to remain faithful to the actual order of events, thereby honoring the way of Jesus. Jesus interrupted and reversed the status quo in order to restore a dying woman. He stopped and asked, "Who touched my clothes?" and with that question radically repudiated the social structure that would silence the woman's voice and the telling of her story. When in doubt, watch Jesus.

But what about this frantic father? Can you just stand there a moment with Jairus? His daughter is dying. He loves his child. He too had heard about Jesus. Faith sent him to seek out Jesus for swift healing mercies. Now instead of continuing with haste to his child, Jesus stops and makes an issue about a woman's touch. Oh, I can imagine the sweat pouring from Jairus's face—fear creeping into his throat, despair entering into his stomach when he learns that the woman has touched Jesus' clothes.

I can see Jairus tripping all over his feet. His plea is inaudible, but can't you feel his anguish and hear what he must have been thinking? "Hurry, hurry

Jesus." Although a synagogue leader, Jairus does not remind Jesus that he has been made unclean. He is an anxious father, urgently in need of a lifesaving miracle for his daughter. That will give you an order of priority all right. However, the neighbors come with heartbreaking news. They tell Jairus to forget about Jesus, saying, "Your daughter has died." Jairus's heart sinks beneath his feet. If only Jesus had gotten there to lay his hands on his child. Jesus looks at Jairus calmly and tells him essentially, "Do not fear. Be cool. Just believe, don't panic, Jairus, just believe." So Jairus falls in line behind Jesus. They arrive at his house. Jesus dismisses the crowd, and in the presence of her parents tells the child to get up. She does. He then orders that she be fed. Twice that day, Jesus reverses death.

Moreover, it is significant that he has earlier used the word "daughter" when addressing the woman with the issue of blood. It graphically illustrates that he who has healed one daughter, who has been dying for twelve years, is able to heal another daughter who has been living for twelve years. Whether it is slow, protracted, living death, or the snatching of a child far too soon, Jesus can and does deal with death.

In the end, this text tells us as much about Jesus in turning around societal norms as it does about his turning around death. The two issues are inseparably linked. So sisters, when culture and conditions require you to crawl, be they medical, social, or the religious gender games of the church, you take your burdens to Jesus and return affirmed, healed, and whole. When gatekeepers claim that your gender disqualifies you from this role or that role, tell them to look at Jesus. Until they do, they do not have the whole story.

And brothers, you go tell the brothers, when Jesus stops by and reverses longstanding socially and ecclesially accepted ways of doing things, don't panic. Just believe. Jesus has blessings abundant for everybody. When God tells you to wait, brethren, or even to step aside for a moment, you do not lose. When God calls you to share power and position, it's all right! It is really all right! God has something better for all of us. We can join hands with this healed sister, and we can celebrate with the father whose daughter is restored to life.

For this hour in our society, we have many dying children whom we must raise in the name of Jesus. Keep your eyes on Jesus. This is why Jesus often put the crowd out, but kept the disciples in. The disciples were to watch and listen and learn from his actions. The disciples were to learn that they should heal and raise the dead in the name of Jesus. So let us keep our eyes on Jesus, for he specializes in radical reversals. He not only repudiates physical and spiritual death, he turns around the social structures of death. Let us watch Jesus and turn our world right side up.

Let us turn around police abuse, child abuse, brutality against women, and brutality against men. Turn around homophobia and xenophobia. Turn around sexism, classism, ageism, and colorism in the African American church and the African American community. Let us turn our world right side up. Then we can join both the wonderful unnamed woman and Jairus. They came to Jesus with a story about death and left with a brand-new story of life—a first-century version of a brand-new song.

> Blessed assurance, Jesus is mine,
> Oh what a foretaste of glory divine.
> Heir of salvation, purchase of God,
> Born of his spirit, washed in his blood.
> This is my story, this is my song,
> Praising my savior, all the day long.

This is my story. This is my story. This is the whole story, hallelujah. Let Jesus turn your encounter with death into life. Keep your eyes on Jesus. Turn things around in his name, by his word, and with his power. Turn our community right side up and make sure you never take your eyes off Jesus. Watch him. Watch him. Keep your eyes on Jesus. Amen.

5

Enabling the Word to Happen

ZAN HOLMES

My method of sermon preparation is primarily shaped by my understanding of the preacher's task. Accordingly, I believe that the major task of the preacher is to enable the Word of God to *happen again* for the preacher and the congregation.

The German preacher-scholar Helmut Thielicke shares the experience of holding his grandbaby before a mirror. When his grandbaby saw the reflected image of himself for the first time, he cried out, "Hey, that's me!" Likewise, I believe that the Word of God happens again for the preacher and the congregation when the preacher lifts up the mirror of God's Word in such a way that both the preacher and congregation are moved to exclaim, "Hey, that's me!"

Also, I believe that if the Word of God does not first of all "happen again" to the preacher, it "may" not happen again for the congregation. Now I must admit that earlier in my preaching ministry I used to think that the Word of God *would not* happen again for the congregation if it did not happen again first to the preacher. However, I confess that since then I have preached some sermons in which the Word of God did not happen again first to me.

Indeed, during those preaching moments I have said to myself, "Surely this sermon will not get off the ground and take flight for anyone's benefit." And yet in spite of my feeble offering on those occasions, some members of the congregation have given me surprising feedback which confirmed that the Word of God did happen again for them! And on those humbling occasions I was reminded that God's grace can enable the sermon to happen again to the congregation in spite of the fact that it did not happen again to the preacher.

So now I am careful to say that the Word of God *may* not happen again if it does not first happen again for the preacher. But I believe that the preacher

74

can make it easier for the Word of God to happen again to the whole congregation if the Word happens again first to the preacher.

Hence, my sermon-preparation method is driven by a process that is designed to invite the Word of God to first of all happen again to me. In other words, I do not believe that much can happen *through* me unless it first of all happens to me!

A few years ago I was eating in a restaurant in Corpus Christi, Texas. I noticed that the man sitting at the table next to me was eating from several dishes of food, whereas I was only eating from one dish. I asked him what he had ordered, and he said that he was tasting everything on the menu. I asked him why he was getting such special treatment. He smiled and said, "I'm in training to be a waiter and I must taste everything on the menu because I can't recommend it to the customers unless I have tasted it first." Likewise, we preachers cannot authentically recommend the items on God's menu to our congregations unless we have tasted them first. The Psalmist said, "O taste and see that the LORD is good" (Ps. 34:8, NRSV).

Therefore, in my desire for the Word of God to happen first to me, my sermon-preparation method begins with a period of prayer and devotion that is focused on the biblical text. I must confess that there was a time in my preaching ministry in which it was difficult for me to read the Bible devotionally. I was so enslaved to the "profession of preaching" that every time I picked up the Bible and read it I was looking for a sermon. I was only using the Bible as a tool of my trade! I was not looking for a Word for the preacher; I was only looking for a Word for the congregation. To be sure, my sermons during that time were finger-pointing sermons that were loaded with "you" language and not much "we" language that included the preacher.

But now I have learned the value of beginning my sermon preparation with a period of prayer and devotions as I sit before the biblical text. I thank God for the text. I thank God for the privilege of proclaiming the text. I then become engaged in a process that I hope will enable the biblical text to happen again to me. I earnestly seek to be convicted by the biblical text. Indeed, I identify with the sermon-preparation method of the slave preacher John Jasper, who said, "First, I read my Bible until a text gets hold of me. Then, I go down to the James River and walk in it. Then, I get into my pulpit and preach it out" (Richard Elsworth Day, *Rhapsody in Black: The Life Story of John Jasper* [Valley Forge, Penn.: Judson Press, 1976], 116).

So the first question that I have learned to ask is, "Lord, what are you saying to me in this text?" However, before I can get the answer to this question I find it necessary to exegete myself before I exegete the text. In other words, I must honestly confront and confess the biases I bring to the text. For example, in what ways do I approach the text with a made-up mind because I am bound by the traditional ways I have preached or heard the text preached in the past? To preach the text faithfully, I must be open to hear the new things that God may be saying to me through the text.

This is one of the reasons that I have accepted the challenge of preaching from the common lectionary. In the earlier years of my preaching I had very much opposed lectionary preaching. I had simply used my own pet texts, which were limited, very limited, and my favorite themes. I began to realize that not only was I limiting my own encounter with Jesus in the Bible, I was depriving my congregation of the fullness offered by a systematic approach to the multiple themes of the Bible and the Christian faith.

In fact, during this time I was team-teaching a course in preaching with a colleague, Virgil Howard, at Perkins School of Theology, where we gave standard lectures on the lectionary each year. He gave a lecture on the advantages of preaching from the lectionary, and I, of course, gave the lecture on the disadvantages of preaching from the lectionary. My standard line was, "Lectionary preaching robs the freedom of the Holy Spirit to move in the selection of sermon texts."

Nevertheless, I accepted the challenge of preaching from the lectionary in connection with a Bible study program in my congregation. But even then I vowed not to become a slave to it. But since I have started using it, to my surprise, I have seldom been moved by the Holy Spirit to stray from it. Even on special Sundays such as Martin Luther King Sunday, I have found a Word there that inspired me to preach a relevant Word, even if it came from one of the so-called hard texts. But regardless of how we preachers choose our texts for preaching, we are challenged to move beyond our biases to enable the sermon text to first happen again to us.

I like to begin the formal exegesis of the sermon text without the use of commentaries for fear that they may inhibit my own insights. When I do finally use them, I seek commentaries that will provide for theological, ethnic, and gender diversity. Indeed, I am aware of the fact that most Bible commentaries are written by white, Anglo-Saxon males. I am also aware of the fact that modern biblical scholarship is being enriched by the published insights of African, African American, Native American, Hispanic, and Asian men and women, Anglo women, and others.

Surely, no preacher's library can be complete in today's multicultural world without the works of these witnesses.

However, prior to any reference to the commentaries, I find it helpful to read the sermon text from several Bible translations. I have also learned the value of addressing some selected questions to the sermon text. For example: Which way is God moving in the text? Does God support the status quo? Or is God calling for a change? Who has the power in the text? Who are the powerless? How do they relate to one another? What emotions does the text call up in me? Does it call up joy, anger, fear, guilt, love, or some other emotion?

My exegesis of the sermon text is also informed by a favorite exercise of trying on all of the characters for size. This exercise is critical because it is tempting and easier for me to identify with the so-called good people in the text. But it is not so easy for us to identify with the so-called bad people in the text. For example, I recall preaching a sermon on the Exodus experience to my predominately black congregation. I said that God calls us like Moses to be agents of liberation who will say to modern-day Pharaohs, "Let my people go." Upon hearing this, my congregation responded with hearty amens!

But then, as I continued I said that we are also like Pharaoh when we cooperate in our own oppression and treat each other like modern-day Pharaohs treat us. I got few, if any, amens from my congregation. They were more accustomed to identifying with Moses than Pharaoh. But chances are the text will not really happen again for us unless we do the radical and unaccustomed thing and try on all the characters for size.

The next step in my process of sermon preparation is to exegete the world that is to be addressed by the Word. To be sure, I believe that preaching that starts off in the Bible, wanders around in the Bible, and ends up in the Bible is not biblical preaching! The Bible was not written in a vacuum! Every word in the Bible was addressed to some particular human situation. Therefore, it is not only important for the preacher to exegete and understand the Word of God, it is equally important for the preacher to exegete and understand the human situation in the world that is addressed by the Word of God.

Gardner Taylor reminds us that we must walk up and down the street on which the text lives. Karl Barth reminds us that we must prepare to preach with the Bible in one hand and the newspaper in the other hand. One of the helpful ways that I exegete the human situation in the world is to practice a process that I describe as "stacking my gallery." It is a process that I discovered while I was a guest preacher at a particular church one Sunday morning. As I met with the pastor in his office prior to the worship service, I noticed a large number of photographs of men on a wall behind his desk. I asked him who they were. He told me that they represented his "gallery of preachers." He said that they were the pictures of the preachers and teachers that he most admired and respected. He said that when he prepared his sermons he was inspired and challenged by the thought that they were looking over his shoulders to keep him honest.

I thought it was a helpful practice. So I have adopted a gallery of people to look over my shoulders to help keep me honest as I prepare my sermons. However, I decided to stack my gallery. Thus, included in my gallery are my favorite female preachers and theologians along with my favorite male preachers and theologians. In fact, I have stacked my gallery to also include my not-so-favorite preachers and theologians with whom I often disagree. For I want them looking over my shoulders to ensure that I accurately represent their viewpoints when I disagree with them.

I include the members of my congregation of all age levels and differing viewpoints. I include persons of all races, political persuasions, and sexual orientations in my gallery. I intentionally stack my gallery to include people who may not be present as well as those who are present most of the time. Indeed, I believe that I am not only called to preach on behalf of those who are present, but I am also called to preach on behalf of those who are not present. To be sure, I believe that if I don't preach on behalf of those who are not present, chances are that they will never come. Indeed I praise God that the gospel we preach is not for insiders only!

After engaging the biblical text (the Word) and the human situation (the world) and enabling them to enter into dialogue with one another, the next step in my sermon-preparation process is to write a *one-sentence* sermon that is a declarative statement of the good news of the gospel. For me this is one of the most difficult and challenging steps in the sermon-preparation process. By the same token, it is one of the most rewarding steps for the sake of the sermon. It helps me to be clear and focused about the one central idea and theme to be presented in the sermon. Thus it protects me from the ever-present temptation to pursue more than one major idea in the same sermon.

The sermon sentence also helps me to select a sermon title that is relevant to the text. My sermon titles are always in the form of a question. I have discovered that titles with questions are more engaging for the congregation because they invite the congregation to think and participate with me as we seek to arrive at an answer to the question. In fact, I always begin my sermons by asking the congregation to repeat the question after I have announced it. I also ask the congregation to address the question to the persons sitting on each side of them. Finally, I ask the congregation to address the question to me. Indeed, this is another way in which I seek to remind the congregation and myself that I expect the Word of God to "happen again" for me as well as the congregation.

Once the sermon sentence is developed, I turn to the task of selecting the support material that is necessary to communicate the sermon. Of course, I am collecting support material all the time. The support material for the sermon is the nitty-gritty stuff of life that we encounter in our daily living. It is the stuff that we encounter within ourselves and in others. It is the kind of stuff we encounter in the continuing struggle for justice and liberation. It is the stuff that we encounter in our exegesis of the biblical Word and the world. It is the stuff we encounter in the political, social, economic, and spiritual issues that affect our congregation and community.

However, in my case I find that most of this stuff will escape me if I do not systematically collect it for my sermon support material. Therefore, I maintain a scrapbook and file for support material that I collect on a daily basis. Now I must confess that my system for collecting support material is not the most elaborate and sophisticated one. I usually place newspaper clippings in a large box under my desk. Thus I often have a hard time finding the particular clipping I'm looking for, but I know for sure it's in that box! Furthermore, often in my search I will come across another one that is more appropriate.

It is at this point that I usually begin to give some careful thought to the structure of the sermon. I am careful not to place a structural outline on the sermon too early for fear that my thinking will be captive to the perimeters of a preconceived outline. Instead, in the early stages of the sermon-preparation process I want a liberated mind that is open to explore the many possible sermon ideas and insights that may be available in the text.

In selecting the sermon outline or shape, I am more concerned about how the sermon moves. I always decide whether I want the sermon to move deductively or inductively. Deductive movement is when I reveal the main truth of the sermon in the introduction and then use the remainder of the sermon to explain how the biblical text supports that truth. Inductive movement is when I do not reveal the truth of the sermon in the introduction but keep the congregation guessing while I invite them to join me on a journey in which I lead them into the discovery of the truth for themselves. I know this form of sermon movement is successful when someone in the congregation will finally say, "Now I see where you're going!"

But whether I choose deductive movement or inductive movement, I always want each movement to be informed and directed by what I call "celebrative movement." Celebrative movement is employed when the sermon slowly builds and ascends to its highest point of celebration. Perhaps it is best expressed in the familiar saying of the African American preaching tradition: "Go slow, rise high, strike fire, and sit down!"

The next step in my sermon-preparation process is the writing of the sermon manuscript. I am a morning person, so I do most of my sermon work during the first hours of the day. I begin each day with a time of personal devotions. Then I engage in sermon work. I do most of my exegetical work on Monday and Tuesday. On Wednesday and Thursday I am working with the sermon sentence and the gathering of support material. Actually, I am doing some writing each day. But on Friday morning I devote a full day to a formal writing of the full sermon manuscript. Even though I am able to preach without the manuscript and do not rely fully on it during the preaching of the sermon, I strongly embrace the practice of writing the full manuscript as a vital step in sermon development.

In writing the sermon manuscript I have learned the important difference between writing for the ear and writing for the eye. For example, I write for the eye if I am writing the sermon to be read. In writing for the eye I have the luxury of writing long and complicated sentences because the reader can see the sentence and review it, if necessary, for clarity. However, this is a luxury that the worshiping congregation does not have because the preaching event is an oral happening. Therefore, my sermon manuscript is an exercise in oral writing in which I am writing for the ear.

I have gladly found that the best way to write for the ear is to *talk* the words onto the paper. In this way the words are tested on my ear, and I write them when I am convinced that they sound right and can be effectively heard in the language of my congregation. Furthermore, writing the manuscript is a rewarding discipline that keeps me on track and helps me to be precise in my selection of words. By the same token I clearly understand that the sermon manuscript is *not* the sermon. Instead, it is a *step on the way* to the sermon. The actual sermon is all that takes place in the actual preaching moment, including the inspiration of the Holy Spirit.

Before final completion of the sermon manuscript, I test it with the following vital questions: Is it faithful to the biblical text and the contemporary human situation? Is it cross-shaped? In other words, I don't ever want to be guilty of preaching cheap grace! I want to be sure that I am preaching both the gift and demand of a liberating Savior who said, "Come take up your cross and follow me."

Is it pastoral and prophetic? Does it contribute to the process of human liberation from sin and oppression? I want to reflect the spirit of Jesus, who said upon the occasion of his first sermon, "The spirit of the Lord is upon me, because he has anointed me to bring good news to the poor. He has sent me to proclaim release to the captives and recovery of sight to the blind, to let the oppressed go free, to proclaim the year of the Lord's favor" (Luke 4:18–20, NRSV). Is the resurrecting good news of a brand-new future celebrated? Does it extend an invitation to Christian discipleship? Does it reveal any evidence that the biblical text has happened again, first of all to the preacher?

Once I am convinced that the sermon manuscript has passed the above test questions, I will put it down and usually will not pick it up again until very early on Sunday morning. I want to give it some breathing room. I have been working on it all week. Now I want to give it an opportunity to work on me. Often when I pick it up on Sunday morning for a careful rereading, some fresh and valuable insights may come that require some additions and deletions.

When the time for worship comes, I enter the sanctuary along with the choir and the other participants in the worship service. I love to worship! Indeed, I participate fully in every act of worship because I believe that preaching is done in the context of worship. In fact, I believe that the Call to Worship is the proper introduction to the sermon and that every other act of worship should be planned and coordinated in relationship to the biblical text to be proclaimed. This is why I meet regularly with the worship ministry of the church to plan the total worship service. I believe that the burden of preaching and worship was never meant to be borne by the preacher alone.

To be sure, I believe that what P. T. Forsyth suggested long ago is still a word to us all: "The one great preacher in history is the church and the first business of the individual preacher is to enable the church to preach" (P. T. Forsyth, *Positive Preaching and the Modern Mind* [New York: Hodder and Stoughton, 1907], 53). This is an insight that is truly confirmed by the black church worshiping and preaching tradition. Through the power of the Holy Spirit, the authentic black worshiping congregation functions as a worshiping and preaching fellowship that uses all of its resources to hold the preacher up and help the preacher in the preaching event.

How well do I remember this! To be sure, I had to learn this the hard way on the occasion of the very first sermon I preached. I was a student in seminary, and I was doing my field work with the late I. B. Loud at St. Paul United Methodist Church in Dallas, Texas. One Sunday morning as we were all standing to sing the hymn of preparation, Loud turned to me and said, "Okay, son, it's yours this morning!"

I was terrified. I had never preached a sermon in my life! I do not remember how I got to the pulpit, but the Holy Spirit must have gotten me there. I was taking a course in preaching, and I suddenly remembered that I had started writing a Lenten sermon on the experience of Jesus in the Garden of Gethsemane. Talking about identifying with Jesus. I had no problem whatsoever! Indeed, I prayed the prayer Jesus prayed when he said, "Father, if thou be willing, remove this cup from me!" But God, being God, just as God was with Jesus, refused to move the cup!

So I started out preaching, haunted by the fact that I had not written a conclusion to the sermon. Well, I got as far as I had written and my mind went blank! But what was more troubling is the fact that I couldn't move! I was petrified. I was embarrassed. I looked at my wife. She was crying! I became angry with God for calling me to preach! I became angry with myself for accepting the call. I became angry with Loud for his impromptu insistence that I preach on this occasion.

But then as I was about to vent my anger on the congregation, a little old lady stood and said, "Help him, Jesus!" Then another dear saint of the church said, "Yes Lord!" Next I heard a male voice from the choir loft saying, "Come, Holy Spirit." Then the people in the congregation began to moan. Some began to shout! Little children sitting on the front pew began to clap hands.

And all of a sudden the entire congregation rose to their feet with shouts of praise and thanksgiving.

Through the prompting of the Holy Spirit that *worshiping and preaching congregation* provided the conclusion to my sermon! Indeed, in that very moment when I was at my preaching worst, that beloved congregation was at its worshiping and preaching best! Indeed, I am so glad that when the Holy Spirit did release me from my petrified state of being I had enough sense not to say another word! I simply turned around, walked to my seat, and sat down. And when I did I became caught up with the congregation in the highest moment of praise and celebration, which continued after I sat down. The Word of God was joyfully happening to the congregation and the preacher!

When I look back, I truly thank God for the preaching lesson of that occasion. Through it all God taught me that I must always remember that I never preach alone. God taught me that I am always accompanied by the power of God's Holy Spirit and the supportive presence of God's worshiping and preaching congregation. God taught me that I can never provide the official conclusion to any sermon. To be sure, I now know that a sermon is never concluded until the preached Word of God happens again to the preacher and the congregation and bears some good fruit in the continuing struggle for salvation, liberation, and justice.

Sermon: Are We for Real?
John 13:34

ZAN HOLMES

> I give you a new commandment, that you love one another. Just as I
> have loved you, you also should love one another. By this everyone will
> know that you are my disciples, if you have love for one another. (NRSV)

Several years ago, I attended a national church meeting in Boston. While I
was there I ran into a friend of mine who had just returned from his very first
trip to Japan. Quite obviously, he was excited about many things that he
had experienced in Japan. But he was particularly excited about the fact that
he had purchased a very expensive $6,000 Rolex watch for the bargain-
basement price of $25!

In fact, as he flashed it before me, I first became envious and then upset
that he had not purchased one for me, since we were supposed to be such
good friends. But later on in one of the sessions of the convention, he and I
sat next to each other. As the session began, we stood to sing a very lively
gospel song. And as we rejoiced and clapped our hands to the beat of the
song, I noticed that a piece of something fell from his arm. Indeed, upon
closer examination, I noticed that it was a piece of his bargain-basement
Rolex watch!

As my friend stooped down to pick up the broken piece, his eyes met
mine. Without any exchange of words at all, we both knew that his bargain-
basement Rolex watch was not for real. Instead, it was nothing more than a
cheap imitation. You see, it was attractive, but it was not authentic. It was
glittering, but it was not genuine. It was pretty, but it was not pure. It was
fashionable, but it was not functioning. It was stylish, but it was not sound.
It was ticking, but it was not true. It was running, but it was not real. Indeed,
he had been sold a false bill of goods.

To be sure, this incident is a reminder to us that we the church are called to witness and to make disciples for Jesus Christ in a society in which so many people have been sold a false bill of goods. In fact, a recent poll revealed that many people say they believe in God, but they are suspicious of organized religion. This is especially the case among the poor and the oppressed. This skepticism is reenforced by the fact that we live in a society in which it is difficult to tell the real from the unreal. In fact, I once saw a woman watering artificial flowers in a shopping mall. Our culture is fascinated with its look-alike contests. The late comedian Groucho Marx said that he once entered a Groucho Marx look-alike contest and came in third. In the eyes of the judges, somebody else looked more like Groucho Marx than he did himself.

Therefore, in a society in which it is often difficult to tell the real from the unreal, we should not be surprised that many people are suspicious of us and are quick to ask the question, "Are you for real?"

They hear our pious platitudes. They see our pretty processions. They read about our promotional programs. They take notice of our prophetic pronouncements. They are impressed with our professional preparation. But they don't care how much we know until they know how much we genuinely care. Deep down within they want to know if our deeds match up with our creeds. They want to know if our love service matches up with our lip service. They not only want to know if we can talk the talk, they want to know if we can also walk the walk.

Indeed, such suspicious people who have been sold a false bill of goods are looking for the real thing. I am reminded of the young man who was seen leaving a church before the worship service was over. An usher said to him, "Are you leaving the church?" He said, "No I am not leaving the church; I'm looking for it."

Now please note that this is not a new challenge for the people of God. Indeed, it was the same challenge that faced Jesus and the disciples in the thirteenth chapter of John's Gospel. Here we find Jesus in the upper room where he was preparing to share the Passover meal with the disciples. To be sure, it was a critical and challenging time because he knew that he would soon be leaving them and that they could no longer depend on his physical presence as their badge of identification.

Likewise, Jesus knew that his disciples would be faced with a suspicious society who had been sold a false bill of goods and would want to know if the disciples were for real, or whether they were nothing more than another cheap imitation.

In fact, Jesus himself was not exempt from the suspicious questions of those who were looking for the real thing. You remember, we are told in chapter 11 of Matthew's Gospel that even John the Baptist, the cousin of Jesus, became so suspicious of Jesus that he sent some of his followers to Jesus and had them ask Jesus, "Are you the one who is to come, or shall we look for another?" In other words, John was asking Jesus, "Are you for real?" Now please notice that Jesus did not try to escape the question. Indeed, Jesus had to deal with the question because he knew it was a legitimate one. So he said to the followers of John: You go and tell John what you see and hear. Tell him the blind receive their sight. Tell John the lame walk. Tell John the lepers are cleansed, the deaf hear, the dead are raised, and the poor have good news brought to them, and blessed is anyone who takes no offense at me.

So Jesus knew that if suspicious people who had been sold a false bill of goods dared to ask him, "Are you for real?" surely his disciples would not be exempt from the same question. Therefore, Jesus wanted to help the disciples "get real." Indeed, he wanted to give them a badge of identification that would clearly identify them as his disciples, and let every suspicious person know that they were truly for real.

But please note that Jesus did not say to them that suspicious people would know that they were for real by what they said. Nor did he say that suspicious people would know that they were for real by how they dressed. Or by what they knew. Or by their religious affiliation. Or by how they sing or shout. Or by their oratorical skills. Or by their degrees. Or by their color. Or by their social standing in the community.

Instead, Jesus said, "By this everyone will know that you are my disciples, if you have love for one another." Now it is important to note that this love command is not new in the sense that it was given for the first time. In fact, in Leviticus 19:18 (NRSV) the law of Israel had long since required love from the Jews: "You shall love your neighbor as yourself." But in our "get real" moments we know that it is difficult for us to love one another, even within the church!

We are not always lovable because we have all sinned and fallen short of the glory of God. Therefore, Jesus knows that we need some divine help if we are to obey the command to love one another. Indeed, that is precisely why the newness of the command given by Jesus is that his disciples were required to have the same kind of love for one another that Jesus first of all had for them. Jesus said, "I give you a new commandment, that you love one another. Just as I have loved you, you also should love one another" (John 13:34, NRSV). "Just as I have loved you" is the enabling act of this new commandment.

You see, Jesus knows that his love cannot happen through us unless it first of all happens to us—until we have first experienced what it means to be loved. First John 4:19 (NRSV) says, "We love because he first loved us." Albert Outler, my former colleague at Perkins School of Theology, often said, "We must stop telling ourselves and others that we must love one another.

Instead, we must tell ourselves and others that we can love ourselves and others because we are loved by Jesus!"

Famous plastic surgeon Maxwell Maltz, has written a book called *Dr. Pygmalion* (Kent, England: Pond View Books, 1958) in which he tells a story that gives us an example of the kind of liberating love that Jesus has for us. He said that one day a woman invited him to her family's home to talk about the medical condition of her husband. As they sat and talked, she told him that after she and her husband married they moved into a new home and he invited his mother and his disabled brother to live in the far wing of the house. She told him that one night a fire broke out in that wing, and his mother and brother lost their lives in spite of her husband's frantic efforts to save them. In fact, she said that her husband was so horribly burned and his face so badly disfigured that, since that time, he had stayed in his room and would not let anyone come near him because he believed that they would reject him because of his ugly features.

Upon hearing this woman's story, Maltz quickly assured her that he could perform surgery on her husband and restore his face. But she said, "You don't understand; he thinks that God disfigured his face to punish him for failing to save his mother and brother, and so he refuses to have surgery." She said: "What I want you to do is to operate on me and disfigure my face like his so that we can be together again."

Of course, Maltz would not agree, but he was moved deeply by that wife's determined and total love. He got her permission to try to talk to her husband. He went to the man's room and knocked, but there was no answer. He called loudly through the door, "I know you are in there and I know you can hear me, so I've come to tell you that my name is Dr. Maxwell Maltz. I'm a plastic surgeon, and I want you to know that I can restore your face."

There was no response. Again he called loudly, "Please come out and let me help restore your face." But again there was no answer. Still speaking through the door, Maltz told the man what his wife was asking him to do. "She wants me to disfigure her face, to make her face like yours in the hope that you will let her back into your life. That's how much she loves you. That's how much she wants to help you." There was a brief moment of silence, and then ever so slowly, the doorknob began to turn. Finally, the disfigured man came out of his self-imposed prison. He was so overwhelmed by his wife's act of real sacrificial love that he submitted to the surgery and was set free to love again and restore his marriage. This is a dramatic example of the saving and liberating power of the real love of Jesus. It is a love that does not depend on who we are, but on who Jesus is. It is a love that does not depend on what we have done, but on what Jesus did on Calvary's cross.

I am told that when some banks train people to recognize counterfeit money, they don't acquaint them with counterfeit money at first. Rather, before they deal with counterfeit money, the banks let them handle real money and get acquainted with all the features of real money. The banks know that when trainees become fully acquainted with the real thing they will not have any problems recognizing counterfeit money. If my friend had had the opportunity to handle a real Rolex watch first and had become fully acquainted with its features, he may have been better prepared to recognize a cheap imitation.

Jesus first of all showed the disciples some real love in the thirteenth chapter of John's Gospel. As he shared the Passover meal with them, he got up from the table, took off his outer robe, tied a towel around his waist, poured water into a basin, and began to wash the disciples' feet and wipe them with the towel that was tied around him. Then he returned to the table and said to them (vv. 14–15), "So if I, your Lord and Teacher, have washed your feet, you also ought to wash one another's feet. For I have set you an example, that you also should do as I have done to you" (NRSV). Then, he summed up his concern for them when he said (vv. 34–35), "I give you a new commandment, that you love one another. Just as I have loved you, you also should love one another. By this everyone will know that you are my disciples, if you have love for one another" (NRSV).

It is an invitation and call for them and us to get real and present a united front to a divided, hostile, and suspicious world by hanging together with acts of love. The challenge is real. Racism is still alive and well. African Americans have the fastest growing AIDS rate, the highest teenage pregnancy rate, the second highest school dropout rate, and the highest rate of drug-driven violence in the nation. There are still more young black men in prison than in college. We are still the last to be hired and the first to be fired. We still have less access to medical care and many social services than others. Yes, in the face of these and all other challenges, the love of Jesus saves and liberates us to get real by hanging together in acts of love.

During one of our Kwanzaa services a few years ago, the story was told of an African village that practiced a principle of hanging together in acts of love. Therefore, it was understood that if any one of the members in the village was in trouble, all were in trouble, and all would come to the aid of that one. One day one village member who lived high on a hill above the rest of the people looked down and saw that a dam was about to break and destroy the lives of the people below. Time was of the essence. He did not have time to go down and warn them, so he decided to set his house on fire, hoping that if they saw that his house was on fire, they would follow the principle of hanging together in acts of love and rush up the hill to help him.

So, upon seeing their brother's house on fire, they followed the principle of hanging together in acts of love. They all rushed up the hill to help their brother who was in trouble. As soon as they got to the top of the hill they heard a loud crash. They looked back and saw that the dam below had broken. They then realized that in hanging together in acts of love to save one of their number who was in trouble, they also saved their own lives.

Therein lies our hope in a broken, hostile, and suspicious world. If there is a problem, by the power of the liberating love of Jesus that enables us to hang together in acts of love, we can solve it together. If there is a burden, by the power of the liberating love of Jesus that enables us to hang together in acts of love, we can lift it together. If there is a mountain, by the power of the liberating love of Jesus that enables us to hang together in acts of love, we can climb it together. If there is a stone, by the power of the liberating love of Jesus that enables us to hang together in acts of love, we can move it together.

If there is a challenge, by the power of the liberating love of Jesus that enables us to hang together in acts of love, we can meet it together. If there is a race, by the liberating love of Jesus that enables us to hang together in acts of love, we can run it together. If there is a fence, by the liberating love of Jesus that enables us to hang together in acts of love, we can climb over it together. If there is a fault, by the liberating love of Jesus that enables us to hang together in acts of love, we can fix it together.

> I was sinking deep in sin,
> Far from the peaceful shore,
> Very deeply stained within,
> Sinking to rise no more;
> But the Master of the sea heard my despairing cry,
> From the waters lifted me,
> Now safe am I . . .
> Love lifted me!
> Love lifted me!
> When nothing else could help,
> Love lifted me.
>   (James Rowe, "Love Lifted Me")

6

Preaching as an Intimate Act

Carolyn Ann Knight

Honesty dictates that I admit as the deadline for this writing assignment approached, the excitement and enthusiasm about participating in this august project began to diminish. There were several reasons for this, the first being that in twenty-seven years of preaching I do not know that I have ever given serious thought to my own process of sermon preparation. This in itself is a dangerous admission for a person whose present vocation is that of a professional homiletician.

It may seem like a great contradiction for a professor of preaching whose daily activity and assignment is to introduce others to methodologies of sermon preparation. This is not to say that I do not have a method for preparing sermons; I just have never systematically thought about that methodology from preparation to presentation. I do know that there is a process in my preparation that moves from text to context; from creativity to chaos; through construction to communication, but I have never given this process any serious consideration. So this project is taking me into unchartered waters of my own preaching ministry.

The second reason for my reluctance is more serious than the first. I consider preaching to be an intimate act. By intimate I mean that in the preparation the preacher has a moment or period of time with God and the Holy Spirit that will result in the Word from God that a particular people in a specific place at an exact time need to hear. The preacher then must have an encounter with God. Preaching is an act of intimacy, a delicate moment between God and preacher, preacher and people.

The preparation for preaching is even more so. In the language or culture of theater and athletics, it is the behind-the-scene activity, the backstage moment, the pregame routine before the sermon is actually spoken. It is particular, peculiar, personal, and private to each preacher. While there are certain fundamentals and guidelines to follow, the preacher, like the athlete or actor, develops a routine or period of preparation that is uniquely his or her own. I would not permit anyone into my living quarters to observe my personal grooming habits, and I have the same reticence about sermon preparation. It is like when the cook, I mean the real good cook, puts everybody out of the kitchen.

There is a third reason. How do I reflect on and write about my preparation process without talking too much about me? Can I reflect on this process without sounding as if I am engaging in an exercise of self-aggrandizement and authority? I do not know. Suffice it to say that I am being faithful to my assignment, and this process of preparation works for me although others may choose to take another route from preparation to pulpit.

First, I believe that it is necessary to talk about my theological view of preaching. I believe that one's view of preaching has an impact on the process of preparation. I believe that preaching is the primary activity of the Christian church. I know that there are many who will disagree with this statement, but for me preaching is the port of entry through which individuals become involved in the life of the church. It is through preaching that most people first encounter God and Scripture, hear the stories of the Bible and the Christian faith statement. Of course, they discover what all of this means in church school, Bible study, and fellowship groups. But it is usually through preaching that individuals gain their initial contact with the faith.

I am affected in a significant way by 1 Corinthians 1:21: "For since, in the wisdom of God, the world through wisdom did not know God, it pleased God through the foolishness of the message preached to save those who believe" (NKJV). In this text, preaching is spoken of as God's way of saving the world. I like that, because I believe this preaching or preparing to preach is where I spend most of my time, attention, and energy. In almost every waking activity in which I am involved, it is getting me ready or developing my preaching. Since I am presently a teacher of preaching, this gives me time to think about my own preaching. I have discovered that in the process of helping my students develop their sermons, I find myself working on or working out some of my own homiletical ideas. While reviewing the exegetical, hermeneutical, and homiletical work of my students, I can tweak or fine-tune my own sermons.

Preaching is never far from my mind. I can find a sermon anytime, anywhere, or in anything. I believe in this day and age there is a great need for those of us in the ministry to realize that we cannot do it all or be it all. We need to learn what our colleagues in medicine or law, discovered many years ago. Find an area of medicine or law, then specialize. I know that not all churches can afford staff persons, but there are gifted laypersons in our congregation who do the work of the ministry.

I am a specialist in preaching. That's what I want to be. I have no interest in being a Jane of all trades. Preaching is my specialty, my primary business. Obviously, when I was serving in the church I had to do other things. But preaching for me is primary. In terms of preparation, I believe that this is the difference between beginning on Monday morning or Saturday night.

Further, I believe that preaching grows out of and is shaped by my theological worldview; that is, I believe something to be fundamentally true about God, humanity, and the universe. I believe that despite the inconsistencies and contradictions inherent in our world and in our circumstances, God is loving and just. Humanity has tremendous potential for good, and the universe is moving toward God's ultimate future. From a theological viewpoint, there is no other way to preach than to have a clear understanding of what God has done in the world and will do in the future.

In preaching, we remind the hearers of our sermons that God has acted in the past, is involved in the present, and is preparing us for the future. So my preaching centers around confident trust; hope and faith; the promise and possibility; the already and the not-yet. I am thoroughly convinced that God is actively involved in the affairs of humankind and is concerned about a harmonious and just resolution to these affairs.

Preaching ought to empower people to do something about their circumstances in this world. Almost since I began in the preaching ministry, this has been the resounding refrain of my preaching activity. While I believe wholeheartedly that preaching at its best reconciles men and women with and to a loving God, I believe further that the way this reconciliation is accomplished is through preaching that addresses the specific social needs of the person and society. I find that this is what Jesus did. Over and over in the Synoptic Gospels and in the Gospel of John, Jesus addressed and responded to the needs of the people and society as a port of entry to personal redemption and salvation.

Throughout my preaching tenure, this belief has been fostered and supported by many persons who have served as my preaching paradigms: the late Barbara Jordan and Samuel DeWitt Proctor; Charles Gilchrist Adams, pastor of the Hartford Memorial Baptist Church in Detroit; and James A. Forbes Jr., senior pastor of the Riverside Church in New York City. For me, the commitment to preaching on the social needs of the person and society was planted many years ago.

While I was a student at Union Theological Seminary in New York City, Professor Forbes, then the Joe R. Engle professor of preaching, invited William Sloane Coffin, his predecessor at the Riverside Church, to address our "Introduction to Preaching" class. At the conclusion of the lecture, I remember asking Coffin what he really expected to happen when he preached. Coffin said to me that if he preached a sermon on "beating swords into ploughshares and spears into pruning hooks," he expected to see the persons listening to that sermon literally going into the streets and doing just that. He further stated that he believed in the power of the message of the sermon to alter events, situations, and circumstances in this world.

This was the birth of my life as a topical preacher focusing on social issues and social situations. This means that the idea or theme for the sermon is usually generated by some topic or issue that is in my head before I have a biblical text, and then I go to the Bible to find a text that will help to illuminate the idea about the theme. At the heart of this idea is the almost unrelenting belief that preaching on social issues is the missing ingredient in relevant powerful sermons today.

When pastors and preachers pound their desks through the week because they realize that their sermons are unimaginative and lacking in interest, they need to consider preaching where the people are. The people who position themselves in the pews of this nation's churches Sunday after Sunday are confronted daily with the harsh realities of a world spinning rapidly and radically out of control. In the face of homelessness, the resurgence of more virulent forms of racism and sexism, an HIV/AIDS pandemic and drug epidemic, and a seemingly insensitive and impotent government, persons coming to church want to and need to hear sermons that assure them that God is involved specifically in the day-to-day activities of humankind.

Preaching is truth communicated through personality. This is what Phillips Brooks said about the preaching enterprise over a hundred years ago. Whether we know it, believe it, or abide by it, our sermons, preparation, and delivery are characteristic of our personalities. Contrary to popular belief that preachers are always talking, I am not really a big talker. So when I am not preaching or giving a lecture or a formal presentation before an audience, I really do not talk much. My personality type is that of an introvert, and I am really not comfortable doing a great deal of talking.

I can keep a sermon in my head and heart for a very long time. Part of my personality is that I am not good at sitting behind a desk for very long. So I can develop a sermon in my head before it is ever written out formally. Obviously, I have to sit down to do the exegetical, hermeneutical, and homiletical work, but mentally I can outline a sermon in the car, in the bookstore, and on the golf course—not written, but thought through, worked through, and prayed through in motion.

I am thinking it through, turning it over, and tweaking it mentally before I ever sit down to write the sermon. I like this mental process because it allows me the opportunity to deal with "Carolyn" and my presuppositions, problems, and prejudices with the sermonic idea before I start to work with commentaries, books, and other opinions. I can have a mental conversation with myself about the idea of the sermon that is not informed by others.

When I am preparing a sermon, I like to envision members of the congregation being in the study with me. The congregation for whom I am preparing the sermon is a mixture of young and old, female and male, working and unemployed. I have married, single, widowed, and divorced people. People across educational, economical, and political backgrounds are all seated before me as I begin to prepare the message.

I have before me young people in various stages of adolescence, rebellion, and confusion, dealing with issues of peer pressure and sexuality. I like to think of these people as being reflective of the entire congregation. As I prepare the sermon, I like to see them nodding their heads in agreement or shaking their heads in disagreement. I imagine where they will have questions or problems with the subject matter of the sermon. I like to look into their faces and see if I am making a connection with the audience.

This may seem somewhat selfish, but my sermons have to make sense to me first. I ask myself as I prepare the sermon: Would I be interested in a sermon on this topic? Would I listen to a sermon on this issue? Does this point make sense to me? How do you expect me to believe that this is what God is really challenging me to do in light of this sermon?

In the area of homiletics there is a tendency to speak about writing the sermon, preparing the sermon, or developing the sermon. However, when preaching on a topic or a social issue for me, none of this terminology applies. The sermonic social issue is a process that the preacher builds over a period of time. When I preach on social issues, the building of the sermon begins, first and foremost, with my decision and commitment to preach on such sermons, and to be faithful to the task of seeing such a message through to completion. After the decision to preach on a topic or social issue is made, I must then determine what issues are important to me and to the community of faith. Next, the process of building begins, but only after the drawing of a blueprint and the gathering of materials.

How I determine what the social issue or topic will be is perhaps the most important step in the process of building the sermon. Several factors must be taken into consideration at this initial step in the procedure. Certainly there is the matter of my own personal preference and choice. This choice is key, because when I select a social issue or topic that is of great interest and concern to me, I bring a considerable amount of passion and integrity to the process. When I believe that this issue or topic is one of significance for the community of faith, the building process will be accompanied by diligent effort and research.

Most important, if I am personally invested in the issue or topic, then I will sense an urgency about hearing from God on the matter. When I am impressed that this is a Word from God for the people of God, I am deeply concerned to make sure that they hear from God on the matter, through Scripture, meditation, and prayer rather than just giving my personal opinion, the newspaper's opinion, or local television stations' opinions on the social issue. I will be able to keep before me always that this is God's Word to God's people with God's resolution.

Second, I ask myself some fundamental questions about the selection of a particular social issue, the most important being: Why is this issue or topic of interest or of importance to me? Other questions are: What factors—personal, professional, and/or political—may be fueling my interest in this social issue or topic? Would I be interested in hearing a sermon on this subject if I were in the congregation? Have I faced squarely and honestly any prejudices and presuppositions that I may have regarding this issue? Can I preach on this issue honestly and objectively, allowing God to speak without imposing my opinion on the issue?

It is also possible that the people will want to hear a sermon on a particular issue or topic. This is a very interesting part of building the sermon. I believe that most preachers neglect the importance of the people in the process of sermon building. For some strange reason, we feel as if we must lock ourselves away in some remote study with Bibles, commentaries, and dictionaries in order to hear from God. I am not discounting this very important part of sermon preparation. However, when one is preaching on social issues or topics, the community of faith—the ones to whom the sermon is directed—can play a very important role in the process.

For instance, suppose I choose to preach a sermon addressing HIV/AIDS. Would not conversations with members of the congregation be helpful in getting a sense as to where the people already are in terms of their knowledge and opinion about HIV/AIDS? It would be helpful to find out if any of the members of the congregation know someone or have known someone living with HIV/AIDS. It would be helpful to know what they already believe about HIV/AIDS from a biblical and theological standpoint. It would also be helpful to know how they feel about persons living with HIV/AIDS being a part of the community of faith, and what they would be willing to do to include those persons in their community.

It would be helpful to know their prejudices and presuppositions about HIV/AIDS. Certainly there are matters of confidentiality in building a sermon in this way, but that is true of every sermon. Inviting members of the community of faith to be a part of building the sermon on social issues can be an exciting and rewarding process.

Often there will be a need in the larger community that must be addressed from the pulpit. When this is the case, I cannot shrink from the task of confronting head-on the concerns of society with God's resolutions. The preacher must always be faithful in the matter of saying, "This is the Word of the Lord" regarding this issue. However, I must be extremely responsible when preaching in this way.

This is not the time for me to "grandstand" or "showboat." This is not the time to try to wax eloquently just because there is an issue that is popular in the culture. Neither is it the time to preach simple solutions, fancy titles, and cute phrases. However, it is a time to bring the light of God's Word into the darkness of public opinion, the uncertainty of competing claims of truth, and the cacophony of diverse commentary. Moments such as these can be real opportunities for me to lift up the claims of God and the cause of Jesus Christ in the midst of our human situation.

Even though I consider myself a topical preacher, the Bible is the primary source for all preaching; that is, in preaching, the preacher must go to the text and discover what God is saying about the topic or social issue. The Bible is the primary tool of the Christian church and of preaching. The Bible is a collection of books that we turn to again and again to discern God's action in the world, and our response to all that God has done in the life, death, and resurrection of Jesus Christ.

But the Bible is also a book of particularity in that it was written in a particular time and place, for a particular people, living in a particular culture and context. This has always been and still is the most critical task and challenge of the contemporary Christian church—to understand and interpret those ancient texts in light of our present reality. Nowhere is this challenge greater than when preaching on a particular topic or social issue. How I link these ancient biblical texts with contemporary times is one of the most important aspects of preaching on social issues.

An accurate understanding and interpretation of the texts reveals God's will for the community of faith. An inaccurate understanding and/or misinterpretation raises more questions than it answers and confuses rather than enlightens. For this reason, the selection of the biblical text in preaching on social issues is critical. The problem with most preaching on topics or social issues is that I already know what I want to talk about before finding an appropriate biblical text. Many times I will already have the sermon roughly outlined in my head before I begin searching the Bible for a text that will fit the subject of the sermon. While this is dangerous, I am not sure that it can be avoided when preaching on social issues.

For this reason, I must rely on careful exegesis of whatever passage is selected. If after reading the passage in the original languages, doing an exegetical outline, and arriving at an exegetical idea I find that the Scripture passage selected is not suited for the social issue, I must abandon the Scripture of the social issue and begin the entire process again. It is absolutely impossible to arrive at the proper homiletical destination using the wrong passage of Scripture. It is important to remember that what the writers of the Scripture passage wrote in their time will be different from what I want to address, because their congregations were different from mine. Surely, the world of the Bible had its challenges, but the writers of those ancient biblical texts were not addressing the issues that we face in our contemporary context.

I must be careful to avoid simple comparisons and associations between the ancient world of the Bible and ours. There certainly may be similarities, but to suggest such things as leprosy in the Bible was the HIV/AIDS of that day, that the man who Peter and John encountered outside the beautiful temple represents the homeless of every generation, and that the Samaritan woman whom Jesus met at the well was a sexually or domestically abused woman is to take liberties with the texts that exegesis may or may not yield.

Whenever I preach on a topic or social issue, the biblical text must be used to show that God is involved in the affairs of humankind, that God was very active in the ancient world of the Bible, and that God is very involved in our contemporary contexts; that the God who spoke and acted in the Bible is acting and speaking to this present generation. Preaching on social issues should direct the listener to a loving God revealed in Scripture, who is concerned about our affairs. The Bible should be used in preaching on social issues to point to a God who is involved in our lives and our affairs in this way. Preaching on social issues should use the Bible to point the world of the ancient culture to the contemporary world.

Preaching does not take place in a vacuum. When I prepare a sermon I am not coming to biblical texts as one who is preaching this text for the very first time. The truth of the matter is that all of the texts in the Bible have been preached many times before. In this way, I am not plowing fresh ground or turning new soil. Someone has been this way before. Knowing this should eliminate any need that I might have to sit before biblical texts, trying to invent an original thought. There are none.

I am looking for fresh insight and information. This frees me to hear from God about the relevance of this text for this time. Preaching on topics and social issues causes me to make proper use of the biblical texts, and to do thorough exegesis, hermeneutical, and homiletical work while making use of other resources during the building of the sermon.

Among these resources are the history of the church. Part of my preparation process requires that I avail myself to the tradition of the church on matters of social issues. It would be both wise and helpful to see what the church's position has been in the past and what the church's position is presently, and then compare how those positions have changed or remained the same through the years. Nowhere is this more true than in the areas of human rights, civil rights, gender rights, and abortion. For years and years, the church has had deep feelings on these issues. To be well equipped to preach on any one of these issues, I must study the findings of denominational commissions and task forces to see what is the prevailing position of the church.

In addition, there are many new issues that the church has recently been called on to study and take a public position on. Among these issues are ageism; health care; child, sexual, and domestic abuse; and the environment. The church has become involved in these issues, and when I prepare to preach on social issues I must not neglect the findings of the church universal. I may or may not agree with these studies or findings, but such research should not be ignored when building the social-issues sermon. I must always remember that the goal of the social-issues sermon is to be objective and clear. It is to bring God's solutions into human affairs.

Not only is there the opinion of the church universal on social issues, but the local church also has an opinion. There may not have been a formal study, nor was a consensus opinion reached; however, I must always be aware that members of the congregation have formed some opinions on every social issue imaginable. I cannot make the critical mistake of neglecting to discover where "the listeners are" before preaching on a particular social issue.

Inviting the listeners into the building process when preaching on social issues does at least two things for me. First, it will help me to determine where their interests are and what they are willing to do about a particular issue after having heard the sermon. Are they willing to bring their response to this issue in line with God's actions? Are they willing to take ownership as a congregation for addressing this issue in the larger community?

Second, inviting the listeners into the building process will avoid unnecessary battlefields and land mines. I will be able to discover early on what the "mood and the attitude" of the congregation is and sidestep any potential trouble spots. Here a word of caution is necessary. The preacher who would preach on social issues is called to a prophetic ministry. To be prophetic is to be unpopular. Therefore, once I determine what "the mood of the environment" is, I cannot abandon preaching on a particular issue just because I sense that it is not popular with the audience or listener. I must keep in mind that this is God's Word for the people, and it must be preached even though it is an uncomfortable Word. The wise preacher on social issues will be able to help the people to see this.

One cannot ignore public discourse when preaching on current topics or social issues. If the church is to be faithful in addressing the issues of the day, it must assume the high moral ground of public truth. It is not enough to talk about a Savior nailed to a cross as the redeemer of a sinful world. The church must enable a fragmented society to see that same Savior as the restorer of wholeness in a broken and disenchanted age. The church and the preacher who would preach on social issues must enable society to see Jesus Christ as the source of ultimate power and transformation.

My preaching on social issues should help people to see that in a pluralistic, multicultural, and postmodern society, God has spoken in a resounding way about the diverse and complex issues of our times. The church's role in assuming the high moral ground cannot be represented as one truth among many; rather, it should be seen as a firm demonstration of the "promise" of God for this moment.

Preaching on social issues requires me to be sensitive to the language of the culture. I must be aware of the conversations that are taking place in the "marketplace of ideas." I must be attuned to the discourse of diverse peoples who are influencing the attitudes of the culture. I often struggle with the question, "How is the preacher then to be heard amidst the many diverse conversations that are transported over a variety of media and communication vehicles?" Fortunately, I can make use of these same vehicles of communication. Television, radio, newspaper, computer, the Internet, and the information superhighway are all available to me as I preach on social issues. In order to affect the culture, I must be aware of what is going on in the culture and the context.

Recently in a class that I teach on sermon preparation and delivery, a student was passionately preaching a sermon about the "last days." He was going on and on about the imminent return of Jesus Christ to the earth to gather the scattered community of saints. Needless to say, there was much talk about those who have not made their commitment to Jesus Christ being cast into the eternal lake of fire. He talked about a day that is coming when we will no longer be able to buy and sell unless we have received the "mark of the beast." Then he produced newspaper article after newspaper article to make his case and support his theory. The problem with this sermon and this type of preaching is that it did not line up with the facts of the newspaper articles or the biblical text.

Perhaps the most critical and crucial element when preaching on social issues is making sure I have all of the facts and that I have accurately reported them. Since preaching on social issues involves dissemination of information, it is important that when gathering statistics, the figures should be the most recent and reliable facts available. Specific numbers and information are important. When preaching on social issues, I find that generalizations do more harm than good. I must take the time to go to the library and gather the most recent information so that I may state accurately the facts of the issue to the listener/audience.

After all of these elements of the sermon have been brought together, I must now decide how I am going to address the issues at hand. Since the purpose of preaching on social issues is to change the behavior or the action of the audience/congregation, I must decide on the type of sermon presentation that will best bring about such a change. Because behavior does not change immediately, but rather over a period of time, I believe the best approach to preaching on social issues is to preach a sermon issue over a period of a minimum of four weeks and a maximum of eight weeks.

Four weeks is a sufficient amount of time to enable me to introduce the issue, disseminate information about the issue, and reveal what the Bible has to say about the issue. Four weeks will keep the congregation members interested in the issue being discussed and expectantly anticipating what their role should/will be. If need be, the series can be extended to eight weeks, only if the social issue itself warrants such a long series. To try to stretch it out when there is no real need will cause both the preacher and the congregation to lose interest, and instead of looking for ways to get involved in the social issue, they will only breathe a sigh of relief when the series is over.

To ensure that the intent of the sermon is communicated through the series, I believe it is important to provide as many avenues for sermon feedback as possible. Although I cannot do this for every sermon, it is crucial for effective preaching on social issues. Again, the purpose of preaching on social issues is to elicit a response and change some behavior in the listener and in the world. Bible studies, focus groups, seminars, public forums, coffee clutches, and talk-backs are all ways to strengthen and clarify the social-issues sermon. It also helps me to determine if the sermon is on target.

I am a social-issues preacher. For me the sermon must speak to the contemporary context in a specific and concrete way. I believe that the preacher in the third millennium must parallel the prophets of the Hebrew Bible. The political incarcerations of Jeremiah, Jonah, and Daniel are vivid case studies of those who questioned and challenged authority in order to announce God's action in the world in their day. And even though the dungeons and the lions' dens may not be the fate of those of us who preach in this day and age, the risks for those of us who preach are enormous.

To preach is to risk; to preach on social needs and social issues is to risk even more. This type of preaching is always risky. But it is not my credibility or integrity that is at risk; it is God's. I preach God's message, but it is God's action. Therefore, it is God's Word and credibility that are on the line. But it is through me that the integrity and credibility of God are manifested.

Finally, a word about prayer and the Holy Spirit in the sermon-building process. It has been said that preaching does not cause Jesus Christ and the Holy Spirit to be present. We preach only because Jesus Christ and the Holy Spirit are already present. The Holy Spirit is involved in the sermon preparation from text to pulpit, start to finish. Often my students will raise a question to suggest that there is some dichotomy in preparation between the preacher's role and the Holy Spirit's role. I find it troubling to think that a preacher can sit cloistered in a study from Monday to Saturday with computer, commentaries, and concordances and labor over a sermon, and then at some magical mystical moment on Sunday morning the Holy Spirit intervenes and takes the sermon and the delivery of it to a place that the preacher did not intend. The Holy Spirit is involved in the preparation as well as the delivery. My strategy for preparation is, "Pray, prepare, pray, preach, and pray!"

Sermon: *When All Hell Breaks Loose*
Job 1:1–5, 13–22

CAROLYN ANN KNIGHT

Sooner or later, it will happen to all of us. All hell will break loose! Personally, I think that it already has. The events of September 11, 2001, and beyond can be described as nothing short of all hell breaking loose. At 8:48 A.M. and again at 9:06 A.M. our lives and the way we live life changed forever. When the Twin Towers of the World Trade Center in Manhattan went down, when the Pentagon in Washington was seriously damaged, and when a fourth plane crashed into a field in Pennsylvania, it set off a chain of events that altered forever the way we live our lives. Planes were grounded. Businesses shut down. Classes were canceled. Malls were closed. Sporting events were postponed. And that is what happens when all hell breaks loose. One cataclysmic event sets off a series of other events equally horrific and catastrophic in nature—all hell breaks loose!

Lives are lost. Families are torn asunder. Dreams are dashed. Hopes are vanquished. Lifestyles are changed. All hell breaks loose. It happens to individuals, it happens to nations, and it happens to churches. Love dies and divorce follows. Cancer strikes and the primary source of income is taken away. An only child turns to drugs. Tragedy strikes. Life falls apart. Trouble comes. Sickness brings us low. Old age replaces youth and vitality. Death comes. All hell breaks loose!

It can and it does happen suddenly and without warning. Just ask the thousands of people whose lives were unsuspectingly caught up in the events of September 11, 2001. Thousands of people got up; walked their dogs; kissed their families good-bye; went out to work; went about their day; bought a newspaper, coffee, and a bagel. All hell broke loose! A normal, routine day turned out to be for many the worst day of their lives. All hell broke loose!

Now for those of you who have a problem with me saying *hell* from the pulpit, you need to know that hell is a fact of our existence. I do not understand all of these saved, sanctified, filled-with-the-Holy-Ghost people who refuse to accept the reality of hell. My theology of hell is that while we are trying to get to heaven we are either experiencing hell, catching hell, or going through hell. It seems to me that if you want to go to heaven, you have got to avoid hell.

The poetic paradigm of the person of Job points to a time in biblical narrative when all hell broke loose. The length of the text and the limitations on our time will not allow me to give a full review of the life of Job, but just let me say this: Job went from riches to rags and from bad to worse in quick time and rapid succession.

The Bible records that there was a man by the name of Job who lived in the land of Uz, wherever Uz was. We learn that Job was a good and decent man, a faithful husband, a doting father, and a successful businessman. In addition to all of these noble attributes, we learn that Job was a man of deep faith and spiritual conviction. He was a righteous man who loved God and would have nothing to do with evil.

Because of all of this, Job was the most prosperous man in the land. The text says that there was nobody greater than Job in the land. He had many cattle, sheep, donkeys, and goats. All of his businesses were turning a profit. His seven sons and three daughters were good kids who loved him and each other. The children of Job were a close-knit group. So much so that they spent time with each other, hanging out at each other's homes. They ate together and they played together. Job's faith was such that on the occasions when his sons and daughters got together he would pray and fast on their behalf just in case they had done something wrong. This is the exemplary life that Job lived.

Now here is where this drama takes off. The action moves from heaven to earth. One day, so the story goes, the Sons of God, an angelic host of messengers, come to present themselves before God, and Satan comes with them. Among this heavenly contingent gathered to hang out with God is Satan, a fallen messenger. We always want to picture Satan as a pathetic, evil, wicked figure, and Satan is that now. But Satan did not start out that way. Satan was an angel in heaven with access and a line of communication to God. But whenever you start to think that you are as big as God, then you are in trouble. And that is exactly what happened with Satan. Satan thought that access to God makes you God. And God had to remind Satan that there is only One God and that God does not need help from Satan.

So even though the Sons of God come to present themselves before God and Satan comes among them, his status and his position has changed. And even in a crowd of angelic personalities, Satan got God's attention. I do not know how. Maybe he was late for the meeting. Maybe he was wearing some strange clothing. Something that Satan did on that day got God's attention. God said to Satan, "Where have you been and where are you coming from?" Satan answered, "From walking back and forth on the earth looking for someone to devour, looking for someone to mess with and mess up." Make no mistake about Satan. Satan has one purpose and one purpose only in this world, and that is to destroy this world, to mess up your life, to ruin your marriage, to break up your home, to wreck this society. That is why we need to be on our guard every minute of every day. We cannot give Satan an inch because he is going to take a mile.

Satan told God, "I have been looking for someone to destroy." Without a second thought God offers up Job. Job is minding his own business, doing his thing, and he is about to become a participant in some divine/satanic, drama/trauma between God and Satan. God said to Satan, "Have you considered my servant Job? He is a good man, one who is into righteous, godly living who will have nothing to do with evil."

Theologically, Satan accuses Job of serving God only because God takes such good care of him. Satan says that the reason Job worships God is because he has a big house, many possessions, and a good family. This argument by Satan is strangely modern in its content, because one is made to wonder whether or not many of us are doing the same thing. Do we worship God because of who God is or because God is taking such good care of us? When I listen to some of our testimonies I wonder if we worship God because he is God and is worthy of our praise, or if we worship God because of where we live or what we wear or what we drive. Satan said to God, "No wonder Job serves you; you are taking such good care of him, but take all of his possessions away from him and he will curse you to your face." God said, "All right, all that he has is in your hands, only do not touch his life." This is the first encounter between God and Satan.

In the second chapter of the book of Job, we see that Satan attacked Job's health as well. Satan's response was, "Show me where I can find him!" God gives Satan these instructions: "All that he has is in your hands, only do not put your hands on him." Off Satan goes and for Job, all hell is about to break loose. Look at what happens in the life of Job. One day a messenger comes and tells Job that the Sabeans raided Job's field and took all of his oxen and donkeys and killed all of his servants and he was the only one left to tell him.

Now the New King James Version of the Bible makes it really interesting. Three times in this text Job received breaking news of one crisis after another. Look at the text—three times it says, "While he was still speaking. . . ." Three servants of Job have escaped to bring him the news that fire fell from heaven and burned his sheep and servants, the Chaldeans formed a gang and killed his camels and his servants, and finally a great earthquake came and fell on the home of his eldest son and all of his children were killed. While Job was hearing the news of one event, somebody was bringing him more bad news. Before he could digest the horror of one report, somebody was bringing him worse news.

We have seen this in recent days. While we have been riveted to our television screens with the tragic news of September 11, 2001, a reporter announces, "We have this breaking news story. . . ." Job was overwhelmed by events in his life and the circumstances that were spinning out of control. Before Job could digest and comprehend the bad news from one messenger, another messenger comes with more bad news. For Job all hell was breaking loose. He lost everyone and everything that he ever had, and there was nothing he could do about it. The text says that Job got up and tore his clothes and shaved his head—an ancient symbol of mourning, pain, and grief—and then he fell to the ground and worshiped God, saying: "Naked I came from my mother's womb, and naked shall I return there. The LORD gave and the LORD has taken away; blessed be the name of the LORD" (Job 1:21, NKJV).

The book of Job, the oldest book in the Bible, has been problematic in preaching and theology for some time because at the heart of its subject matter is the age-old dilemma of "Why do bad things happen to good people?" The oldest book of the Bible calls into question our simple, comfortable notions of good and evil; of God versus Satan. Nevertheless, we must deal with Job's dilemma, because Job's dilemma is really ours. Just like the blessings of God are a part of our life, so is the suffering and pain that we must endure in this life, and the book of Job teaches us about the nature of suffering, the power of faith, and the wisdom of God in human life.

I

The first thing that we must come to grips with in understanding the book of Job is that living an exemplary life of faith does not exempt us from suffering and trials in this life. Living a life of faith will not prevent hell from breaking loose in your life. Come to church 365/24/7, pray six times a day, fast five times a week. Be a preacher, an usher, a choir member, a tither, a prayer warrior. None of these things will prevent hell from breaking loose in your life.

Our faith in God is not immunization from the storms of this life. In fact, the opposite may be the case. God offered Job to Satan because Job was the best that there was. He was a good man, a loving father, a good church member. He was an honest man of integrity and credibility. And in God's eyes that made Job a leading candidate to go through hell on earth. God knew that Job had been to every practice, he was in game shape, he had studied the play-book, he knew the game plan. And that is what is needed when you go through hell. When trouble comes into our lives it may be because we are living right, not because we are doing anything wrong. Trouble comes to the best of us, the strongest among us, the most faithful.

Let me illustrate that. This summer I was playing golf at the Pinehurst Golf Club in North Carolina. Yes, that Pinehurst. One of the greatest courses in the world. We were playing—and I was playing well—when it went from a sunny day to a stormy day. The clouds rolled in and it began to thunder, followed by lightning. We needed to run for cover. Having never been in this situation before, I ran toward the tallest tree on the golf course, when suddenly my golfing partner grabbed my arm, snatched my collar, and directed me toward a tree that was not much more than a shrub. I said, "What are you doing? This tree is not even going to stop us from getting wet let alone prevent us from getting struck by lightning." My playing partner said, "Carolyn, you're a new golfer and you need to know that lightning always strikes the tallest tree."

When trouble comes to us, it is not necessarily because we are the worst. Sometimes it is because we are the best that God has to offer. Don't you know that in a world such as this, in a day such as this, in a time such as this, God needs some people who are doing something right? God needs people who are keeping the faith, who are standing for truth, who have not sold out to this casual Christianity that will not change anything, will not lift anyone, will not deliver us, and will not save us. God needs some people who are famil-iar with the game, who can go in and score. This is not a day to bring people up to speed. We need people who know that they know that they know what they know. We need people with a witness, with a song, with a prayer, with a testimony, with a word, with a walk, and with a will. Job got the call to go through hell because he was the best that God had to offer.

II

Another thing that we need to know about going through hell is that Satan's access in our life is limited by God's sovereignty over our life. Wake up and write that down because I just said something. Satan's access in our life is limited by God's sovereignty over our life. Satan has some power in this world, but God has all power over the world. I don't know how bad things are in your life or in this world, but God is going to let Satan have only so much power, so much access. He took Job's possessions, he took Job's chil-dren, he inflicted Job's body with disease, but right before he took Job's life God stepped in and said, "Wait a minute, you did not give him life and you have no power to take his life." God allows Satan to have access in the world and in our life, but he can only come so far. Satan did not make this world and Satan will not be able to destroy this world. He can only do so much damage, he can only wreak so much havoc, he can only cause so much terror. He can only strike so much fear. God lets Satan have his way and have his say and have his day.

God lets Osama bin Laden bring a nation to its knees, but the bin Ladens of this world can only go so far, they can only do so much damage. I know that it looks like he is winning right now. People and preachers are scared to fly. People are buying gas masks and Cipro. People are afraid to leave their houses and go to public places. People are afraid to buy stocks and spend money. I know that it looks like he is winning now, but it ain't over until God says it is over. It ain't over until God decides that it is over. Everybody has been asking the question, "What was God doing on September 11?" The answer to that question is easy: God was doing whatever you were doing. Wherever you were, that is where God was. We are God's representatives on this earth. We are God's hands and feet and eyes and ears. God goes where we take him.

One of my former students has a fiancée who is a lawyer at a major law firm. I mean this sister is on the rise like the clouds in the sky. She is a major attorney in the firm. I try to treat my students well because it just may pay off down the road and in this case it did. In August the PGA championship was in Duluth, Georgia, and I really wanted to go. Everybody who is anybody in the world of golf was going to be there: Tiger Woods, David Duval, Phil Mickelson, Vijay Singh (these names many not mean anything to you, but in the golf world this is the dream team). The event started on a Monday and ended on the following Sunday. I really wanted to go. Monday, no ticket. Tuesday, no ticket. Wednesday, no ticket. Thursday, no ticket, but the phone rang. Doc, we have something for you.

Thursday night I had my ticket to the PGA championship—not just a normal ticket but one that granted me "all access." I could go to the clubhouse and the Wannamaker Club of the Atlanta Athletic Club. I had access to the practice tee and the press room. I was free to mingle with the big shots. But even though my ticket said "all access," it was limited. My ticket did not allow me access to the players. I could get close, but I could only get so close. I could not touch the players. I could not yell at the players. I could not distract them from their purpose and goal of winning the golf tournament.

God has given Satan access to the world, but God has not given Satan sovereignty over the world. God will allow only so much confusion, chaos, and challenge in your life. In this world, God will step in and get this world back on divine course. God will not allow trouble to last always, sickness to linger for long, evil to destroy us, darkness to overshadow us, or death to defeat us. Yes, wickedness is wide, but God's mercy is wider. God loves us too much to leave us in the control of Satan's devices.

III

Finally, God is not going to explain himself while you are going through hell. But I do know this: God is going to reveal himself while we are going through hell. Why does God do it even for a season? I don't know. Preachers, philosophers, theologians, poets, and scholars have been puzzled for years trying to answer that question. Read the book of Job from front to back; back to front. Read it over and over and over again. God never explains to Job why he must go through hell. Never gives him an explanation, never gives him any warning that he is going through hell. Never gives him any notice that hell is on the horizon. It has blown the mind of people who read the book of Job that God never explains to Job why all of this trouble came to him. God never even gave Job a warning that it was coming.

Everybody and everyone had an opinion about Job's predicament except God. His wife said that he should curse God and die. His three best friends accused him of some secret sins and said that he should repent. Everybody had something to say but God. Job cried out in violence and God still never answered him a word. In fact, even when Job was asking God some questions about the situation, trying to get to the "why" of his situation, God summoned Job into the courtroom of human existence, not to answer Job's questions but to ask some of his own: "Come here, Job, where were you when I laid the foundations of the earth? Who determined its measurements? Who laid the cornerstone of the earth? Where were you when the morning stars sang together and all the Sons of God shouted for joy? Where is the way to the dwelling of light? Do you know the time when the wild mountain goat bears young? Have you entered the treasury of the snow? Or have you seen the treasury of hail?"

God reveals to Job and to us that he plays in a different league than we do. God operates from a different book of directions than we do. God's ways are not our ways. His thoughts are not our thoughts. His actions are not our actions. Our attempts to extract explanations from God only frustrate our faith, because God is just too deep for us. So God need not explain himself to us, but this is what God does. God reveals himself to us. All of you who need an answer to the "why" of September 11, one is not coming, at least not from God. We know that bin Laden hates us. America has enemies. Terrorists are on the rise. Hate is wide. Evil is deep. Sin is wicked. That is the only explanation that is coming, and that is the only explanation that is needed.

But you need to know and believe and trust this. In the midst of our trouble, in the midst of going through hell, in the face of great evil, God shows us his power, his wisdom, and his love. God is not dead. God is not absent. And God is not silent. God is working it out. God is listening when we pray. God is still blessing. God is moving even now. For whatever reason, we must endure this trouble right now. There have been long periods of prosperity in this nation. We have had many happy days in this life when our marriage was happy. We loved our job; we had money in the bank and in our pockets. We have enjoyed year after year of good health. And now if we must go through this deep darkness we know that God is able to see us through. This is no simple theology. This is faith at its best. Read the entire book of Job.

Job never lost his faith. He maintained his integrity. His testimony got stronger. He said, "All of my appointed time I will wait until my change comes. I am going to watch and wait and see what God is up to. . . ." God has a purpose. God has a plan. He's working it out for my good and for your good. It may look chaotic now, but turn the tapestry over and see the beautiful design that God has for your life and for this world. Job said, "When he has tried me, I shall come forth as pure gold."

I may be going through hell now, but I am coming out of it too. And when I come out of this hell that I am in, I am going to be better because of it. I am going to trust God even though I am going through hell. Even though all hell has broken loose in this world, I know that God is able to deliver me from hell or he will deliver me in hell. God is keeping me even while I go through hell. God is providing for me in the midst of my hell. I will be stronger because I have been through hell. I will praise better while I am in hell. I will preach better when I come out of hell.

7

The Gloom, Glamour,
and Glory of Preaching

JOE SAMUEL RATLIFF

The assignment to address the preparation and delivery of sermons is not as simple as it appears. I was surprised at how difficult it was for me to formulate and then communicate how this frequently romanticized enterprise has evolved in my life. I've chosen to hang my thoughts around the gloom of preaching (text selection, personal devotion, discernment of congregational needs), the glamour of preaching (delivery of sermon, approach to Scripture, discernment of congregation's immediate response), and the glory of preaching (the role of the invitation to action and application of the gospel in the daily life of our congregation).

THE GLOOM OF PREACHING

I've been touted as an effective church administrator, so I'm often invited to do workshops, lectures, and sermons. Ralph West, the pastor of the "Church without Walls," in Houston, Texas, often remarks "that people by the thousands don't return Sunday after Sunday to see and hear an administrator. There must be some preaching happening." Believe me, the agony begins with a love for the people. Melvin Watson, the retired chairman of the department of religion and philosophy at Morehouse College, in Atlanta, Georgia, often challenged me with the question, "Who are you trying to impress?" As a result, I narrowed my preaching focus to the people present, not my professors or family but to those who are drawn to the church I serve.

I rise daily around 5:00 A.M. and spend quiet time at home praying, reading, and seeking what to preach. I must admit that my greatest challenge is what not to preach. There are so many needs in my congregation that I must agonize over what should be prioritized in my preaching. This occupies much of my praying time. Consequently, I've emerged as a planned thematic series preacher. This has been true for the last five years. Before that time preaching for me had a hit-or-miss approach. Now I am able to print and mail to the congregation two months at a time my preaching schedule, sharing text, subject, and focus for each Sunday. This requires a lot of discipline, but it also frees me of the tyranny of Saturday night or even Sunday morning scrambling and assembling of messages.

My formative years in the United Holy Church of America fueled my love for and dedication to Bible reading and memorization. There was this constant caveat to avoid reading too many books about the Book and not reading the Book. My impatience with poor reading and callous exegesis of Scripture has not waned over the years. This may explain my frequent use of textual and topical sermon presentations. The gloom of preaching is intensified by the desire to be true to the text and God. An atlas, concordance, and lexicon have become my standard equipment. My undergraduate degree is in history, and my love for geography and history causes me to weave such information more frequently in my delivery than the sermon often demands.

I am not a lectionary preacher, but I have found the seasonal preaching around Easter, Thanksgiving, and Christmas most enjoyable. I often avoid occasional preaching such as Mother's Day, Father's Day, Women's Day, and so forth. Because of my planned series preaching, I've found other ways to incorporate family issues and social-justice agendas in my preaching schedule.

The duties of the pastorate are so overwhelming at times that the priestly, kingly, and pastoral duties drain me of time and energy to the point that there is little time left for the preparation of the prophetic proclamation. So the early hours of each day become precious and protected. Routinely on Wednesday I begin to focus my thinking for Sunday preaching. First comes the biblical review and prayerful exploration for insights not seen in previous readings. This involves a continuous process of input, injections, and redactions.

This nonstop flexibility and fluidity may reflect my pentecostal urgings to leave room for the Holy Ghost to speak. This process has proven to be most rewarding and beneficial to the hearers. I have to admit that some of the most memorable and often quoted phrases by congregants were those "injected by the Spirit" and not from the prepared notes.

When dry spells occur in my preaching, I can almost without fail trace them to my poor prayer life and to a relaxation of devotional activity. Many of the men and women preachers I was exposed to in North Carolina during my youth were seminary or Bible college graduates. I was impressed with the oratorical excellence of the Baptist preachers, the narrative eloquence of the Methodist preacher, and the celebratory, yet always substantive, delivery of the holiness preachers. I yearned to blend the three if I ever preached. That desire became a reality when I accepted my call to ministry the summer following my junior year at Morehouse College. Thus began my journey to emulate the best of each tradition.

THE GLAMOUR OF PREACHING

The glamour of preaching for me is measured by one's ability to present a word that will reach a people and move them to want more. This sounds like entertainment, but it is far from it. I so want to find examples, illustrations, and other slices of life for my sermons that will endear me to my hearers. I search for them everywhere—in human-interest articles, conversations, the hip-hop language, slang, dialects, music, and television.

This makes for excellent intergenerational preaching. To use the various mediums and translate them to the listening audience in such a way that all can understand has become my personal obsession. Harry Emerson Fosdick, Robert Schuller, and Samuel DeWitt Proctor were the practitioners of illustrations and profoundly influence my attempt to achieve their excellent skill in this area. I feel that the introduction to a message is critical to how it will be received. I try to offer a proposition on or focus for every message at the very start. I try to capture the audience's attention immediately and lead them to where I am trying to go. The introduction is the key!

I don't use a manuscript in the pulpit. I sketch an outline and intentionally include phrases or quotes I may forget and that I want my audiences to remember. I tape each sermon and then send it to a company to be transcribed. Upon its return I edit the transcription and place the final draft in my file.

The closing for me is equally intentional. If you've grabbed them at the beginning, then the release must be equally graceful, complete, and memorable. I try desperately to summarize points made and offer challenges for the hearers to act upon. Celebration takes varied forms. There is not always the traditional whoop. I would if I could—I've been known to fake one from time to time.

I've been blessed to use various sermon forms from Sunday to Sunday. I feel strongly that the substance of the message should dictate the form. If it demands a holler, then so be it. If not, then none should be attempted. I have not preached my sermons more than once at home, but I repeat them frequently on the road or away in revivals. Occasionally I will ask the congregation to request favorite sermons and will preach them in a series called "Most Often Requested Repeats." The brevity of the sermon is also a trademark and aim that makes thirty minutes the amount of time I believe it takes to cover a subject and for the average congregation to enjoy.

THE GLORY OF PREACHING

Having described the gloom and glamour of preaching, I will simply rejoice in the fact that the glory of preaching is manifested in the invitation. This is a good point in this essay to submit my theological conviction that evangelism is at the heart of all preaching. To win someone to Christ or to provoke and engage someone to action on his behalf is the ultimate goal of preaching. I plan my preaching in such a way that the denouement or climax is the invitation.

I have grown to the point where at least two invitations are extended after each sermon. The first one is to seek a commitment or a decision by the hearer/congregant in response to the proposition of the message. Often in the past I have preached sermons about stewardship, led people to feel guilty, and then gave the benediction. Now I preach the same sermon, extend the first invitation to respond to the stewardship question, and then extend the traditional invitation to discipleship. This has proven to be an effective method to crown my preaching.

Finally, the gloom, glamour, and glory of preaching permits me to reach people, develop believers, and thrust disciples forward to mission action. I enjoy preaching and recommit daily my passion for it and a compelling compassion for his people.

Sermon: Manipulated Blessings
2 Kings 5:15–27

JOE SAMUEL RATLIFF

How many of us are truly blessed by the Almighty God? You may have a nice house, drive a nice car, and have great employment, wonderful finances, and other material goods, but does that mean you are blessed by God? Many great leaders and persons across this nation have manipulated many material goods and called them blessings. Many of us sitting here in the sanctuary today have driven cars that God has not given us, married people God has not sent to us, and bought homes that God did not navigate us to and have been identified as blessed individuals. However, I am certain, without a show of hands, that if you have something that God has not ordained in your life, although it may look good, sound good, or even feel good to others, it has become a burden or a curse for you.

Whenever you are a child of God, you do not have to manipulate your blessings; what God has for you, it is for you. I have come to learn that a blessing is a supernatural favor from God. In essence, it's asking God to do something that is impossible when left in the hands of humanity. To be blessed is to experience more than the ability to wake up in the morning—that's grace. It's more than just being forgiven for our evil ways—that's mercy. But when you are blessed, you can examine your life and see the fingerprints of God time after time painting his approval on the canvas of your soul. That is why as the golden queen of the day continues to set, I ask God, "Give me grace and show me mercy, but please don't forget to bless me and bestow your supernatural favor upon me."

Second Kings describes a people without direction, leaders who failed to lead and a God who was forced to discipline his rebellious people. The text informs us that Naaman had been healed from leprosy by Elisha as a result of dipping in the pool seven times. As a result of his blessing and his transformation, he desired to be a blessing to Elisha. Naaman was a leader who was moved from arrogance to humility. His transformation externally resulted in a transformation internally. His heart was softened and his spirit was elevated. He was excited about the reality of his blessing because he knew personally that it had to have been God. There was no medical attention given, no prescribed drugs consumed, no forms to complete—simply obedience.

Can you imagine Elisha walking away and Naaman asking, "What can I give you or what can I do for you? I was cursed, but now I am healed. I was strong in my position but weak in my body and you healed me; just allow me to pay you or even open doors for you."

But thanks be to God, Elisha knew that he was called by God for a specific task and he did not have to rely on the blessing from man. Elisha had an opportunity to manipulate Naaman because of his vulnerability, but he decided to focus on God. There may be someone today whom God has used to be a blessing to many people, and you have contemplated manufacturing your blessings through the vulnerability of weak saints who have been touched as a result of God's anointing on your life. I caution you, if God has called you to preach, teach, or heal others, that is all he has asked you to do. People do not owe you money, dinner, or any material gains when you are working for the Lord. What God has for you he will give freely.

But there was a man named Gehazi who could not comprehend why Elisha was denying Naaman's offer. Elisha said, "I don't need your silver, your talents, or your garments. There is nothing you can do in this cosmological world to suffice the debt of heavenly blessings. Thus, just thank God for your blessing and continue obeying his voice." The pericope tells us that Gehazi was not content with where he was and what he had. He decided that he was going to send two men to retrieve the silver and bring back his gifts from Naaman.

Isn't it strange how people have a way of using others only to benefit themselves? It's a dangerous commentary when we as blessed individuals of the Almighty become narcissistic in our existence. God created us to be servers of others and not manipulators. We ought to be willing to bend our knees, sacrifice our time, spend our finances, and render our talents in an effort to become first in his kingdom. When we as people of God are willing to sacrifice time to be a blessing to others, there will never be the need or desire to contemplate the possibility of manipulating something that is not ours. Gehazi thought he had to get what Elisha had missed. It was only because he had lost his focus on God that he could not hear the Lord for himself.

When we have lost focus on God, our comprehension and direction for our lives become cluttered and we cannot hear the audible voice of God. We begin to ask God to bless us because of what we see others with and what others may possess. Our identity is soon determined by our social setting and not our spiritual connection to the Trinity. And too often we settle for less and miss the opportunity to be truly blessed by God. God wants to take us to higher levels in life, but because we are looking with our natural eyes we determine that our destiny is what we can see and we become satisfied with mediocrity instead of experiencing the supernatural favor of God. It is in the text—it says Gehazi was cursed as a result of pursuing something that he did not have.

Notice, if you will, the text did not say that he did not obtain what he pursued or that he did not have it, but it says he was cursed. My brothers and sisters, there may be some curses in our lives as a result of the ungodly possessions that we have. If we plan to experience the full revelation of God, we need to ask God to remove whatever or whoever he has not placed in our lives and to place whoever or whatever he desires in our existence. When we become fully available to God and able to hear his voice, blessings will begin to flow and his hand will begin to navigate to places and spiritual levels that we have never imagined.

Gehazi was cursed, as a result of his sin, with leprosy. He was cursed because he disobeyed God. He was cursed and doomed to die. But I am certain that as we hear this word today, we, too, can testify that we have manipulated things in our lives and called them blessings. We, too, have used people to benefit us. Because of the sovereign will of God who decided to send his Son as our redeemer, we have a chance to return to God and truly experience his blessings.

I close by sharing a story that took place in my family. My uncle Reginald was a drug addict who was smoking in my deceased grandfather's home. He must have dropped the pipe and dropped the match, which resulted in the house catching on fire and being consumed. Everyone knew it was a crack house, everyone knew that my uncle was using drugs, and everyone concluded that nothing would be done in an effort to repair what had been burned down. It was a result of negligence, which would automatically release any insurance company from supplying any funds.

When the insurance adjuster arrived, there wasn't anything I could do or say to imply that I was deserving of finances. The adjuster just kept on looking around. But thanks be to God, as God would have it, she noticed a photo of my grandfather still hanging in the midst of the fire on the wall. She stated his name for validation. Then she begin to testify to me and share how he was a blessing to her in many ways. She said, "Mr. L used to drive me to school, feed me when my parents were gone, and take care of me. He was a great man." She then turned and looked me in the face and told me, "You are not supposed to get anything as a result of your uncle's negligence, but because of what Mr. L has already done, I am going to give you as much as I can."

I don't know about you, but we as sinful finite humans are not entitled to have any blessings from the Lord because of our inherited curse. We have sinned before God, lied to our neighbors, disrespected our elders, manipulated our friends, and performed countless acts of ungodliness that should have exempted us from being restored time after time. But we have been blessed because of one man, who was born in a manger, who healed the sick, raised the dead, and gave sight to the blind. One man, who is omnipotent, omnipresent, sovereign, and divine. One man, who walked on water and fed five thousand. Help me, Holy Ghost—one man! His name is Jesus. Yes, you may have manipulated your blessings in life. Yes, you may have the Gehazi spirit. But thanks be to God, if you confess your fault and seek ye first the kingdom of God, I am a witness that he will transform you inside and out. And you will be able to say, "The things I used to do, I don't do any more. The place I used to go, I don't go any more, since Jesus has come into my heart."

Because when Jesus comes in your heart, there's no need to manipulate what you already have. Well, what do you have? The saints of old would say:

> This joy I have, the world didn't give it to me.
> This peace that I have, the world didn't give it to me
> And the world can't take it away.

8

Preaching with Passion

CHERYL SANDERS

My aim is to share a few reflections and insights from my own experience as a preacher in order to communicate my interpretation of what it means to "preach with passion." Since I began teaching ethics at Howard University in 1984, I have had occasion to do research, writing, and lecturing on the subject of preaching, as well as to preach my share of sermons during weekly chapel services at the School of Divinity and on Sunday mornings at Rankin Chapel on the main campus. Since 1995 I have preached most Sundays from the pulpit of Third Street Church of God, where my two pastoral predecessors, Elder Charles T. Benjamin and Dr. Samuel G. Hines, established a noteworthy tradition of preaching excellence over a period of nearly nine decades. I offer my reflections along three lines: preaching as conversation, with conviction, and for conversion.

PREACHING AS CONVERSATION

Homiletics is the art of preaching as a subject of theological study. The term *homiletics* translates from the Greek as the "art of conversing" or "a conversation with the crowd." The preacher undertakes numerous tasks in the course of carrying on a conversation with the crowd, engaging the listeners with words of exhortation, affirmation, rebuke and critique, the exegesis and interpretation of Scripture, storytelling, teaching, and testimony (Sanders, "God's Trombones," 10).

Preaching is first and foremost a conversation with the crowd. However, in most of our Christian traditions this conversation is more like a monologue than a dialogue—preachers seldom, if ever, pose questions or make statements with the expectation of verbalized response. Even in the black church tradition, where call-and-response affords the congregation permission to give verbal feedback to the preacher during the course of the sermon, there is a limited lexicon of response, which affirms the preacher but does not afford true dialogue in the sense of equal voice and participation in the conversation. So if the preacher has sole control of the terms of the conversation, the listening audience must look to the preacher for a clear sense of where the conversation is going. In my opinion and experience, the best way to accomplish this is to offer some sort of structure at the beginning of the message so that the hearers can know what to expect, that is, what is going to be the scope of the proclamation. To fail to provide such a signal is to impose a heavy burden upon the listener, who is then challenged to guess what direction the conversation will take and how long.

My solution to this problem is to list a succinct number of points or themes at the outset of the sermon in order to offer the listener a structural scheme for hearing and processing the message. In this essay I have at the outset signaled my intention to address three themes in relation to preaching with passion: conversation, conviction, and conversion. Admittedly, alliteration may sometimes come across as contrived, but this and other literary devices can be employed to great effect as aids to memory and retention.

To illustrate further, in a sermon I preached titled "Hearts Aflame," based on the story of the journey of two disciples with the resurrected Lord on the road to Emmaus as recorded in Luke 24:13–35 (KJV), I set forth three keys to hearing the text: (1) the dialogue of open minds, "while they communed together and reasoned, Jesus himself drew near, and went with them"; (2) the discipline of open Bibles, "beginning at Moses and all the prophets, he expounded unto them in all the scriptures the things concerning himself"; and (3) the discernment of open eyes, "did not our heart burn within us, while he talked with us by the way, and while he opened to us the scriptures?" The point is to offer the listener some scheme that is not too elaborate or esoteric to bear in mind throughout the listening experience, and that will empower the listener to organize and process what is being heard. In other words, the preacher should structure the conversation so as to give the hearer both the fruits of proclamation and a "basket to put them in," to borrow a phrase from the homiletical instruction of Professor Krister Stendahl of Harvard Divinity School.

My own penchant for numbers leads me to employ short, odd numbers of points when crafting a sermon, not fewer than three and not more than five or seven. Too many points make the presentation hard to follow, unless one is taking notes, and can create a preoccupation with keeping track of the numbers instead of the content. However, the most important consideration here is to attempt to represent faithfully and coherently the actual facts, insights, or mandates of the biblical text. The three or more points should also be carefully ordered so as to enable a progression of interest and intensity—the final point should be stronger and more compelling than the first point. Yet, in the interest of coherence, each point in succession should build on or grow out of the content of the previous points.

Preaching with passion does not preclude logical coherence. It is imperative that the sermon have a thesis, that is, a proposition that is clearly presented, supported in the text, and illustrated in terms that are comprehensible to the listening audience. Without a thesis or basic argument, the listener is left wondering: "What is the point of what is being said? Why is this important? What should I be listening for in this message? Can I trust this preacher to have thought through what is being said to me?" *Thinking through* the sermon means that the preacher has studied the text carefully, discovered some underlying truth or message, and organized the proclamation to enable others to share the light that the preacher has unveiled in the text. It is this moment of illumination that fuels the passion of the conversation between preacher and audience.

In addition to structure and content, consideration must also be given to form as an essential component of the conversational dynamic in preaching. Any sermon form can be preached with passion. The choice of sermon form should be influenced by the preacher's assessment of the expectation and interest of the listening audience. In his book *Designing the Sermon*, James Earl Massey presents a helpful discussion of the various forms of sermons ranked in terms of relative popularity. The most popular and traditional sermon form is the topical sermon, which highlights the truth or importance of a topic or theme, letting the logical points or facets of that topic control the sequence of treatment and timing of the application. The topic can be chosen from any one of a number of sources, but it is usually backed or supported by a related scriptural text (Massey, *Designing the Sermon*, 21).

Ranking second in popularity is the textual sermon, in which the sermon is designed to follow the divisions or sequences of thought in the scriptural text. Third, the expositional sermon addresses an extended passage of Scripture, centering attention on some one emphasis in that passage, "purposefully treating a teaching, an insight, a promise, a hope, a warning, a character, an experience, a meaning, a prophecy, a virtue, a key word, and so on" (Massey, 23). A fourth sermon form is the narrative sermon, which treats some biblical story with particular concern for atmosphere, character, plot, tone, and movement. Both in content and in form, the narrative sermon is centered on the telling of a story.

Whatever form the sermon may take, the one thing that distinguishes preaching from other forms of public address is the focus on the Scriptures. A passage from the Bible ought always to be the centerpiece of the conversation. This is not to say that the biblical exposition is the preferred form for the sermon. Rather, it is to suggest that the "conversation with the crowd" is always enriched by the literal and figurative opening of the Bible in view of both preacher and listener. The audience has every right to assume that the preacher has devoted adequate time and attention to repeated readings of the text prior to attempting to preach it.

It is very disconcerting for me as a listener to have a preacher draw my attention to a text and then never get around to reading or discussing it because the proclamation has wandered off in some other direction. Sometimes preachers overwhelm their audiences with too many Scriptures, quoting passage after passage strung together with the intention of reinforcing some point or insight, but with the result of creating the impression that the preacher has nothing of significance to say about any of them. If a text is to be cited, it ought also to be dealt with and addressed in light of the central theme or message. Otherwise, the audience may feel lost or misled.

Another obstacle to effective conversation in preaching is to select a passage of Scripture that is too long. Just to read aloud (or hear read) more than ten or twelve verses is a serious challenge to the attention span of most audiences. Moreover, if the passage is too long, it becomes difficult to establish and maintain focus on the message being elicited from the text.

Whatever the length of the text selected, reading with passion enables preaching with passion. Whether the text is read at the beginning or at some later point in the sermon, it should be read with an intensity of expression and degree of accuracy that are indicative of the preacher's excitement about how and what that passage speaks to the hearers today. Sometimes the simple act of reading the text effectively will prime the listeners to be receptive to the voice of God in their own lives. After all, the test of good preaching is not the points or the polish or the performance of the preacher, but rather the retention of the message.

It also makes a difference when the preacher is willing to think and speak inclusively with respect to such identity markers as race, class, age, and sex. Insensitivity to these factors can offend the hearers and obstruct the conversation. One approach is to bear in mind the interpersonal dimension of conversation, so that the central dynamic is not the word "I" speak to "them," but rather the word "we" hear together as a faith community listening to the voice of God. This requires a profound sense of empathy on the part of the preacher, that is, to discipline ourselves mentally to imagine how what we are speaking from the pulpit sounds to those in the pew. Although the use of generalizations is unavoidable in preaching, we ought not overdo it by presuming that any and every listener is included in the "we."

If I am to be passionate about communicating a message to an audience, I must be extremely cautious about using words, expressions, stories, and illustrations that may be familiar to my culture, my race, my class, my generation, but not to theirs. At the same time, I must take care not to be condescending in presuming to speak of some experience or in some vernacular peculiar to an identity category of which I am not a part. It helps to use inclusive language and biblical translations (for example, using "humankind" instead of "mankind," brothers *and* sisters, men *and* women) where possible in order not to contradict the notion of equality to which most of us subscribe in the modern world.

It is imperative to conduct the conversation with genuine respect for the hearers, even if we are required to suppress or disregard the mutual feelings of contempt that can arise between audience and preacher because of differences in race, sex, age, and/or class. This is especially a challenge for women ministers, who on occasion must stand before listeners who question the qualification of women to preach or have strongly preconceived ideas about how a woman's preaching style and performance should differ from a man's. The burden of preaching in the twenty-first century remains as it was in biblical times, namely, to find a language with which to communicate the message of the gospel to this generation. Let us be instructed by the soul-searching sermon Peter preached to Cornelius after overcoming his own prejudices and growing into a deeper awareness of the inclusive ethic of the gospel:

> I truly understand that God shows no partiality, but in every nation anyone who fears him and does what is right is acceptable to him. You know the message he sent to the people of Israel, preaching peace by Jesus Christ—he is Lord of all. . . . He commanded us to preach to the people and to testify that he is the one ordained by God as judge of the living and the dead. All the prophets testify about him that everyone who believes in him receives forgiveness of sins through his name. (Acts 10:34–36, 42–43, NRSV)

PREACHING WITH CONVICTION

The fundamental wellspring of passion in preaching is the preacher's conviction concerning the call to preach, the content of the message, and the urgency of communication in the preaching context. The call to preach is grounded in the conviction that God has designated certain individuals among us to be gifted and empowered to proclaim God's Word. Conviction unleashes the energy of the message in concert with the articulation of its content, signaling that the preacher is fully convinced of the urgency of the preaching task, that is, the pressure to deliver a particular word for a particular audience at a particular moment.

Conviction goes beyond emotion: it engages heart, soul, and mind toward the end of revealing the seriousness of purpose embedded in the proclamation of God's Word for the benefit of God's people. Depth of conviction is measured not in decibels, but rather by the intensity of the preacher's struggle to disclose the Word that God has spoken into his or her life with the mandate to illumine that life for others. To preach with passion is to convey a message with conviction. If people are not convinced by the cogency of the preacher's propositions, they ought to be persuaded by the sincerity of the preacher's convictions. Any preacher who has no convictions in this regard has perhaps missed his or her calling.

Preaching under conviction does not relieve us of the obligation to tell the truth. Corresponding to truthfulness is a second obligation not to be boring. In other words, preaching ought to bear the twin fruits of veracity and relevance, authenticity of both content and delivery. One of the worst errors a preacher can commit is to misrepresent God's Word to the hearers as irrelevant and/or unreliable. The preacher has no right to stretch the truth in order to make the sermon sound more interesting, nor to lose sight of the listening capacity and attention span of the audience. No statement or claim should be made whose authenticity has not been examined. Ideally, the audience should be given the opportunity to hear the preacher's own questions come to light in the sermon.

My rationale for treating truthfulness and relevance in tandem is based on my awareness of a typical problem in preaching. On the one hand, one can preach credible content without sufficient attention to how effectively that content is being communicated and received, which is the recipe for boredom. On the other hand, one can preach a perfectly engaging message that is entirely devoid of evidence that what is being stated has been subjected to the scrutiny of critical thought and interpretation. To preach with passion is to ascribe priority to achieving clarity of expression that effectively conveys to the listener the relevance of what the preacher has felt and heard and experienced. But the credibility that conviction builds can be undermined by the dangerous assumption that what is being said is so obviously true and relevant that no further effort is required to convince the hearers. Therefore, there needs to be some element of debate and challenge in the presentation of the sermon, so that the listeners are aware of the effort being undertaken by the preacher to persuade them to envision something new and different in their relationship with God. This presupposes that the preacher has deeply engaged his or her own convictions beforehand in the preparation of the message, and can bring a measure of renewed confidence and courage to the proclamation of the Word.

My emphasis here on conviction is not intended to imply an obsession with the self in the preaching performance. On the contrary, I am convinced that to preach with passion is to approach the pulpit with a healthy dose of self-denial and a corresponding affirmation of the transformative purpose of God at work in the lives of those who listen. The preacher who has said "Yes" to God in private moments of conviction acquires credibility in the public domain of preaching to encourage others to say "Yes" to God, by affirming or renewing faith in specific response to the preached mandate or teaching or narrative.

Thus, the ultimate effectiveness of the proclamation is not based on the force or eloquence of the preacher's delivery, but rather on the impact the preacher's convictions bring to bear on the hearers' faith commitments concerning that message. Indeed, there are moments in ministry where we experience the outpouring of God's grace and approbation as the preacher preaches and the congregation responds. Thus, our goal in preaching is to seek this level of anointing, as we stand united in awe of the presence and power of God. The apostle Paul expresses this sense and power of preaching with conviction in his first letter to the Corinthians:

> When I came to you, brothers and sisters, I did not come proclaiming the mystery of God to you in lofty words or wisdom. For I decided to know nothing among you except Jesus Christ, and him crucified. And I came to you in weakness and in fear and in much trembling. My speech and my proclamation were not with plausible words of wisdom, but with a demonstration of the Spirit and of power, so that your faith might rest not on human wisdom but on the power of God. (1 Cor. 2:1–5, NRSV)

Throughout my quarter century of preaching ministry I have remained keenly aware of the particular challenges faced by black women who pursue the call to preach with passion. One of my first scholarly publications was an article titled "Woman as Preacher," which appeared in the *Journal of Religious Thought*, a publication of the Howard University School of Divinity. I studied and compared thirty-six published sermon manuscripts preached by African American male and female preachers. My analysis led me to the conclusion that women and men preach the same types and forms of sermons, from similar selections of biblical texts, but differ slightly in their choices of themes and in their understanding of the tasks of preaching.

I devised an extensive list of seventeen tasks undertaken in preaching, each of which has some bearing on the articulation of passion in preaching. These tasks include:

1. Affirming—speaking in positive, encouraging terms to an individual or group, usually with reference to a declaration of belief of commitment in solidarity with others
2. Celebrating—calling attention to the joy of worshiping and praising God
3. Criticizing the church—pointing out the problems and shortcomings of a particular body of Christians, or the church at large
4. Criticizing the society—pointing out the problems and shortcomings of the society and especially the unjust social structures and systems
5. Exegeting Scripture—performing a critical analysis or examination of biblical texts
6. Exhorting—admonishing the hearers to act or to exhibit some virtue
7. Interpreting Scripture—expounding the significance of a particular text with an emphasis on application
8. Inviting hearers to Christian commitment
9. Observing a liturgical event such as the Lord's Supper or Pentecost Sunday
10. Proclaiming an eschatological vision—announcing what the future holds in an ultimate sense, usually with reference to heaven or to some notion of the reign of God
11. Quoting lyrics of hymns in order to create a certain effect or to convey a particular mood in keeping with the sermon's message
12. Quoting lyrics of Negro spirituals to illustrate that suffering and the struggle against injustice remain central to Christian faith
13. Quoting the works of great poets and playwrights to amplify the essence of the thought being communicated in the sermon
14. Telling stories from the Bible or from human experience to make the sermon's message come alive
15. Teaching—setting forth a structured presentation of information within the sermon
16. Testifying—offering a personal word of witness to the self-disclosure of God, usually with reference to the preacher's own experience of conversion or healing
17. Translating Scripture into the vernacular, the standard language of a particular locality

(Sanders, "Woman as Preacher, 6ff)

None of these tasks is exclusive to African American preaching; indeed, every preacher stands before the listening audience with the intention of performing certain tasks or achieving specific outcomes. And each task performed within the preaching moment bears potential as a vehicle for passionate preaching within and beyond the African American context. Any of these tasks can be employed as a means to interject passion and energy into the practice of preaching. The delineation of discrete tasks here enables assessment of passion in the content of preaching, and not just as a feature of preaching performance.

My analysis of homiletical tasks in the comparative survey of the content of sermons preached by men and women revealed that women tend to emphasize the personal tasks (such as testifying and storytelling) and men the prophetic tasks (such as critique of church and society). I concluded that men and women have something to teach and to learn from each other with respect to passion in preaching. Women's sermons can teach men to temper social criticism with compassion. At the same time, women can learn from men how to sharpen their own testimonies and calls for Christian commitment with the cutting edge of prophetic indignation (Sanders, "Woman as Preacher," 22).

PREACHING FOR CONVERSION

> I appeal to you therefore, brothers and sisters, by the mercies of God, to present your bodies as a living sacrifice, holy and acceptable to God, which is your spiritual [or reasonable] worship. Do not be conformed to this world, but be transformed by the renewing of your minds, so that you may discern what is the will of God—what is good and acceptable and perfect. (Rom. 12:1–2, NRSV)

I will conclude with a few comments about the role of passion in preaching for conversion, with a view toward critical thinking, social transformation, and soul salvation.

In the Church of God, preaching is almost always oriented toward response. Typically, our sermons conclude with an altar call challenging the hearers to make a decision to follow Jesus, that is, to become converted to Christian faith, or to seek the baptism of the Holy Spirit. Sometimes at the end of a sermon the worshipers are invited to pray, to seek healing from their diseases or deliverance from problems such as troubled relationships and addictions. In the black church tradition, preachers also tend to close with a call to discipleship or the opening of the doors of the church, with the added expectation that the listening audience will have already responded with verbal feedback throughout the sermon and will not just wait until the appeal at the end to respond.

By contrast, in many white churches verbal feedback is rendered only after the worship has ended, in the narthex or during the coffee hour, as the case may be. Notwithstanding the preacher's race or denomination, however, response-oriented preaching is likely to be passionate preaching, because preachers tend to employ emotion and energy when making a conscious effort to elicit some response from the hearers.

Paul's appeal to the Romans to live sacrificially in the presence and worship of God assumes intellectual assessment of what "reasonable service" requires. Paul also speaks about being transformed by the renewing of the mind, an allusion to the experience of religious conversion, which for Paul is the aim and purpose of the preaching of the gospel of Jesus Christ. But the active agent at work in the transformative process is changed minds more than

charged emotions. And in order to become discerning of the good, acceptable, perfect will of God, the mind must become engaged in critical thinking,
and be willing to raise critical questions in order to make critical decisions.
This transformative process is not devoid of emotion, but the engagement of
thought and reflection emerges as the higher goal of the preacher.

Paul's warning not to be "conformed to this world" should not be seen as a
prescription for otherworldly or escapist religion. Rather, it presupposes a critical assessment of the social order, as well as a heightened attentiveness to injustice and unrighteousness. Passion empowers the social-ethical dimension of
preaching. Perhaps the most impressive single example of passionate preaching
for social change known to the American public is the sermon Dr. Martin Luther
King Jr. preached on the steps of the Lincoln Memorial during the 1963 March
on Washington. As an activist, theologian, and preacher with deep roots in the
black Baptist churches of the South, King found in passionate preaching the
ideal vehicle for public proclamation of his ethical ideas with regard to the pursuit of human and civil rights. For nearly forty years his sermon has been con-
tinually cited, replayed, and analyzed as a nonpartisan ode to the most cherished
values in American civil existence—freedom, justice, and equality. King used the
rhythmic refrain "I have a dream" to set up a string of rich incarnational images
of the ethic of racial reconciliation (Sanders, "God's Trombones," 158):

> I have a dream that one day on the red hills of Georgia, sons of for-
> mer slaves and sons of former slave-owners will be able to sit down
> together at the table of brotherhood. I have a dream that one day, even
> the state of Mississippi, a state sweltering with the heat of injustice,
> sweltering with the heat of oppression, will be transformed into an
> oasis of freedom and justice.
>   I have a dream my four little children will one day live in a nation
> where they will not be judged by the color of their skin but by the con-
> tent of their character. I have a dream today.

King's purpose in this proclamation was to present a riveting image of a
transformed society to be embraced by men and women of all races, cultures,
and ages. His words helped to galvanize a mass movement committed to the
implementation of the ideals of freedom, justice, and equality.

In 2001 the French telecommunications firm Alcatel launched a television
advertising campaign featuring an excerpt from Dr. King's sermon, with the
video image altered to show him standing alone at first, then with the crowd
of people appearing at the end. The ad makes a point about the importance of
communications: "for passion to inspire a nation, it has to reach the nation."
Alas, the preacher's passion is used to pitch a product.

Elizabeth R. Achtemeier has observed that "the purpose of preaching is so
to frame human words that God may use them to create new persons in Jesus

Christ " (Achtemeier, "Canons of Sermon Construction," 68). In my experience, when preaching with passion it is essential to maintain the intent of ministering to the human soul; not to disregard the mind, of course, but to be consciously aware of all that the preached word can potentially bring to bear on the condition of the soul—liberation for souls in bondage, forgiveness for souls full of guilt, salvation for souls in anguish. So to preach with passion in the ultimate sense is to preach with a passion for the well-being of souls. A story Massey shares in his book *The Burdensome Joy of Preaching* will suffice to illustrate the challenge:

> Alexander Whyte once reported a woman's comment to her minister on one occasion: "Sir, your preaching does my soul good." And her minister never forgot the grave and loving look with which that was said.

Not only did that preacher remember those warm words, but often when selecting what to preach, his heart and conscience always asked him, "Will that do my friend's soul any good?" (Massey, *Burdensome Joy*, 34). Passionate preaching does the soul good—the soul of the hearer as well as the soul of the preacher!

In my holiness tradition, the focus of our preaching and teaching is the salvation of the soul, and we borrow freely from the words of the apostle Paul in Romans:

> The word of faith, which we preach: that if you confess with your mouth the Lord Jesus and believe in your heart that God has raised Him from the dead, you will be saved. For with the heart one believes unto righteousness, and with the mouth confession is made unto salvation. For the Scripture says, "Whoever believes in Him will not be put to shame." (Rom. 10:8–11, NKJV)

How then will they call on him in whom they have not believed? How will they believe in him whom they have not heard? And how will they hear without a preacher? How will they preach, unless they are sent?

How can we preach with passion in the twenty-first century? By taking seriously our tasks and responsibilities in dialogue with those who listen, by owning and expressing our deepest convictions in our sermons, and by envisioning preaching as a vital path to personal and social transformation. For our passion is but a faint reflection of the immeasurable compassion of a God who seeks and sends preachers. Holy fire, ignite the dynamics of conversation, the courage of convictions, and altars of conversion throughout God's church; restore to the souls of the preachers passion for the souls of the people, that they may be brought to salvation and nurtured for wholeness, in this life and the life to come. Amen.

REFERENCES

Elizabeth R. Achtemeier, "Canons of Sermon Construction," in Barry Callen, ed., *Sharing Heaven's Music: The Heart of Christian Preaching, Essays in Honor of James Earl Massey* (Nashville: Abingdon Press, 1995).

James Earl Massey, *The Burdensome Joy of Preaching* (Nashville: Abingdon Press, 1996).

———. *Designing the Sermon* (Nashville: Abingdon Press, 1980).

Cheryl J. Sanders, "God's Trombones: Voices in African American Folk Preaching," in Callen, ed., *Sharing Heaven's Music.*

———. "Woman as Preacher," *Journal of Religious Thought* 43, no. 1 (spring-summer 1986).

Sermon: The Parable of the Sower
Luke 8:5–8

The parable of the sower develops the kingdom principle of planting, growth, and harvest further and in more detail than any other parable of the kingdom. This is the only one of the parables of Jesus where we get a full explanation of its meaning in the text. It begins as a story about seeds:

> "The sower went out to sow his seed; and as he sowed, some fell beside the road, and it was trampled under foot and the birds of the air ate it up. Other seed fell on rocky soil, and as soon as it grew up, it withered away, because it had no moisture. Other seed fell among the thorns; and the thorns grew up with it and choked it out. Other seed fell into the good soil, and grew up, and produced a crop a hundred times as great." As He said these things, He would call out, "He who has ears to hear, let him hear." (Luke 8:5–8, NASB)

With these words Jesus describes four different outcomes of harvest based on the particular conditions under which the seeds are planted and attempt to grow: (1) the wayside seeds neither grow nor produce a harvest because they are stepped on and eaten up by predators; (2) the seeds on rocky ground wither away and produce no harvest because they lack roots and moisture; (3) the thorny seeds are planted and grow up among weeds, so the harvest is overtaken with weeds; (4) only the seeds that fall on good ground are successfully planted, and grow up and produce a harvest.

Jesus' interpretation of the parable relates each of these four conditions and outcomes to the preaching and hearing of the Word of God, and the success or failure of the harvest in the lives of the hearers. So Jesus uses a story about seeds to illustrate how the effectiveness of the ministry of the Word depends on the responsiveness of the hearers.

In his interpretation there are four categories of hearers corresponding to the variety of conditions for planting seeds:

1. There are those who hear the Word, but fail to understand it. Therefore, the Word has no effect, and is taken away from their hearts by the devil, who robs them of their opportunity to believe and be saved. These hearers lose out because they are not mentally ready to receive the Word; the devil's inroad is their lack of understanding.

2. The second category of hearers is illustrated by the seeds falling on stony ground. They receive the Word with joy, but fail to apply it when they get in trouble, because they are not emotionally ready to receive it. Temptations, adversity, affliction, persecution easily offend them, and they literally stumble away from God. The devil's inroad is their emotional immaturity.

3. The third category is represented by the seeds sown among thorns, believers whose spiritual growth is stunted and damaged by the cares and riches and pleasures of life; thus none of their fruit matures. These hearers are not spiritually ready to do ministry because they are too busy making money, pursuing pleasure, and seeking status. The devil's inroad is their love of money.

4. The fourth and final category of hearers are like the seed that was planted and grew up in good ground. They possess an honest and good heart, so whenever they hear the Word, they keep it, they hold on to it, "and they persist until they bear fruit" (Luke 8:15b, TEV). The devil has no inroad here, because these people are mentally, emotionally, and spiritually ready to receive the Word—not only to receive it, but also to spread the Word, so that other people's lives are touched and blessed.

I believe Jesus' interpretation of the parable of the Sower was especially directed to his disciples, a small company of men and women who had committed themselves and their substance to following Jesus and supporting his ministry. This was a special gathering of disciples—the women with testimonies of healing and deliverance who ministered unto Jesus out of their substance, and the twelve men whose testimony was spoken by Peter, "Lo, we have left all, and followed thee" (Luke 18:28, KJV). What message, what meaning, what mandate, beyond the basic story and its interpretation, does the parable of the Sower convey to the disciple who is committed to the kingdom?

One mandate we hear is to "plant the seeds." If you want to see the kingdom of God flourish and grow, don't just hold the seeds in your hand. Scatter the seed everywhere you can—even by the wayside, on the rocks, among the thorns—but try to cultivate the good ground to bring forth the best results. A very basic biblical principle applies here; if you sow bountifully, you will reap bountifully; if you sow sparingly, you will reap sparingly.

Plant the seeds, preach the Word, teach the Word, spread the Word, as broadly as you can, even under the worst of conditions, in season, out of season. Clearly we ought to seek the best conditions, the good ground for planting the seeds, but don't feel sorry if a few of the seeds fall by the wayside, or on the rocks, or among the thorns. Because it just may happen that some of those mentally deficient, emotionally immature, materially obsessed folk will catch on to the seeds that you scatter their way. Plant the seeds, in your preaching, in your prayers, in your worship, in your work, in your leisure, in your casual conversation. The more you sow, the more you will reap.

A second mandate is to "pull the weeds." Just as in your garden, if you just clip and snip at the weeds, they will just grow back thicker. You have to pull them up by the roots. Don't leave them lying around where they might take root again and grow back. Get rid of them. In the parable the thorns choke the harvest. What we must guard against is the encroachment of materialistic preoccupations as our African American people and our churches face a new century of increased and unprecedented affluence, prosperity, and economic opportunity. Many African American Christians are enjoying increased access to luxuries and leisure, the finest accommodations and automobiles, and are devoting more time to the pursuit of these things.

But the key warning that occurs in the telling of the parable is a warning not to be inhibited by the cares of this world, but to seek first the kingdom of God. Those thorns represent the devastation brought on our ministries, our churches, our families by the unbridled pursuit of pleasure. Don't let the weeds take over. Better still, don't sow all your seeds in weeds, because the weeds will win, and the word will suffer loss.

A third mandate we observe is to "give back"—the key to reaping the harvest. The women disciples who heard Jesus tell the parable of the Sower—Mary Magdalene, Joanna, Susanna, and the others—these were people who had learned the grace of giving back, people whose prosperity did not inhibit but rather enhanced their commitment to the gospel of Jesus Christ. Their testimonies of healing, deliverance, and support showed that God will produce a rich harvest from the generosity of God's people.

Right at the point when he finished telling the parable of the Sower but before he gave the interpretation, the Bible says that Jesus cried, or called out, "He who has ears to hear, let him hear" (Luke 8:8b, NASB). Then he spoke to his disciples what might be regarded as the most awesome word of all—"To you it has been granted to know the mysteries of the kingdom of God, but to the rest it is in parables, so that seeing they may not see, and hearing they may not understand" (Luke 8:10, NASB).

Thus the key blessing that accrues to the disciple in this parable is the blessing of enlightenment—not only understanding God's Word intellectually (don't be afraid of that word; we are all creatures of intellect, and God gave each of us a brain with the intention that we should use it), but also from the heart being touched and formed by it, so that the labor of love flows readily from your life, because you are walking in the light.

What makes the difference between hearing and not understanding, seeing and not seeing? Who can know the mysteries of the kingdom that lie beyond what is expressed in parables? What makes the difference? How can we position ourselves to have ears to hear? The parable says we must be mentally, emotionally, and spiritually ready to receive the Word, with honest and good hearts, if we would desire the Word of God to bear fruit in our lives and in our ministries.

The blessing, the warning, the promise of this passage merit our special attention as we contemplate the future of our African American churches in the twenty-first century. It is time for us to turn the corner in our understanding of God's Word as empowerment to our lives. Let us hear the warning and the encouragement, let us be attentive to the thorns and the fruit, let us receive the promise, all God offers to signify our inheritance. Plant the seeds. Pull the weeds. Meet the needs. Give back.

9

How Can They Hear
without a Preacher?

J. ALFRED SMITH SR.

I always prepare a sermon with deep concern for the sermon hearers. Who are these people? Why have they come to hear me preach? Are the listeners diverse academically, culturally, economically, ethnically, and theologically? What expectations are they bringing to the sermon event, and how much do they know about the Christian message? What do I need to know in order to communicate effectively to this specific audience? After discovering the social location of the people to whom I will be preaching, as well as the purpose for the sermonic event, I move from the stage of audience inquiry through the following seven stages: invocation, selection, meditation, separation, organization, internalization, and proclamation.

INVOCATION

The stage of invocation takes me into the consciousness of the presence of God who calls and sends women and men to preach to every generation and to every historical situation. This stage has two dimensions. First, I seek personal cleansing. I ask for God's forgiveness and for the consecration of my thoughts so that I can be focused in the preparation endeavor. Alien thoughts need not distract or destroy the concentrated, cognitive activity of prayerful reflection.

Second, I pray for the guidance of the Holy Spirit in selecting a biblical passage that will address the head and heart of the audience. The action of the Holy Spirit is needed in sermon preparation, as well as in sermon delivery. Unless the church calendar dictates the choice of Scripture, the selection of the preaching message is guided by the revelatory activity of the Holy Spirit, who not only selects, but also unveils the interpretive meanings that are hidden in the invisible layers of textual structure.

SELECTION

From the pre-exegetical phases of inquiry and invocation comes the exegetical phases of Scripture, of which the first is the phase of selection. I experience three stages in the phase of selection. First, I select a text or a narrative to exegete so that the sermon will be a biblical sermon that will not misuse the text as a pretext. Second, I cull from the preaching passage selected the subject that is the central and controlling idea of the text. That idea could, for example, be prayer, discipleship, stewardship, evangelism, or social justice. Each of the ideas mentioned are too broad to adequately address in any one sermon. Thus, in the third phase I narrow the focus to a single thematic emphasis. Instead of preparing a sermon on a broad subject that emanates from the biblical passage on prayer, I take an aspect of the subject, such as productive prayer or passionate prayer.

Upon the selection of the biblical pericope, I am tempted to read commentaries in order to reach an early and painless conclusion as to what the Scripture means. I overcome this temptation by moving from selection to meditation.

MEDITATION

There are seven steps in the meditation process:

1. Read the passage several times and brood over its meaning.
2. Read the passage in several translations.
3. Read the background material, which provides the history, theology, and sociology of the text.
4. Read the word studies and the exegetical conclusions of textual scholars.
5. Ask questions of the preaching passage, such as what? when? why? and how?
6. Allow the text to interrogate the preacher. How does the preaching passage comfort or challenge the preacher?
7. Formulate the meaning and message of the preaching passage for responsible living in today's world.

Each sermon has a different purpose. That purpose can be evangelistic or it can be instructive in matters pertaining to discipleship, stewardship, missions, Christian ethics, spirituality, or Christian education. Its purpose can also be simply to lead one to a deeper commitment to Jesus Christ and his church. One hopes that each sermon will be both informative and inspirational. The fruits of prayerful and critical meditation usually provide far more data than I can use for the sermon.

SEPARATION

All of the ideas and insights that are obtained in the meditation stage are treasures. Therefore, extra material not used in the sermon that is being prepared can be placed in a file for future preaching. Culling extraneous material is necessary because no sermon presentation should be a lecture that offers an information overload. The sermon is designed to transform the lives of persons so that they can become new persons in Jesus Christ.

ORGANIZATION

The next logical step is organization. I strive to organize the gathered material in such a manner that the thoughts flow smoothly and logically. Proceeding from my introduction or from the world of the text, I create a transition sentence, which serves as a bridge. The transition from one idea or one paragraph to the next idea or paragraph should be done in a logical, sequential manner. Deductive, inductive, or narrative sermon designs require methodical and common-sense transitions. Great teachers help me in this struggle for logical coherence and clarity.

David Buttrick has helped me to see that biblical passages are not always open to a three-point development. Therefore, I strive to develop the logical moves that occur in the biblical passage, much like the movements in a symphony. Frank Thomas, in *They Like to Never Quit Praisin' God*, helped me to use the three steps of situation, complication, and resolution in preaching the narrative. Eugene L. Lowry's *Homiletical Plot* has five stages for developing the narrative: (1) upsetting the equilibrium, (2) analyzing the discrepancy, (3) disclosing the clue to resolution, (4) experiencing the gospel, and (5) anticipating the consequences.[1]

Wayne McDill, in *The 12 Essential Skills for Great Preaching*, suggests that a narrative plot should consist of the following five phases: situation, stress, search, solution, and new situation. However, my personal approach is similar to that of Frank Thomas. I move from a tear, which is bad news, to a smile, which is good news. Then, I try to give the listener something to do. My organization and

design for the sermon is based on what I am attempting to accomplish in each
sermon. The basic controlling principle for sermon organization and design is
in line with Cleophus J. LaRue's thesis of two fundamental questions:

1. How do I demonstrate to God's people this day through the proclamation
   of the Word the mighty and gracious acts of God on their behalf?
2. How best do I join together Scripture and their life situations in order to
   address their plight in a meaningful and practical manner?[2]

In the sermon introduction, I strive to get the attention of the audience at
once with a captivating sentence. In the conclusion of the sermon, I strive to
bring home the central purpose of the sermon in both a challenging and celebrative manner. Both the sermon introduction and the sermon conclusion are
brief in length.

In following the example of my elders, I also strive to preach narratives
from both the Bible and literature. The Christian message is not a litany of
abstract philosophical ideas, but an expression of God's love in the concrete
experiences of people who see God's face in the loving face of Jesus Christ. A
narrative in preaching uses the plot, imagery, color, and an appeal to the senses
and imagination in bringing home to the hearers the meat and message of the
sermon.

The parables, as well as biblical biography, are excellent sources for narrative preaching. In preaching the narrative I always remember that the sermon
is always a present-tense telling of a story. I strive to be the main character who
thinks, feels, speaks, and acts just as the biblical narrative suggests. Other
times, I am a first-person observer, who simply describes from my imagination
how it was when Joseph's brothers sold him into slavery or the holy awe that
John experienced when he was in the spirit on the Lord's day while on the Isle
of Patmos. Sometimes in preaching a biblical narrative I will identify with a
single character and allow that character to give her or his angle of vision on
the events in the pericope.

At other times, I have several characters sharing their mood and message as
active participants in the biblical narrative. However, after organizing the sermon outline in an inductive, deductive, or narrative manner, the most painful
task for me is the next phase of writing a full sermon manuscript. When the
writing task is complete, it is always helpful for me to allow my mind to rest
before reading the manuscript for revision and the second writing.

Writing for me is slow, painful work that requires analysis and a search for
words that will clearly express the emotions and will artistically paint the visual
images through the skillful use of figures of speech. Preparation time is never
long enough for me to adequately prepare a preaching manuscript that reflects
literary elegance and oratorical excellence.

In my work *Preach On*, which is a concise handbook of the elements of style in preaching, I make fifteen suggestions on the study of word choice:

1. In the choice of words, let the paramount consideration be exactness.
2. Seek to have at your command more than one expression for the same thing.
3. Cultivate the habit of observing the derivation and history of words.
4. Enlarge your vocabulary by diligent study of usage by the best writers.
5. Beware of words too new to have a recognized place in the language.
6. Be sure of ample justification before coining new formations or compounds.
7. Be suspicious of current newspaper and colloquial terms.
8. Do not, out of mere affection, indulge an ancient word or archaic term foreign to the background of your audience.
9. Do not employ words peculiar to a limited section of the country, unless you are speaking in that region and are confident that you will not insult the hearers by using those words.
10. Do not use technical terms where they are not likely to be understood.
11. Do not use an unnaturalized foreign word unless you are sure it expresses an idea for which there are no fitting terms in English.
12. Use no expression thoughtlessly.
13. Avoid the use of clichés and timeworn expressions or slogans that have been overused.
14. Enlarge your speaking vocabulary by reading excellent literature and by cultivating a taste for the meaning of words.
15. Keep in mind that a study of poetic and prose diction will add color and richness to your own use of words.[3]

I have tried to study classic African American preaching mentors, such as our departed preaching masters of elegant language; namely, J. H. Jackson, Sandy Ray, Benjamin Mays, Timothy Moses Chambers, Thomas Kilgore, Manuel Scott, Charles Satchell Morris II, Samuel D. Proctor, Henry C. Gregory III, and T. S. Boone. Present teacher masters who influence me are Gardner C. Taylor, Charles Adams, Prathia Hall, Renita Weems, Emilie Townes, C. L. Franklin, Ella Mitchell, Ernestine Cleveland Reems, W. A. Jones, Wyatt T. Walker, Otis Moss Jr., A. Louis Patterson, William Lawson, C. A.W. Clark, E. K. Bailey, Nelson Smith, Jeremiah Wright, F. D. Haynes Sr., F. D. Haynes Jr., Charles Booth, Otis Moss III, Carolyn Ann Knight, and my own son, J. Alfred Smith Jr.

Hearing these preachers, I would be remiss not to study their word choice, poetic diction, and preaching styles. I would be very poor as a person and as a preacher. As it relates to sermon structure, no one is more skilled than Princeton Theological Seminary–trained Manuel Scott Jr., who has been an influential preaching coach across the years. Miles Jones, of Virginia Union, continues to provide me with corrective and constructive criticism in the use of correct exegetical methodology and the use of elegant language. The creative imaginations of both James Perkins, of Detroit, and H. Beecher Hicks, of Washington, D.C., push me never to give up on polishing my phases of sermon preparation.

Every young preacher needs to know that role models are available to pattern excellence in the preparation and delivery of sermons. When I discover that my academic tastes are making me too sterile and lifeless in the writing of a sermon, I turn to preacher-scholar Fred Lofton, of Memphis, to study his art of making the abstract touch the person in street-corner society. No one of us can travel the road of excellence in sermon preparation without critically and carefully reading the homiletical works of Henry H. Mitchell, Warren Stewart, Frank Thomas, James Harris, and Olin P. Moyd.

I am learning that as the artist skillfully uses paints, pigments, and brushes, I, too, must use the tools of my trade—words—in order to paint a fitting picture in the minds of the listening congregation. Clear, convincing communication employed by the selectivity of a sensitive and trained spokesperson constitutes a combination of exegetical mastery, skill in the organization of sermon content, excellence in word choice and poetic diction, plus the artistic articulation of vocabulary in the delivery of the sermon.

INTERNALIZATION

However, before the sermon manuscript is ready for delivery, I must internalize the sermon so that it will be alive in my heart and active in my memory. A written manuscript is not ready for preaching. The material on the paper must take up residence in both the cognitive and affective dimensions of the soul of the preacher. This calls for serious communion with the sermon so that it is not a separate entity apart from the preacher. The sermon should soak the soul of the preacher, until it has become a part of the preacher. The sermon is the preacher and the preacher is the sermon. The sermon is not a speech the preacher has written. The sermon is the essence of who the preacher is and what the preacher believes. Charles Bugg reminds us that:

> Preaching is more than a craft or an art or a profession. It is more than the shaping of some words designed to dazzle the ears of hearers. Preaching grows out of the minister's own experience with the Living God. As preachers, we stand inside faith. We are not objective. We bear witness to what has changed our lives.[4]

When the sermon emanates from the head and the heart of the preacher, sermon hearers are motivated to incorporate the essence of the gospel into lives of reconciling action in an unreconciled world. The gospel message preached becomes the living good news in a bad-news world. As Clyde Fant would say:

> "What can preaching do?" It can send the church into a real world, a world of starving children and murderous competition, of lonely rooms and smug clubs, of shattered dreams and burned out hopes. This is the final mark of true preaching, to send the church into the world. For that is where the Christ of the church is: "He goes before you into Galilee: There you shall see Him." Mark 16:7[5]

After I have internalized the sermon manuscript so that it is a part of me so much so that it has the potential to motivate others to hear good news and to be good news in a bad-news world, I am ready to preach the sermon.

PROCLAMATION

Proclamation has three steps:

1. The practice step is the trial step, when I preach the sermon in the privacy of my home or in the privacy of the church auditorium.
2. I actually preach the sermon before the audience for whom it was intended.
3. I evaluate how well the sermon was organized and preached. Since there are no perfect preachers, I always see areas where improvement is necessary. After critically examining these areas, I strive to improve the sermon for future preaching opportunities.

CONCLUSION

These eight stages used in my personal sermon preparation address the mechanistic aspect of methodology. They provide a brief road map of how I journey from the start to the completion of the sermon manuscript. However, sermon preparation must address not only the "how," but also the "what" of preaching. What do we preach to a nihilistic community? Olin P. Moyd points out in *The Sacred Art*:

> Some members of the household or the family transmitted these religious values among the non-churched, as well as among the churched. This tradition is not prevalent today as it was two or three decades ago. Today, we have in the African-American community second and even third generations of family who are non-churched.[6]

Young people listen to the profane lyrics of the gospel of rappers. Hip-hop culture has replaced the sermons preached to the youth who attended churches that employed youth ministries. Illegal drugs, violence, and the rise of AIDS among African Americans are adversely affecting families. Too many single mothers are struggling to rear children while working long hours on low-paying jobs. Resources for senior citizens are diminishing. Affordable housing is in short supply. Unacceptable numbers of children live in homes where health care is nil. The public schools are filled with children who perform far below their grade levels.

Personal immorality and social injustice helps to erode traditional moral, ethical, and spiritual values. Racism, sexism, classism, ageism, and the values of economic exploitation challenge the African American pulpit. Racial and cultural diversity creates (within the memberships of all American churches) the need for preachers in pulpits who know how to speak and lead in a multi-cultural world. Many African American churches are slow in welcoming to their pulpits women clergy who are generally college- and seminary-trained. While mastering the "how" of sermon preparation, African American preachers who are true to their long prophetic preaching legacy will be on guard to preach as did Amos of Tekoa about the holiness of a God who requires us to plead for justice to run down as waters and righteousness as a mighty stream.

Actors in the theater master their craft of drama. These actors may play many parts during their careers, but you and I who preach cannot afford to be simply play actors. In our time of ongoing or never-ending preparation to proclaim the gospel, you and I must always remember that since we speak for God, what we speak is as important as how we speak. Preaching is serious business.

Sermon: Foundations of Our Faith
1 Corinthians 15:12–18

J. ALFRED SMITH SR.

INTRODUCTION

We live in earthquake country. At any given moment our foundations can be shaken. Our possessions can be shattered. Without warning you and I can lose every precious presence or any potential ever promised. Foundations that we thought to be secure can crumble into dust beneath our feet. When the recent Loma Prieta earthquake surprised us on the eve of an opening World Series baseball game between the San Francisco Giants and the Oakland Athletics (As), freeways fell, cars were crushed, buildings burned, lives were lost, and the foundations for the future of many persons were flung far away into the land of nowhere. After some two decades, buildings and bridges that were damaged by the Loma Prieta earthquake are being retrofitted.

The foundations were not only shaken on the West Coast by the Loma Prieta earthquake, but on September 11, 2001, the foundations were shaken at the Pentagon, in Washington D.C., and at the World Trade Center, in New York, as a result of the action of terrorists.

Our spiritual lives are lived under the constant threat of earthshaking realities. Our foundations are in danger of being destroyed by disease, death, disappointment, divorce, and destruction. Today is God's time to retrofit the feeble and fragile faith of persons whose foundations have been or may be fractured by the earthquakes of life. In 1 Corinthians 15:12, spiritual engineer Paul sets out to retrofit the faith of all Christian believers. He asks, "Now, since our message is that Christ has been raised from death, how can some of you say that the dead will not be raised to life?" (GNB). Paul calls attention to the "if" of doubt.

THE "IF" OF DOUBT

"If" is a word of possibility. Possibility can be either positive or negative. You and I are called as Christian believers to be possibility thinkers and cleave to the sunnier side of doubt. It was Alfred Lord Tennyson who made us look positively at the sunnier side of doubt in his work *The Ancient Sage*.[7] Because the Christians of Corinth were those who saw doubt through the lenses of negative possibility, they confronted the apostle Paul with the words, "If Christ be not risen. . . ." They doubted the testimony of their peers and predecessors, who preached the resurrection of Jesus Christ. Paul therefore reminded them that Christ appeared to Peter and then to all twelve apostles. Then he appeared to more than five hundred of his followers at once, most of whom are still alive, although some have died. Then he appeared to James, and afterward to all the apostles. "Last of all," said Paul, " he appeared also to me—even though I am like someone whose birth was abnormal" (1 Cor. 15:5–8, GNB). Yet, some of the Corinthians gave a negative response to many positive testimonies that Jesus Christ has been raised from death. They raised the word of denial, defeat, and despair. Their cry was, "If Christ be not risen. . . ."

If Christ be not risen, then gospel preachers are masquerading clowns of foolishness. If Christ be not raised, then for centuries the Easter observance is the possible deception of a gullible public by pulpiteers of deceit and prophets of damnation. If Christ be not risen, we who preach are tragic imposters, terrible inciters of false hopes, and treacherous frauds of history. On the other hand, since our message is true, then those who are guilty of the "if" of doubt must logically embrace the death of hope.

THE DEATH OF HOPE

> If our hope in Christ is good for this life only and no more, then we deserve more pity than anyone else in all the world. (1 Cor. 15:19, GNB)

Listen to the rap artists. Hear the lyrics of popular, secular music. Read popular novels. Critique the plays on the stage. Sample only a small viewing of television talk shows. Your heart will feel a heavy burden for a generation starved for hope. Because the present has failed to give them what they want or what they feel they deserve, they have closed the door of constructive responsibility on the opportunity for beautiful lives. We are miserable without hope. When hope dies there is no sense of right or wrong, good or evil, because everything goes. Nothing is off limits. When hope dies, the grave is a dead-end street. Death is an evil intruder, a heartless monster, a cruel joke, and a robber of earthly joys. Without hope there is no heavenly city, no new world a-coming, nothing eternal to look forward to experiencing. A hopeless world is a heartless world without compassion, a hellish world, where goodness is wasted work, and a helpless world where there is no amazing grace to save sinners like you and me. But thanks be to God who has given us the victory over the "if" of doubt and the "death of hope," with the reality of the Resurrection Christ, who retrofits our faith's foundations.

In a century when AIDS seeks to destroy Africa and African Americans, hope is a tiny sprout growing in cracked concrete. In a world where our youth live by the secular gospel of rappers, who profane the holy with cursed speech, hope lives. In a sensate culture where pleasure-intoxicated persons live from their waist down, rather than from their shoulders up, hope in Christ is present for the preservation of the moral fiber of society. In an era of racism, ageism, classism, and homophobism, hope survives in the name of the Living Christ, who has torn down and continues to tear down the devilish dividing walls of Lucifer, the evil one. In an era when the privilege, power, and purses of countries defy environmental health, because they value capitalistic greed far more than the ecological harmony bequeathed to us by God, our originating, sustaining, and continuing Creator. The slave owners thought our slave parents had hope projected into another worldly future. They sang, "I am a poor pilgrim of sorrow. I'm in this world alone. No hope in this world for tomorrow. I'm trying to make heaven my home."[8]

But Frederick Douglass sets the record straight. He said:

> We were at times remarkably buoyant, singing hymns, and making joyous exclamations, almost as triumphant in their tone as if we had reached a land of freedom and safety. A keen observer might have detected in our repeated singing of O' Canaan, sweet Canaan, I am bound for the land of Canaan, something more than a hope of reaching heaven. We meant to reach the North, and the North was our Canaan.[9]

Hope, crucified and buried, rose again in the bosom of elders whose salty tears and moaning voices were cleared away with the reality of the resurrected Christ in their midst: This mystical Christ continues to retrofit the faith of faithful followers in every generation. Retrofitted faith is God's way of empowering each generation with stability during times of volcanic upheaval and vicious earthquakes in our social order. Let the earth shake.

Let foundations tremble. There is the activity of God, who has a glorious record in the retrofitting business.

THE RETROFITTING OF RESURRECTION FAITH

God continuously retrofits the foundations of our faith conversion. Conversion is not a once-and-for-all experience in our salvation history. Conversion is the act of sanctification, where God continues to call us from corruption to a clear lifestyle of thinking and living. God continuously retrofits the foundations of resurrected faith with a commission. God commissions cowardly disciples with a history of denying Jesus into becoming courageous witnesses of the power of Christ's resurrection and the richness of the fellowship of Christ's suffering. Christ becomes the companion of those who have been retrofitted with foundations of resurrected faith. Like the apostle Paul, those who are companions of the Christ are able to say, "I can do all things through Christ who comforts me, who consoles me, who counsels me. Christ is the one who gives me the courage to stand with the minority against injustice and oppression in society. Christ is living in my convictions, Christ is living in my conversations, Christ is living in my commitments, and because Christ lives in me, I will courageously face my future, because all fear is gone. All fear is gone, because Christ holds the future. Christ is Alpha! Christ is Omega! Christ lives!"

THE OFFER OF EARTHQUAKE SECURITY

Christ who lives today offers you earthquake security. You can accept his offer of protection today; death did not destroy the Lord Jesus Christ. The grave could not hold him. Doubters, unable to blot out the name of Jesus from the blackboard of history, come and go. Their names are forgotten in the graveyard of generations past and present. But there is a person who is the same yesterday, today, and tomorrow. He is your resurrection and your life. He converts you from corruption. He cleanses you from guilt and self-condemnation. He communes with you through prayer. He counsels you with his word. He commissions you to serve him in a compassionate ministry to those who need help and healing. He retrofits your faith for times of trouble, trial, and testing. Through the Holy Spirit, he gives you courage for every challenge, comfort for every crushing earthquake, and in the end when death has brought your early life to a conclusion, Jesus Christ offers you commencement in a place he has prepared for prepared people.

NOTES

1. Eugene L. Lowry, *The Homiletical Plot* (Atlanta: John Knox Press, 1980).
2. Cleophus J. LaRue, *The Heart of Black Preaching* (Louisville, Ky.: Westminster John Knox Press, 2000), 19.
3. J. Alfred Smith, *Preach On* (Nashville: Broadman Press, 1984), 21–22.
4. Charles B. Bugg, *Preaching from the Inside Out* (Nashville: Broadman Press, 1992), 12.
5. Clyde E. Fant, *Preaching for Today,* rev. ed. (San Francisco: Harper and Row, 1987), 20.
6. Olin P. Moyd, *The Sacred Art: Preaching and Theology in the African-American Tradition* (Valley Forge, Penn.: Judson Press, 1955), 2.
7. See Henry Van-Dyke, *The Gospel for an Age of Doubt* (New York: Grosset and Dunlap Publishers, 1896), 2.
8. James H. Cone, *The Spirituals and the Blues* (New York: Seabury Press, 1972).
9. Frederick Douglass, *Life and Times of Frederick Douglass* (New York: Collier Books, 1962), 159.

10

A Holy Pursuit

GARDNER CALVIN TAYLOR

THE PREACHER AS AMBASSADOR

LaRue: Dr. Taylor, to what end do we preach? Why do we do this at all?

Taylor: I think it starts from the Godward side. We are ambassadors of God's kingdom and we address the terms and the ultimatums of that kingdom which we represent—the kingdom of the Lord. I think many of us who preach—I think I fall into that—fail to have that sense, not of importance so much, but of significance. Often I see Mr. Colin Powell in Israel representing our government and this is wonderful. But he is representing a very temporary kingdom. Ours is not. Ultimate authority belongs to our king and we are his ambassadors. We bring to a recalcitrant creation the promises and the ultimatums of our God. This is our job.

Now I think we can get presumptuous in this, and I think one ought to try to do this with fear and trembling because it is an awesome kind of idea, and the worst thing we can do is to be filled with self-importance in doing it. But at the same time we do need a sense of the importance of it, and therefore gain by ourselves a significance in doing it lest we be overwhelmed by all of this panoply of apparent power and glory that we see so prominently displayed in our morning newspapers. When you look in *The New York Times*, almost the first whole page is devoted to the glory of this government. At best, any government is a temporary passing. We are ambassadors of Christ.

---

*Editor's Note: Gardner Taylor, pastor emeritus of the Concord Baptist Church of Christ, Brooklyn, New York, agreed to a taped interview and thus the necessity for the question-and-answer format. Every effort has been made to preserve the tone and richness of Taylor's speech.

THE DISCIPLINE OF SERMON PREPARATION

LaRue: How does the preacher strike a balance between study time and the pressing needs of community life? You said once that your wife told you your preaching got very thin when you got too involved in politics.

Taylor: Yes, my wife Laura said that it got very thin. I hope that was an excessive statement. [*laughter*] But I think there must have been some validity there because Laura had a very keen insight. But of course it is difficult to maintain this balance in public life. As you well know, preaching that is going to have any element of creativity to it takes time. You just cannot throw it together. It's not just the writing of it, but the brooding, the waiting on it. And that, I think, is the problem.

LaRue: With respect to the amount of time preaching takes, you mentioned in an earlier article that preaching had lost some of its appeal among the young and for this reason they concern themselves with matters other than sermon preparation.

Taylor: I have said that, but I never wanted to say that in the sense of denigrating civic responsibility and civic participation. I think we have made a mistake when we have made that the primary and almost exclusive theory of what we try to do. The preacher has a responsibility to participate in the life of the community, and his or her preaching is immeasurably aided by that kind of participation. The problem of our whole enterprise is the question of whether the church is going to be baptized by the secular society, or whether secular society is going to be baptized by the church, and it is very easy to be bewitched by all of this. I was a member of the Board of Education for the city once and I had a limousine and it can dazzle if you are not careful; it can confuse your priorities and your values.

LaRue: What do you make of preachers who study so little of the Bible because they say they see so little of their lives in the Bible?

Taylor: There is not only an abysmal intellectual ignorance of the Bible but a terrible emotional ignorance of the Bible—so much so that we do not get into the Bible as we should. I think that is one of the problems in our preaching facing all of us. I did a commencement for a school where I was talking about God and Paul. I find it exciting that he would get hold of this man who had some feeling for Greco-Romans, and I also find it exciting to think about how bad it would have been for Peter to go to Athens. All of these things are in Scripture, and they are so contemporary. I don't understand how anybody could say that they don't see the relevance of Scripture to their lives. My God!

LaRue: How can the preacher make the Scriptures live again for him or her?

Taylor: My God Almighty! I think the first thing a person ought to do is just go back and start reading the Scriptures imaginatively. Adam Burnett years ago said that one ought to walk up and down the street on which the Scripture lives. Catch the atmosphere—cloudy or sunny. What are the neighbors like? Get into it that way.

LaRue: How did you find time each week to prepare a well-crafted sermon? Did you block off a certain portion of your day, like the early morning hours?

Taylor: I think people who do such things as that are right in their intentions. Unlike almost any other work, pastors can decide when they are going to do a lot of things. You don't have to see sick people in the afternoon; you can see them in the morning. You can have office hours when you want. But time can be found to do the work of sermon preparation. I think we who preach overemphasize how busy we are. I don't think we are that busy. A large part of sermon preparation involves allotting time and using time wisely. But there is another element to this allotment of time, and it is this informal brooding. Alexander Maclaren spoke about a sitting silent before God. It means that a lot of people like you and me spend part of our day doing nothing. And sometimes even we say to ourselves, "I ought to be doing something." But this sitting silent is the gestation period required of all good preaching. I can't explain it any better than that.

LaRue: Does sermon preparation become any easier with disciplined study?

Taylor: I think so. I try to devote my mornings and late nights to some kind of formal study because I don't go to sleep before one or two o'clock in the morning. I think you need the time for the formal study. But beyond that you need time for informal reflection and brooding. I find it very interesting that the Scripture said the Spirit of the Lord God brooded over the water. The Spirit is just sitting around, just thinking. Now, it isn't, as we say, just "sitting around," although it is "sitting," but not just "sitting around." It is something else. In such an environment, a lot of things come to you. I have great admiration for Paul Scherer. In fact, Scherer liberated my blackness for me in preaching. I am almost embarrassed to say that, but going to a seminary in the North, I came to a feeling of uncertainty about my background as a preacher, but I heard in Scherer some of the imaginativeness, I guess, of black preaching, and it gave me a certain confidence. It's a shame that I had to wait for that, but I did. Scherer's brooding imagination and creativity helped me tremendously.

LaRue: This sitting silent before God, is that why you seem ill at ease in the company of others at times? One had the sense that there were times when you simply preferred to be alone.

Taylor: I hope I didn't show that, but sometimes I guess I did. I am embarrassed for two reasons: My wife Laura taught down at Southern University for a while. She said of the former president there that he always seemed to focus intently upon anything anyone said to him. I have another acquaintance of whom it was said that he seemed completely absorbed in anything anybody was talking about. Well, I wanted to be that way, and never could. You have embarrassed me this morning.

STEPS IN THE WEEKLY TASK

LaRue: Let's talk about the specifics of your sermon preparation. What do you do on Sundays when you are done preaching? Do you start then and there to think about the next sermon?

Taylor: People often ask what I do when I'm done preaching. I say to them, "I rest!" I rest and prepare to preach again. I think there is an informal preparation going on constantly. We are having it now. I don't think the preacher has to be forever scurrying around looking for something to preach about. One has to be open to the experiences of life, and the preaching will come out of that together with a knowledge of the Scriptures. One of the sad parts of the lives of seminary students, and in my own time too, is that they study so much about the Bible and not enough of the Scriptures. I am not sure that you can simply study the Bible and get what I am talking about. I think you can get the raw material out of the Bible, but I think one's own being has to be stamped on, and even more than that, stamped into the Scriptures, and the Scriptures have to be stamped into your personality so that one lives in the then and the now, in the Scriptures and then in what's going on now. And I don't think you can ever separate them.

LaRue: How do you move from an initial idea that comes to you to the finished sermon?

Taylor: I would want to think that a sermon idea has been decided for me, rather than I just decided it. I think that goes into that brooding. I shy away from the notion that it is all self-generated. And here we come upon the inexplicable. I was talking with Albert Einstein one morning in Princeton, and he said during the course of our conversation that an idea came to him. I didn't challenge him on that, but I did raise the question about how ideas came to him. He said that the idea of relativity came to him. We cannot know what he meant, but I think he meant something like what happens to all of us—that you are thinking about brooding and then something comes. Now is that self-generated? I don't think so. Maybe a part of it rises out of us, but a part of it comes down upon us. It's not just a matter of me deciding, and that is the mystery of it.

LaRue: You rest and prepare? What do you do on Monday?

Taylor: Monday, well, you know I play golf a lot. I will go to the theater and I will sit around and talk. And I am not scurrying, I am not looking for what I am going to preach about. I found when I was preaching every Sunday in the same pulpit that about Tuesday something would begin almost invariably to deal with me more and more. By Wednesday or Thursday I was pretty well set on the direction I wanted to go. I found something else very interesting, that as the idea was taking shape—things I read, conversations I had, television I watched—all seemed at some point or another to contribute to what I wanted to deal with.

LaRue: What about Tuesday? Where do your ideas come from? Do they come from Scripture? Do they come from reading? Do they come from life experiences?

Taylor: I think they come from all those places. And that brings me to something that we ought to mention. There ought to be disciplined reading of the Scriptures. I was in Louisville many years ago and heard a preacher say that nobody ought to live without having read through the Bible at least once. That thing stuck with me and I started doing just that—reading a chapter from each Testament. Every morning I plowed through a lot of arid, dry, desert material but also through a lot of rich material. I won't do it now, but I went through the Bible three or four times, and I practiced jotting down in the flyleaf things that struck me. I don't like to call them ideas, because idea is too cerebral.

LaRue: Why not call it a fruitful possibility?

Taylor: Yes, that's it. A fruitful possibility gets hold of you. I would jot that down. Sometimes I would come back to it and sometimes I wouldn't. I found, living in the Scriptures—and I don't mean here a slavish literalism—but living in the sense of the Scriptures you get a different outlook on life.

LaRue: How many hours per week do you spend in preparation?

Taylor: You know [Harry Emerson] Fosdick used to say for every minute in the pulpit, spend one hour in the study, but I never put any stock in that. I put stock in this: I think we've spent all too few hours in preparation. Like I said, I do morning reading; I try to read an hour in the morning and at least an hour or so at night. I am afraid my reading is not as systematized as it might be, as it ought to be. But I just read and read. As I said earlier I find a lot of things from *The New York Times'* theatrical section, its book review section, from this, that, and the other. All these things sort of dovetail into my preaching.

LaRue: On an earlier occasion you said by Tuesday or Wednesday you turn to some commentary or word study?

Taylor: By Tuesday or Wednesday I turn. I don't want to make too much of that or too little of that. But I turn toward some idea on which to brood, for I would not look at a commentary right away. I want the idea to, as we say in the South, "percolate." Then I want to compare what I saw in the text with what the commentary had to say about it. Sometimes I have to abandon what I thought the text was saying and sometimes not. It is a terrible thing for us to be dishonest in ideas and dishonest in words, because words are the only thing we have to work with. So the quest for the right word to say what we are trying to say is a holy pursuit.

LaRue: When you finally turn to the commentaries, what kind of commentaries do you use?

Taylor: I look at Alexander Maclaren's work, Calvin's *Exposition of Scripture*, Barclay's commentary, Joseph Parker, and others. Sometimes I get a blending of my ideas and theirs. Other times I take much of what they said. I never have any mathematical formula for how much I used from other people. I think the preacher has to have some sense of proportion about that, but never a fixed formula. Fosdick saying he spent so many hours in preparation is a legalism. Now you can make a lot of excuses and cop out and take a cheap flight from reality by avoiding legalism, but you can also be enslaved by it. I never had a fixed formula for how long I studied and how much I used or did not use from others.

LaRue: In my mind when I think of your sermon-preparation process, I see you in a very deliberate, pronounced manner trudging up the stairs to your study every day at a certain hour for a certain amount of time. Is that the case?

Taylor: Yes, sir, I do that. And I have been blessed with two wives, neither of whom has trespassed upon that time I spend there. I still do it. I was up there last night—I'll be up there tonight, it's my place. I will show you my study table. It's in awful disarray for you, but not for me.

LaRue: Does that process guarantee that your creative juices will flow?

Taylor: No. But even in the doing of that one must remember that creativity is not systematic. You cannot dictate to it. You cannot subject creativity to a sundial or a clock. The wind blows where it will. But it is your responsibility to place yourself in a position to evoke the creative process.

LaRue: When would you begin actually to jot down what you wanted to deal with and how you wanted to deal with it?

Taylor: Rarely before Friday night. But I spend all night Friday night, if necessary. I've seen the sun come up many a morning sitting at my study table. But by the time I sit down on Friday evening I pretty well know which way I want to go. You know I've got a theory about preaching. People often ask me, "How do you preach without notes?" I think if you can decide where you're trying to get, and where you're going to start, and the route you're going to take, you've got it.

LaRue: I've often heard you speak of that process as a journey. Is that how you view it?

Taylor: That is exactly what it is. I used to know a man at Yale who would often hear me outline my preparation process and he would say to others, "I hope none of you all believe that's all there is to it." But that is generally what it is. Know where you want to get, where you are going to start, and how you are going to get there.

LaRue: What motivates you toward such diligence and faithfulness in your sermon preparation? Is it the waiting congregation?

Taylor: That's part of it. I don't know whether anybody else sensed it, but I tell you in Concord Church there was almost a tense expectancy among those people for the gospel. Sandy Ray and I would often talk about it, and he said he had experienced the same thing. It made it an exciting kind of thing, this digging for the people. I miss that tense expectancy.

LaRue: You say you miss it, and yet you stepped down. No one forced you out.

Taylor: No, not yet. I had a lot of lessons in that, too, and here again I think we are called upon to take lessons from experiences and conversations. I was in Dayton, Ohio, with the pastor of the Tabernacle Church. I was I guess fifteen years away from retirement. But we were just talking. He was an older man. He had been in the church forty years. He said, whether it was true or not, that he was walking through the kitchen area; two ladies were preparing food, and one said to the other, "How long has the pastor been here now?" and the other said "Too long." Well, that kind of thing settled into me. And my mother said to me, when I was a very young man, "Gardner, when you get old, don't be putting yourself on the people. Try to get out."

LaRue: So, Friday night you stayed up all night if you had to? Were you at a typewriter or writing with pencil and paper?

Taylor: I wrote those manuscripts with pencil and paper.

LaRue: Did you erase or mark through a lot? Did you ever ball up a piece of paper in frustration and throw it in the trash?

Taylor: Very rarely. Very rarely. I would just write and somehow it would come together.

LaRue: Did you ever have the sense that you were running out of time?

Taylor: No, because I knew I had Friday night and Saturday so I never worked under that pressure of time. At least I don't remember doing so. I'm sure it must have come to that on some occasions, but I don't remember times when I was up against it on Saturday.

LaRue: Were all of them publishable?

Taylor: Well, you might ask the other question: Were any of them publishable? Who knows? But they were what I wanted to do and what I tried to do. On Saturday I would go over them two or three times, but very rarely would I make any corrections.

LaRue: When you say, "go over," what were you doing in your mind?

Taylor: I would read them not to memorize, because I didn't memorize them. I would read it over several times in order to get a sense of it. And I come back to that thing that we spoke about earlier. I would remember my starting point, where I was going, and where I would conclude. I followed those thoughts in my mind. Now I would lose a lot of material which I thought was wonderful but perhaps it wasn't. Maybe it needed to be lost. But I also picked up material that I had no notion about when I was preparing the sermon. This new material would come in the actual preaching of the sermon.

LaRue: I suppose that's one of the benefits of a long pastorate—that you feel the freedom to do that sort of thing in the pulpit?

Taylor: Oh, my God, yes. Oh, my God, yes.

LaRue: In preparation for Sunday I know you guarded your time so much so that you did not attend Saturday functions at your own church.

Taylor: That is right. I guess people talked about it but they never said anything to me about it. For twenty-five years I never went to anything—a wedding or a funeral, yes—but a social event or a club thing, no. I tried to say to them that if you expect me to come to you on Sunday morning with the best that I can give you, then I've got to be free on Saturday. And that was a kind of oral contract that I had with them. Of course, I have said in lectures that I think the people need to see some evidence of your not having been available on Saturdays. I wouldn't go anywhere else on Saturday either. My wife and I would go to a movie or something like that to try to settle my nerves. I almost had a nervous breakdown in the first year or two of my pastorate at Concord. I'd never been in a church like that. I was about thirty, coming loose, and scared to death. I was scared to death and this is why I said to you earlier, I think preachers, particularly young preachers, have to, without gaining too much self-importance from it, need to have a sense that they are ambassadors from another world. I had to find a way to settle my nerves.

THE PREACHING LIFE

LaRue: What does the preacher need to do in order to keep himself or herself in a state of readiness for sermon preparation?

Taylor: I don't believe that a preacher ought to try to stay in a state of readiness. Jesus taught, healed, ministered, preached, and went away, and came back. So there was alternation. Frank Boreham was the premier preacher of Australia in his generation, and he was a great fan of Australian cricket. James Stewart was the most marvelous preacher of his generation, and he was a chaplain of the Scottish football team. He actually rode on the truck to the field with the football players. J. H. Jackson of Chicago was a marvelous preacher and he loved baseball. I think you need something that is not this. I think that my game (golf) is the closest to it because the Scots invented it with their almost morbid sense of penalty and individual responsibility and all that kind of thing. [*laughter*]

LaRue: Did you experience dry spells or momentous changes in your preaching?

Taylor: Very much so. My wife Laura called those "preaching plateaus." She said in education there are plateaus. But, yes, indeed that happens. But I think what the preacher has to do is to wait on the vision; it will surely come. A. J. Gossip said in his day that he preached through his dry time because everybody goes through it. And so he sought the spiritual value and instruction that there might be in those periods. Yes, I went through that. I think it is inevitable.

LaRue: Did a sense of unworthiness ever come over you in your preaching or preparation for preaching?

Taylor: I lived with that. That's why I keep saying—I've said it to myself—the preacher has to get a sense, without too much self-importance, that he is an ambassador from another kingdom. I don't think anything takes the place of that. But there is the danger of self-importance and pomposity, but I am coming from another kingdom.

LaRue: In your lectures you talked about a "humbling negative" in the preacher's life. May I ask you to expand on that, without being too specific?

Taylor: To be quite honest with you, I was haunted by the fear that I would bring discredit not so much on myself, but upon the congregation I served, and more than that upon the Lord. I knew my own proclivities and tendencies, and that haunted me, yes.

LaRue: But you kept going?

Taylor: Yes, and the Lord did it with me. I spoke one Sunday not long ago, and I was saying that as I looked back how thankful I was for one thing: that in the building of Concord Church and in New York politics, that twenty-four angels could not say anything was passed under the table or that there had been any shady deals. I said I made some mistakes, some of which I regret and some for which I don't feel sorry. Scandal worried me, but I am thankful I have been able to go on. Of course, I have reached the age now where very few things that are bad could happen to me. A very few. I beat the devil running.

Sermon: Look Up!
Luke 21:25–27

GARDNER CALVIN TAYLOR

The guide leading his tour group on some narrow ledge of the Alp mountains, or some other high place, will say to them every so often, "Do not look down." At the same time, in a high place those of us who suffer from fear of heights find it the hardest thing in the world not to look down. The moviemakers have many devices and ways in which they build suspense and instill terror in those who watch their pictures. One time-honored device is to appeal to our fear of heights, which comes of looking down. They will picture someone perched on the narrow ledge of a skyscraper, seventy or a hundred stories from the ground.

This does not frighten us as much, for in theory if the ledge is wide enough to stand upon, there is no difference between a sidewalk on the ground and a platform a thousand feet in the air. The moviemakers send chills through our spines by first picturing the person up on the ledge and then playing the camera down all the way to the street, where traffic is moving. This makes some of us want to scream. It is the downward look that is so terrifying, so chilling, so almost unbearable.

Well, life can be pretty dreadful if we spend our time looking down. Now, I am not saying for a moment that there is not the strong temptation to look down, to look for the worst. And heaven knows there is enough, more than enough, that is low and distasteful and destructive and discouraging in this day and age in which you and I are called to live our lives.

A true and honest and Godly faith will not deny that there are dreadful and frightful realities, facts, in life. The faith of Christ truly stated is forever against those "lavender and lace," "tea party" readings of life even when they are speaking in the name of Christ. Jesus never claimed that things cannot be bad, terribly, tragically bad. He rather made large and ample place for the things that are destructive and harmful, the devilish, demonic powers that are loose in the world. If you are going waltzing and prancing through the days making believe that life is one grand round of lovely parties with no gloom and no grief and no trouble, then go ahead, but in the name of God and in the name of truth, do not do it in the name of Jesus.

I want you to hear the bad things, the frightening, chilling list, the devastating catalog, the withering rundown of formidable, cruel, ruthless forces driving against our lives and playing havoc with our dreams and our hopes. In these words of Jesus which I propose now to repeat, you can hear the roar and crash of a great storm with its screaming winds passing through life, leaving a fearful and empty silence in its wake. Let the Lord speak. He says that we "shall hear of wars and commotions . . . Nation shall rise against nation, and kingdom against kingdom: And great earthquakes shall be in divers places" (Luke 21:9–11, KJV). On and on he goes about outside conditions, "signs in the sun, and in the moon, and in the stars" (Luke 21:25, KJV). How accurate a description this seems for our own time. There seems so little decency left anywhere! We have the notion even in high places that if an act is not potently illegal, it is all right. Ought not people in high places think not only of "evil" but of the very "appearance of evil"?

Now Jesus does not stop with his recitation of external calamity. He probes at the internal batterings and sieges to which the soul is liable. Jesus says that under the pressure of outside forces a person's spiritual defenses may crumble like the Maginot Line before the Nazi blitzkrieg. This is really the crunch and the greatest of the terrors. You and I can stand anything if our faith holds fast. If an anchor holds within the veil, then never mind how strong and contrary the winds might blow. If, on the other hand, our inner defenses fall and our spiritual fortress is breached and overrun, then all hope is lost.

Jesus spoke of it in these awesome words: "men's hearts failing them for fear." Among so many of us there has been that worst loss—"a loss of nerve." Things can go so awfully wrong that those central confidences upon which life is built begin to quiver and totter. The night of sorrow or pain can be so long and so lonely that it seems that all about us there is only insanity and there is only ugliness.

The temptation is to look down. That is what we are getting all around us. We see such violations of honor in places of public trust and responsibility. Many people have decided that everybody is a crook in public life. The temptation is to look down. Those of us who love the church and the gospel and the role of the preacher see so much that is discouraging. So many of our churches are little more than social clubs or places for purposeless emotional orgy. Too many of us who preach seem to have little else in mind except how much we can get, how much money we can filch and scheme out of people for our own comfort and luxury. It is easy to cry, "A plague on all your houses of worship." I am ashamed of some things I see being done in the name of Jesus. I blush at some of the schemes and methods some of us practice who are supposed to be the shepherds of the people of God. I blush. I blush. With so much that we can do and so little that we do do, is it any wonder that men and women say honestly, "To hell with your churches."

It is easy to look down, but Jesus says that at such a time, "Look up. Lift up your head." Do not look down where all is ugly and corrupt and mean. Yes, people all around us seem so low, so conniving and so selfish. On the other hand, do you not know some people whose hearts beat not just for themselves? Fix your mind and heart on them, not on the lowest and dirtiest. Look up! The divorce rate seems forever to climb, and many people seem not to care a snap of their finger for the vow "till death do us part." Sometimes, I almost choke on those words at marriage ceremonies. There is nothing to marriage, you are likely to say. Don't look down! I know of people who have this year celebrated their fiftieth wedding anniversary in joy and happiness.

Don't look down! Look up! A black architect who grew up in the shadow of this church has designed that building next door (the 120-bed Concord Nursing Home), which will stand when these vultures and parasites, these bloodsuckers and community-ruiners are gone and their work but an ugly memory. Look up!

You and I must want to be one of those examples upon which others may look and from whom other pilgrims may take strength. There are such people. I have known, still know some in this church whose example gives us courage, whose dauntless faith inspires our faith. Look up toward such examples. I have known people here who lived such giant lives in Christ that we can scarcely hope to have all of their gifts and graces. They are like a man I did not know, but of whom I read and who fell asleep the other day. Someone who knew him wrote for all who were blessed by the brightness of his faith and the dedication of his life to Jesus Christ:

> "His mantle was too great," we said. Not one of us
> so tall and grown up in the ways of God could wear that great cloak of
>   him now gone. Not one could pick it up and wear the whole. And so
>   with one accord
> We thought to share it while we're growing. "Mine the corner made up
>   of love," one cried—"his love for everyone he knew."
> "Give to me the portion of his gentleness to soften my harshness," begged
>   another.
> So on through the list we made our choices,
> His intellect, his humor, his compassion,
> Generosity, awareness, understanding.

Each one making claim according to his deep-felt need.
It was not a dividing
But the wrapping of his mantle of greatness
Around so many
Had drawn us together in a closeness
Never quite achieved before.
Now as with bowed heads we close the grave
Of the one gone from us,
And share the mantle he left,
May we grow in stature beneath its folds
Until we all attain a measure of the
Godliness, compassion, love,
Gentleness and all the other characteristics
That made up the warp and woof of that beautiful garment.
Worn so easily, yet so regally
By our Elijah.

Look up! Lift up your heads! Your redemption draweth nigh. Jesus still lives, the Holy Spirit is yet at work, God is still on the throne. Things may go so terribly wrong that the holiest center of life seems violated and defiled and spoiled. Look up! This is the worst and most sinister danger, that we, looking down, will be content to live in the lowlands of doubt and fear and defeat. Some of you may have come to that really desperate and terrible place, to that awful night of the soul where you suspect that there is no God anywhere in all the thick and starless night through which you are passing. Some of you sitting out there may be at the place where you wonder if trying to be decent and honest is at all worthwhile, that right and wrong are just words that people use. When that kind of terrible doubt grips you by the throat and starts choking you, scramble loose, look up! God lives and is on his way to relieve and rescue you right now.

Looking up, you may well climb above the clouds and mists and rains that have now blinded your view. Once years ago I told here of an illustration I once heard my father use in the pulpit of a little church in a Louisiana bayou village to which I had driven him. He repeated an incident in which Charles Lindbergh, the first man to cross the Atlantic alone in a plane, told of his lonely flight to Paris. I remember it as if it was yesterday: my father saying that Lindbergh reported running into a blinding storm out of whose thick clouds lightning flashed. The pilot looked to his right, but the clouds and the storm seemed to extend as far as he could see to the right. He looked to his left, but, again, the storm seemed raging as far as he could peer to his left. The clouds seemed to hover ever lower. The pilot said that he knew his little plane would never stand that buffeting wind and those sharp lightning bolts for long. There was just one thing to do. The pilot tilted the controls upward, and the little plane trembled and shivered and climbed until it shot through the clouds and out into the bright sunshine of a cloudless sky.

The clouds may be heavy where you are traveling. Look up and, by faith, face skyward. Above the clouds the sun is shining; somewhere kind winds are blowing and the skies are cloudless and clear. Up above the clouds of gossip and meanness there is a fellowship, a joy divine. Look up. God lives and by faith, looking up and climbing up, you may see the blessed sunshine and move in the calm, pure atmosphere of the Holy Spirit. Look up!

11

Whence Comes the Sermon Idea?

WILLIAM D. WATLEY

I will address the issue of sermon preparation in two ways. First, I will discuss the matter of where sermons come from, or where the preaching idea or the subject matter of preaching comes from. Then I will give some suggestions, based on my own method of sermon writing, on how we should prepare for public presentation or discourse the message that God has laid on our heart to deliver to the people of God. Let me say at the outset that I write not as an authority, but as a student of preaching. I do not speak ex cathedra. Rather, I approach this subject from the posture of a lifelong student and learner. Preaching for me is an ongoing process of learning and experimentation. I do not have a surefire method for successful preaching, however success is defined. I present one approach among many to a great undertaking and one answer among many to a great question.

Whenever we frail creatures of the dust, we "earthen vessels," dare to speak for Almighty, All-Glorious, and All-Righteous God, we should always do so hesitantly and with a spirit of humility. When we consider the variety of need as well as the depth and complexity of both pain and experience that are present in any given congregation of worshipers on any given day, at any given preaching moment, we are made acutely aware that we need more than our own wisdom and experience to adequately feed the flock of Christ. Thus, each preaching moment is as unique as the congregation to which it is addressed. It will never be repeated in the exact same composition and moment in time.

Where, then, do sermons come from? One hopes that the ongoing and standard answer to that question will always be the Holy Spirit. One hopes that the Holy Spirit is the primary and ultimate source of all preaching. However, most sermons do not fall straight from the Holy Spirit already packaged and prepared for delivery. In my experience, most sermons, while having the

Holy Spirit as their ultimate source, come to us as seed or as spark or as sperm in the midst of our own work and warfare, struggles and strife, agony and anxieties, experiences and ecstasies, fallings and risings, stumbling and recoveries, and require some participation and input from us to produce a finished product. How, then, does the Holy Spirit speak to us in the midst of daily living? How does the Holy Spirit move in the midst of our mess to produce the miracle of preaching?

As I ponder this issue, I have found the paradigm suggested by Grady Davis in the classic text *Design for Preaching* to be helpful. Like Davis, I believe that sermons can be life led, subject led, or text led. I believe it was Confucius who said that beauty is all around us but not everyone sees it. In the same way, I believe that sermons are all around us but only the eye of the preacher can see them. Where do sermons come from? They come from the everyday events and experiences of life. They come from the traffic that we are stuck in that reminds us that we cannot always have things our way and that there are some things over which we have no control. They come from our taking out the trash, which reminds us that we must deal with the ordinary and mundane things of life no matter how spiritual we are.

They come from commercials and advertisements and songs and television. They come from casual remarks made to us when we are standing in the checkout line at the grocery store or when we're at home. They come from lessons that we have learned from our successes and our failures. Sermons come from everyday occurrences that happen to us personally. Sermons also come from pivotal experiences and seasons that mark certain moments of transition and serve as rites of passage on our faith journey.

Nature all around us provides a good source of sermons. As a "city boy," I used to envy my colleagues from the country, who could draw so many illustrations from the nature that they observed as a normal part of growing up. Then, I discovered that one does not have to be from the country to learn the lessons of nature. If one subscribes to *National Geographic*, or if one watches the Weather Channel, the Discovery Channel, or Animal Planet, one can glean many lessons from nature. Or one can just observe the rotating patterns of the seasons and note how things grow in the spring, flourish in the summer, begin to wither in the fall, and die in the winter.

However, in the spring, when the resurrection happens, one observes the cycle and pattern of the Christian life and hope. If we look at fresh flowers in a vase and understand that they don't have much life because they have been cut off from the stem, then we understand what the Lord meant in John 15:4 about "abiding in the vine." However, if those flowers are fake, they look good but they do not have any fragrance.

When we look at the beauty, the patterns, and the variety of life found in nature, that's all preaching stuff. Psalm 8 (NRSV) declares:

> O LORD, our Sovereign,
> how majestic is your name in all
> the earth!
> You have set your glory above the
> heavens.
> Out of the mouths of babes and
> infants
> you have founded a bulwark
> because of your foes,
> to silence the enemy and the
> avenger.
> When I look at your heavens, the
> work of your fingers,
> the moon and the stars that you
> have established;
> what are human beings that you are
> mindful of them,
> mortals that you care for them?
> Yet you have made them a little
> lower than God,
> and crowned them with glory and
> honor.
> You have given them dominion
> over the works of your
> hands;
> you have put all things under
> their feet,
> all sheep and oxen,
> and also the beasts of the field,
> the birds of the air, and the fish of
> the sea,
> whatever passes along the paths
> of the seas.
> O LORD, our Sovereign,
> how majestic is your name in all
> the earth!

Psalm 19:1–4 (NRSV) reminds us that:

> The heavens are telling the glory of
> God;
> and the firmament proclaims
> his handiwork.

Day to day pours forth speech,
and night to night declares
knowledge.
There is no speech, nor are there
words;
their voice is not heard;
yet their voice goes out through
all the earth,
and their words to the end of the
world.

Since many of the Psalms emerge from David's own trouble and his experience, they also demonstrate how the issues, questions, and struggles that we encounter in our own faith journey can serve as sign and shadow or even source and substance for preaching. Listen to David in Psalm 27:1–2 (NRSV): "The LORD is my light and my salvation; whom shall I fear? The LORD is the stronghold of my life; of whom shall I be afraid? When evildoers assail me to devour my flesh—my adversaries and foes—they shall stumble and fall." That's personal and that's preaching. Not only is preaching prophetic and pastoral, it is also personal. Preaching cannot escape the personal as the man or woman of God looks at the meaning of life through the lenses of his or her own faith journey and still affirms that "God is . . ." That's the life-led sermon—when we look at something small or large, trite or tremendous and sense a message and see and hear a word from the Lord. In the life-led message, we move from life to the biblical text.

There is also a subject-led sermon. Subjects may come from life, from the Scriptures themselves, or from supplemental reading. Even though the text of life is the steering wheel, the sermon is guiding the car. However, even when a sermon is subject led or life led, the integrity of the biblical text must be respected. I have discovered that when one is preaching on a regular basis to the same congregation, thematic or series preaching is very helpful in providing focus to both the preacher as well as the congregation. Preaching that is based on what I refer to as the hunt-and-peck method—in which there is no consistency and no connection between one Sunday to the next—is like fast food as opposed to planned meals. Fast food and even junk food can be very filling and satisfying. However, growth comes when one carefully plans and prepares meals to make sure there is proper balance and a variety of food.

As preachers, our goal should not be congregational maintenance but congregational growth. I would caution us that even in this day of the sixty-second sound bite, we must be careful about choosing subjects that are sensationalistic but that have very little substance. It is still possible to choose subjects that are both exciting and excellent, that have meat as well as milk, that have power as well as pabulum, that are catchy without being crass. The pulpit is no place for the trite but for truth.

Thematic preaching helps develop discipline even if one is not preaching on a regular basis. If you are not a pastor and there is a series evolving in your soul, you should go ahead and preach it. Even if you preach only once a month, continue to prepare and write the series that you feel within. Sermons have what I call a *shelf life*. If we do not at least prepare what is evolving in our souls and resonating within our spirit within a certain period of time, while it is *on the shelf*, then what is in our souls will leave us. The fire will diminish. The season will pass. The urgency in our spirit will leave. It doesn't matter if we cannot preach what we prepare right away and we have to revise it when the opportunity presents itself. Because we have written down the message we felt burning within, we would not have lost the message reverberating within our spirit.

Sometimes, we will be assigned a theme or a topic to preach from that is too long, too convoluted, too dull and that makes no theological or even logical sense. Sometimes, we will be assigned a topic or a Scripture that we are just not "feeling." I believe that when one is assigned a theme or a passage of Scripture, then one should try to respect the brainchild that has been submitted by some well-intentioned committee or pastor who is attempting to be relevant, chic, or deep. However, I would be cautious about preaching where the Holy Spirit has not led and what the Holy Spirit has not given. We cannot get others to feel what we are not feeling ourselves. We cannot excite others about something we are not excited about ourselves. After making the effort to address a theme, if nothing comes to us, then my advice is to follow where the Holy Spirit is leading us. As an act of courtesy, we may be in touch with those who invited us to let them know that, while respecting their theme, we are led another way.

Text led—that's when you're reading the Bible and something comes out; the passage grips your spirit. That is the text-led sermon. My daddy used to say, "It's like there are neon lights around a particular word." Whether we are life led, subject led, or text led, we should not force a text. The text must fit into what we are saying, or what we are saying must fit into the text. The best habit that any preacher can have is the development of a regular, not crisis-oriented, devotional life.

The study of the Word should be consistent and personal. There is no substitute for a sustained devotional life. Not a day goes by that I am not in my Bible. I have several types of Bibles that I use. I read one for my devotional life and travel with one because it's small and easy to pack. There is also one I preach from. I sometimes read from them all. I spend time in prayer every day, and I study. I stay with my main resource, which is the Bible. If you read the Bible every day, it will take a year to complete the reading. You have to know your Word. Some people know it and live it better than you. It doesn't mean that you will always quote or recite a passage, but you should know the difference between truth and error. You have to stay in your Word. You can't live, preach, or minister without staying in your Bible. Don't tell me how busy you are. You can never be too busy to read and study the Word of God.

My preaching is planned. I think about the series, and the text will come to me. If you are having problems finding something to preach about, that means you are not reading enough. You have to stay with it and read. Devotional books and commentaries are good. However, there is no substitute for the Bible. When you stay in the Bible, things will come out at you, and you must read and write those things down.

Life led, text led, and subject led. If you select a text and it hits you, the first thing you want to do is read the text and see what it tells you. Self-applications come first, then you go to the commentaries. I read other people's sermons—Gardner C. Taylor, T. D. Jakes—and I put my children through school with the royalties that I received from books on sermons. A sermon is not a testimony. A sermon must flow. It must have a beginning, a middle, and an end. Organize your thoughts. In the black church, we end up on a high point and celebration. I personally resonate to the method espoused by Taylor: "Start low, go slow, get high, strike fire, and retire." Create a design. If you have one point, wear that one point down. Taylor says that some sermons will be like the walls of Jericho: you will march around them, and march around them until they fall.

I outlined my sermons until my father stopped me. I preached from John 14—"Make Ready and Make Way." My father told me that I better not preach without writing it out first because I didn't know enough about preaching. If you have an idea of what you are going to say and never write it down, then people will leave with the idea that you never developed. If you outline only, certain notes that you write will grow cold and their significance or meaning will be erased from memory.

Writing your message out allows you to convey, in language that is crystal clear and precise, what you are trying to say. Some of us never state the point when we use an outline. When we write everything out, we can develop a point. All of us need to write out our sermons word for word. It helps us to familiarize ourselves with the message. There will also be nuances that would not have come forth if you had put your sermon in an outline only. Gardner Taylor was one of my first instructors, and he stated that you should write your sermons up to your first twenty-five years of preaching. I have found out from my experiences that when I write my sermons, major points come out that ordinarily would not have come out. Do not confuse the two. You can develop an outline from the written sermon. It's okay to be a manuscript preacher, and it's okay to deliver a sermon from an outline.

Preparation time is very important. If you have to preach Sunday, do not start on Saturday night. You dishonor the Lord and the Word. Start preparing early enough. Sermons are like children: no two are alike. Some sermons will come to you easily within two hours, and some may take an entire day. I usually start to think about my sermon on Tuesday morning, and then I commit to a sermon-writing day on Thursday. I commit the entire day to preparing my sermon for Sunday. Always prepare for sermons, and if you must err, err on the side of preparation. After you have given your best and do your best, that's all you can do.

Sometimes, even with the most consistent and thorough preparation, you will still flunk. Get familiar with "Flunkersville" because you, like every other preacher, will visit there. Sometimes, the preacher is the reason, and other times the worship context or setting, the length of the service, all that has taken place before the preaching moment, "the spirit" or issues in the congregation itself, the tiredness of the audience, and various distractions over which you have no control will be major contributing factors to one's visit to Flunkersville.

Let me say two things about Flunkersville. First, a visit to Flunkersville does not mean that it has to be our permanent address. When we visit Flunkersville, we should learn from our mistakes, seek repentance from God for not doing justice to the Word or the people of God, and make every effort not to do the same thing again. Second, remember that everything that looks like Flunkersville is not Flunkersville. There have been times when I have bombed so badly that I wished the ground would open up and swallow me, or that I could go somewhere and hide and never show my face in public again.

There have been times when I have flunked so badly that I wondered if I was really called to preach. And during those moments (not every time, but often), someone will invariably walk up to me and say, "Thank you, Reverend, that was just the word that I needed to hear." Or months or even years later, I hear someone quote from the sermon that I thought was so poor. Whenever instances like this happen, I am reminded again of how imprecise a craft the preaching enterprise is and how often God gets the victory in spite of those of us who preach. Like the seed growing secretly, many times God is working when we are not aware of the movement of God's hand and power. Often, God is speaking mightily even when the response to a sermon was not what we had wanted or had imagined, or what our own egos told us it ought to have been.

Whenever I visit Flunkersville, in reality or in my perception, I am humbled indeed, and reminded again of the truth that the preaching enterprise is really not about *us* but about *God*. Every preacher who attempts to declare God's Word should always remember Paul's statement in 2 Corinthians:

Therefore, since it is by God's mercy that we are engaged in this ministry, we do not lose heart. We have renounced the shameful things that one hides; we refuse to practice cunning or to falsify God's word; but by the open statement of the truth we commend ourselves to the conscience of everyone in the sight of God. . . . For we do not proclaim ourselves; we proclaim Jesus Christ as Lord and ourselves as your slaves for Jesus' sake. For it is the God who said, "Let light shine out of darkness," who has shone in our hearts to give the light of the knowledge of the glory of God in the face of Jesus Christ. But we have this treasure in clay jars, so that it may be made clear that this extraordinary power belongs to God and does not come from us. We are afflicted in every way, but not crushed; perplexed, but not driven to despair; persecuted, but not forsaken; struck down, but not destroyed; always carrying in the body the death of Jesus, so that the life of Jesus may also be made visible in our bodies. (2 Cor. 4:1–3, 5-10, NRSV)

Sermon: Healing Shadows
Acts 5:14–15

WILLIAM D. WATLEY

Peter had surely come a long way since that incident recorded in Luke 5 when the Lord taught the crowds that gathered along the seashore from Simon Peter's boat. Then the Lord told Peter to let down his nets, and even though Peter had fished all night long and had caught nothing, he still obeyed the Master's instructions. Peter received such an abundant catch of fish that he fell down on his knees before Jesus and said, "Go away from me, Lord, for I am a sinful man!" Peter had come a long way since Jesus had first called him and had invited him to be a fisher of people. Peter had surely come a long way since the night that Jesus was betrayed and tried. He had come a long way since he had forthrightly declared at the Last Supper that he would follow Jesus even to death. He had come a long way since he had pulled a knife later that same evening and had cut off the ear of the high priest's servant in a futile and unnecessary effort to save Jesus when the Lord was arrested. He had come a long way since he had cursed and sworn that he didn't even know Jesus still later that same evening. He had surely come a long way, when upon realizing what he had done, he went off to himself and broke down like a baby and wept bitterly.

Peter had even come a long way since his restoration beside the Sea of Tiberias when Jesus charged him to "Feed my lambs . . . Tend my sheep . . . Feed my sheep." From hesitant self-confessed sinner, to overconfident saint, to fallen saint, to restored and humbled church leader, Peter had surely come a long way to reach the point in our text when the sick believed that God's power was so heavily on him that if his shadow simply fell on them as he passed by, they could be healed. If anyone had seen Peter on his knees before Jesus that day when he first met the Master, begging the Lord to go away from him because of his sin, or if anyone had seen him pulling a knife to attack an enemy or cursing and swearing and denying Jesus, if anyone had seen him crying with remorse because of his shameful actions, no one would have ever guessed that this same Peter would have such an anointing upon his life that people would believe his very shadow contained healing properties.

At what point did Peter emerge into such a spiritually powerful personality? The New Testament doesn't record any one defining moment in which he became the person we see in the text whose shadow was believed powerful enough to heal. The New Testament records the moment of his call and his confession of faith in Jesus as the Son of the living God. The New Testament records some of his mistakes, and some of his greatest ups and lowest downs. The New Testament records some of his miracles, but at no point does it say that at this moment Peter became holy, or at this moment Peter became spiritual, or at this moment Peter became an anointed healer whose shadow was believed to have healing properties. Perhaps there was no defining moment in which Peter crossed the threshold from being unholy to holy, or nonspiritual to spiritual, or an ordinary believer to a person who could cast a healing shadow. Perhaps with Peter, it was all of his experiences—his highs and his lows, his victories and defeats, his progress and his retrogression—which when added up, made him the spiritual healing giant that we see in Acts 5.

Perhaps there are persons who have a defining moment in which they can consciously recall, in which they can say that at this minute or hour or during this experience I crossed the threshold from weakness to strength, or I grew from an infant or adolescent believer to a mature Christian. However, I am inclined to believe that most of us are like Peter, that holiness, being strong, or loving, or faithful is not something that we consciously reach, like we know when we arrive at a destination such as church or home. It is not something that we achieve, like an award or a diploma or a degree, when we know that it has been bestowed. I am inclined to believe that with most of us, holiness, strength, growth, becoming a new person is something that just happens to us as we daily follow the Lord and faithfully serve him, and go through our ups and downs, our sorrows and our celebrations, our failures, our frustrations, and our triumphs.

While a number of us are looking up in the sky waiting for some great sign or happening to occur that lets us know that we have been changed and then feel disappointed because we don't have some great life-changing, foundation-shaking story to tell or experience to relate, every day God is working in our lives to make a new person out of us. With every failure or mistake, God has a lesson for us. With every triumph and victory, God confirms his Word for us. Day by day, trial by trial, and triumph by triumph, God is building us into a person with an unusual love, or unusual commitment, or an unusual gift of generosity or encouragement or service. We don't know when the moment of our maturation or development occurs. All we know is that we find ourselves in a mess, and we can remember a time when we wouldn't have been able to take it or make it. But now miraculously we find ourselves able to endure stuff and bounce back stronger, facing something that would have turned us around or crushed our faith a while back. When did we get so strong? We really don't know; we just looked up one day and saw a shadow of strength beside us.

We can remember a time when some things would have upset us to no end. We would have lost our religion and almost our mind. Now, we pay no attention to talk and things that used to upset us. We don't know when we learned to be so calm and quit allowing things to upset and get next to us. We just looked up one day and noticed a shadow of peace walking beside us. We can remember a time when we would have carried a disdain for certain people for the rest of our lives. We can remember when we would have spent time and energy trying to get even or at least thinking about how to get even. We can remember a time when the very sight of them upset us. We can remember a time when we would have talked them down to everybody we met. Now we can forgive them and bear them no ill will. We don't know when our feelings changed. We just know that we looked up one day and saw a shadow of love beside us. Before we were aware of it, God's grace had cast some healing shadows of strength, faithfulness, joy, peace, and love upon our lives.

How did Peter develop his healing shadow? If you had asked Peter, he wouldn't have been able to tell you if his very life had depended on it. He couldn't tell you not because he didn't have spiritual depth. Peter couldn't have told you how he developed a healing shadow because he didn't give it to himself. God gave Peter his healing shadow as he faithfully followed and served the Lord Jesus Christ. We cannot manufacture a shadow. Shadows only show up when the conditions are right, when the lighting is right. When I was a little boy growing up in St. Louis, every Sunday afternoon after church I would listen to the radio to hear my favorite program, "The Shadow." The Shadow was just what the name implies: a shadow. In the radio program, the Shadow was a mysterious phantom crime-stopping presence on the order of Superman, or Wonder Woman, or Batman, or Flash. I never knew where the Shadow came from or where it went with its bone-chilling laughter; I just knew when the conditions were right, when he was really needed, the Shadow would always turn up to save the day.

As believers, it's all right to have an image of holiness or of what it means to be a true Christian. But we need to understand that we cannot make ourselves holy, or a Christian, or anointed, anymore than we can will our shadows into existence. God produces holiness or greatness or strength when the conditions are right. Let me just say to our young preachers that you don't make yourselves into great preachers. You don't become a great preacher by listening to tapes or by watching television. You don't become a great preacher by trying to copy somebody else's style. You don't become a great preacher by sitting down on somebody else when they are trying to preach or by criticizing somebody else. You don't become a great preacher by being jealous or resentful of somebody else's gifts or opportunities or growth. You don't become a great preacher by becoming sullen and resentful because you are not being given all the preaching opportunities that your ego tells you that you deserve. God will make you a great preacher when the conditions are right.

First, God has to give you the gift, and then you have to develop that gift through prayer, study, submission, obedience, and trying to walk your talk. You have to have a love for God and a hunger and thirst for the Word of God. You have to have a passion for lost souls. You have to understand that this thing called preaching is not about your being in the spotlight but about the glory of God. When the conditions are right, God will provide you with opportunities for you to develop into the preacher that God wants you to be.

You don't become a Christian on your own. That's why some of us are so frustrated in our efforts to be Christian. We think that we can make ourselves into one by dressing a certain way, looking a certain way, talking a certain way, and having a certain self-made and manufactured aura of holiness. We don't give ourselves the Holy Spirit. We don't teach ourselves how to shout or dance. We don't come up with our own tongue based on what we have seen or heard others do or say, or what somebody has taught us. Our job is to just love God and to remain open to God doing something new in our lives. Our job is to have the desire to grow deeper and reach higher. Our job is to study the Word of God so that when God does begin to move in our lives we will understand what is happening. Our job is to surrender ourselves for service to others. Our job is to be faithful. And when the conditions are right, being Christian will emerge as effortlessly as rainbows after the storm or as springtime's flowering after winter's barrenness. We can't scream the Holy Spirit down or force it down or command it down or play it down or shout it down or preach it down. When the conditions are right, the Holy Spirit will come forth with the fruit and the appropriate gifts. If I read Acts 2 correctly, the church gathered in the upper room did not bring Pentecost. God sent the Holy Spirit when the conditions were right. God will cause the appropriate praise to spring forth from your life when the conditions are right.

You can't make others respect you or give you what you think is your proper deference. But if the conditions are right, if you walk humble before the Lord, if you seek to serve and not be served, if you manifest the fruit of the Holy Spirit which begins with love, when you don't take yourself or your title too seriously, when you are not always fighting for recognition, when the conditions are right, God will bring forth respect, admiration, and love from people.

We can't even make ourselves into a tither. All we can do is surrender all that we are and all that we have to God. When we truly surrender ourselves to God, when we truly love God with all of our hearts and all of our souls and all of our minds, then God will bless us with the proper giving spirit. Love for God, surrender to God, gratitude to God, trust in God—those are the conditions for a tithing spirit. That's why some of us are having such trouble with tithing. We have not truly surrendered our whole hearts to the Lord, for where our treasure is, that's where our hearts are also. But when we say, "I'm yours, Lord, everything I am, everything I'm not, everything I've got. I'm yours, Lord, try me now and see, see if I can be completely yours," when we say that and mean it, God will give us a spirit of tithing. "That's too much money to give to the church," some people say. What's too much to give to the work of the One who has given us our life, our health, our families, and whatever success we have had? What's too much to give to the One who has answered our prayers, made ways out of no ways, and kept enemies at bay? What is too much to give to the One who has brought us through messes, brought us out of mud, and delivered us when our own foolishness, flesh, and shortsightedness could have destroyed us?

Peter was able to cast a healing shadow. Shadows, as I have said all through this message, emerge when the conditions are right. There must be light to see a shadow. If there is only darkness, the shadow may be there but we can't see it. And a shadow is not a shadow unless you can see it. For the shadow to emerge, there has to be some light. And when the light is present, when the conditions are right, you can't stop a shadow from showing up. The psalmist has said, "Your word is a lamp unto my feet and a light unto my path." When we walk in self, that's darkness. When our theme song is "I did it my way," that's darkness. When we walk in sin, that's darkness. When we walk in ignorance, that's darkness. When we walk according to the wishes of others, that's darkness. But when we walk in the Word of God, that's light. Tithing is the Word of God, and that's light. Obedience and surrender are the Word of God, and that's light. Service is the Word of God, and that's light. Justice and truth are the Word of God, and that's light. Enlightenment is the Word of God, and that's light.

Peter was able to cast a healing shadow because the light hit him the right way. To cast a healing shadow, a powerful shadow, an anointed shadow, we have to walk in the light. Jesus said, "I am the light of the world. Whoever follows me will never walk in darkness but will have the light of life." If we walk in Jesus, we will cast a shadow of healing. If we walk in Jesus, we will cast a shadow of love. If we walk in Jesus, we will cast a shadow of faith. If we walk in Jesus we will cast a shadow of strength. If we walk in Jesus, we will cast a shadow of peace. No wonder George D. Elderkin wrote:

> Walk in the light, beautiful light;
> Come where the dewdrops of mercy shine bright
> Shine all around us by day and by night,
> Jesus, the light of the world.
> > (from "Jesus, the Light of the World")

12

Weaving the Textual Web

RALPH WEST

How would you like to write a biblical sermon with relevant applications? Anyone who has attempted this task knows all too well that the preparation process is demanding. If you have the responsibility of preaching weekly to the same congregation, you have undoubtedly learned two important lessons. The first is that the longer you occupy the place of principal preacher, the more demanding the responsibility to preach relevant messages becomes and the more difficult it is to remain fresh. The second is the sense of urgency created by the breakneck speed at which time elapses between Sunday and the next preaching weekend.

The longer the pastorate, the more insistent these realities are. If you have a family, making time for them while staying with the modus operandi of church affairs is challenging. Add to these the interposition of other important matters—current events, exercising, reading, and community involvement. Of course, one cannot relinquish the indispensable several rounds of golf! How you manage your time in terms of sermon preparation is critical.

The purpose of this chapter is to share with those who read it the method that I use in writing a biblical sermon. This may be helpful to preachers seeking a primer on the elementary principles of sermon preparation and a method to help busy pastors craft messages creatively. Preparing a sermon is like weaving a web from many components, much like a textile crafts worker weaves multicolored fabric from single fibers. Just as weaving is an intricate process, so is the writing of a sermon.

Consider the question King Zedekiah posed to the prophet Jeremiah in a time of national crisis: "Is there any word from the LORD?" (Jer. 37:17, NKJV). A similar query falls from the lips of congregants who have battled all week in the marketplace, in their homes, with families, in relationships, and with the various issues of life. They are asking if there is any news from another network.

They are seeking directions for life and declaratives that cannot be found in the self-help section of the local bookstore.

People are yearning for something to satisfy their longing for purpose and meaning in life. This is evident in our culture's fascination with materialism, hedonism, and relativism. People do not know how to satisfy their deep longings. Yet they do know that what they are consuming does not meet their needs. Fortunately, a favorable consequence results—people are discovering that these superficial and ultimately meaningless diets cannot satisfy their deepest spiritual longings. A line from the popular hymn "Lift Him Up" says, "Oh, the world is hungry for the living bread, lift the Savior up for them to see." Therefore, the apostle Paul's imperative, "preach the word" (2 Tim. 4:2, NKJV), becomes the preacher's mantra.

The Christian preacher is under biblical mandate to feed God's sheep. The food for nourishment is Scripture. The preacher's essential task is to communicate the Word with the centrality of Christ in proclamation. Unfortunately, ours is a time when the phrase *the Word* is thrown around with the velocity of a fastball that breaks like a slider. There is a sect in the community of faith that promotes itself as "preachers of the Word." The definition of a "Word preacher" is as difficult to define as the term *postmodern*.

SELECTING THE THREADS

It is Monday morning and you are haggard from the previous day. The next Sunday's text is staring you squarely in the face, that is, assuming you have a text. The quest for a text can be harrowing. Series preaching may prove helpful here. It works well for me. I am currently preaching a series from the book of Nehemiah titled "From Ruin to Renewal, the God Who Rebuilds Broken Lives." Individual sermons in this series cover all or portions of chapters and have such titles as "Caring Enough to Pray" (1:1–11), "Matters of the Heart" (2:1–10), and "Dealing with Discouragement" (4:10–23).

Series preaching, however, does not have to be limited to biblical books. A good series could involve themes in the Bible, for example, "The Glory of God." This thematic series could commence with the Exodus narrative with Moses' request to see the glory of the Lord (Exod. 33:18). Isaiah 6 could be a subsequent delight in preaching this series. The New Testament story of Jesus' transfiguration could be next, with the series culminating in the Jude doxology.

Series preaching is an effective approach to selecting a text because it is consistent with the way the culture thinks. The media lends much that is useful in preaching. For example, a person sitting at home during the day becomes addicted to the soaps. These melodramas develop a plot and draw it out. A person can return to them after an absence of weeks or even months without losing the story line. Similarly, a person looks at Oprah Winfrey's or some other talk show. Although the themes on these shows change from day to day, the basic formats remain the same. The faces are the same. The audience sounds the same. Therefore, selecting books of the Bible, biblical characters, and biblical themes is a helpful approach. I mention these methods because with a week to prepare for worship, I need to reduce the amount of "treasure-hunting time" as much as possible.

Often, I am asked how long a series should last and when it should end. My response is that it depends on your congregation and on your popularity within the context of your pastorate. I will normally preach a message series ranging from four to eight weeks. I have occasionally preached four months on one theme or from one book in the Bible.

I start early when looking for texts to preach. I use the month of December to plan this phase of sermon preparation. I have to balance between an abundance of Christmas cheer and attending to the preaching load of the coming weeks. Therefore, I rest during the first week, taking advantage of walks in the park, strolls through Houston's Galleria, and drives in the country. I use this week to center down, to detox spiritually and physically as I clear my thoughts. During this time I do not think much about preaching.

I spend the second week reading the Bible and praying about where God is leading the church. I am keenly sensitive to the Holy Spirit's guidance and direction. I look at themes. I pay attention to our congregational life. I listen to what the people are saying and the questions they are asking about life. I factor conversations and events as well as social and political happenings into the text-selection process.

During week three, I read, look, and listen for the Spirit to speak to me regarding what he wants me to say to the congregation. I am careful to consult with the Holy Spirit, for I am in partnership with him in shepherding the sheep. During this week, I select the material I will use to develop my sermons. Usually, I prepare four, five, and as many as six weeks of sermons at a time. I determine the texts, theses, and titles and submit them for printing and to the worship leader for planning the music, Scriptures, and prayer. By week four, I have completed at least two manuscripts and developed thesis statements for others. This process is repeated in the summer for the fall months of September to December.

During December, I also prepare the next four to six months of preaching. My goal is to plan ahead to the month of May. May is a difficult time for me because my biorhythms change and I begin to slow down. This is when I start planning for the month of June and for the rest of the summer. My preaching load is reduced during July and August. These are the months that I do academic study and take vacation.

Monthly Preaching Schedule

December	Advent Messages, Christmas, Watch Night (December 31)
January	The Lordship of Christ (During this time the people make commitments)
February	Black History Month (Messages, however, do not focus on black themes)
March	The Family
April	The Cross

Some people have voiced concerns about the efficacy of selecting texts weeks ahead of time. They inquire about the role of the Holy Spirit. They ask, "How do you know that the Spirit will not change the message?" My response is that it is his church. He can alter the preaching format any way he chooses. My aim is to give the Spirit something with which to work. Accordingly, I plan early, but if I have to delay preaching a text or abandon it altogether for the sake of some special event—for example, the September 11, 2001, attack on America—I will. Fortunately, I did not have to do so in this case.

As I was working on my preaching patterns for the fall in the summer of 2001, the book of Nehemiah was given to me, "From Ruin to Renewal, the God Who Rebuilds Broken Lives," mentioned earlier. Ordinarily, I choose the particular book of the Bible or series of messages, but in this case Nehemiah chose me and placed a demand upon me to preach it. With no foreshadowing of the events to come, I could not have asked for a better book to be preaching through! Following September 11, I heard the report given to Nehemiah: "The survivors who are left . . . are there in great distress and reproach," and I witnessed what Nehemiah saw, "the wall . . . is also broken down, and its gates are burned with fire" (1:3, NKJV). I wept when I saw the ruins. As one dear lady in our congregation commented, "If you had started the series two weeks later, it would not have the impact it is having in our church." That was one of those "ah-hah" moments in preaching.

TREATING THE TEXT

I carefully select the beginning and ending of my pericope. This prevents my wandering about the chapter. My text is that portion of Scripture I will be treating in detail. Although the text may be located in the middle of the chapter, I read it contextually with a sense of what is taking place before and after my preaching passage. A well-apportioned pericope retains the contextual integrity of the text.

It is important to me to read the pericope in its original language and in a good English translation. Since I am familiar with the languages, I read the text in Greek or in Hebrew. This helps me to get a feel for how the author wrote the passage. Although this exercise can be laborious, it yields valuable fruit. If you are not skilled in biblical languages, a good English translation will prove to be most helpful. It is advisable that you read several translations to better exegete the text.

I practice reading and rereading the text many times. This disciplines my observation and allows me to look at the particulars of the text to see where they lead before I form conclusions about them. I continue to read silently and aloud until I can sense the movements within the passage. I want to experience what the writer's intentions are. I pay strict attention to the words, phrases, and nuances within the text. I want to see how the author uses these words and phrases elsewhere in the biblical text and how other biblical writers use them as well.

I closely observe particular terms and grammatical and literary relationships. I note such usages as "like," "for," "because," "therefore," and "so that" because they express relationships between words. I look for relationships that contrast, form comparisons, progress along a continuum of thought or climax. I look for hinges in the text, pivots that swing the thought in other directions. I try to detect the tone of the text. I determine if the author is encouraging, rebuking, or instructing his listeners. I pay attention to signs of approval, displeasure, or indifference in the general atmosphere of the text. These literary relationships help me "see" the text and prevent me from reading my own thoughts into it.

With a blank sheet of paper before me, I write down each verse and record my best thoughts on the text. At this point, I am not attempting to write the sermon—I am merely engaging these initial stages of my detective work. By now I have a grasp of the setting of the text, who the characters are, and why the author wrote it. I also know what the author is communicating to the recipients of the text and why he chose to use certain terminology in this passage.

Though this method is initially tedious, what I am establishing are the historical-grammatical and theological perspectives to the biblical text. I am rescued from eisegesis and a privatized interpretation. The phrases that we often hear, such as "The Lord just dropped this in my spirit" and "You have never heard this before," may not be compliments. If an idea is novel but cannot be substantiated by Scripture and two thousand years of church history, its "revelation" is insupportable.

The Bible demands my best as I approach it. I value being able to work through the text in its own literary, historical-cultural, and theological context as I allow it to speak to me. I utilize scholarly commentaries, but only after I have done the grunt work of investigating the text on my own. Neither can I, nor any other scholar, dictate what the text says. My aim in reading commentaries is to ascertain what other investigators see in the text, noting where they agree with me and where they disagree. This enhances my observation, analysis, and interpretation of the text.

Following this exercise I am ready to write the preliminary page (see the sample page, below). This involves establishing the movements of the message. The first entry on this page is a concise interpretive sentence of eighteen words or less of what the text means in past tense. This is called the "Central Idea of the Text," or CIT. The CIT provides the historical intent of the text. This is most important in shaping the sermon.

The second entry is the "Main Objective of the Text," or MOT. Here, I ask if the text is doctrinal, ethical, consecrative, prophetic, exhortative, or pastoral. Once I determine the text's objective, I start thinking about how I might want to treat this message. I find it quite useful to understand the genre in which the passage is written. For instance, I ask whether the text is historical narrative or report narrative, poetry or wisdom, prophetic or apocalyptic. The genre determines how the message is to be repeated. One does not tell a story by saying, "Once upon a time in the West, first there were . . . then second there were . . . and third it so happened. . . ." Stories are told and each movement identified without numbered statements sequencing the events that take place.

I write the thesis next. The thesis is the sermon represented in a concise statement. Every word hinges on this one statement. It can be a question, a sentence, or a problem that needs to be resolved. It can be simply a rewriting of the CIT in present tense, or a new statement. In most instances, I write a completely different statement. I work diligently to word and reword the thesis until it flows naturally.

The "Main Objective of the Sermon," or MOS, follows the thesis. I record what I expect from the sermon. I ask the following questions: What do I want the hearers to learn? What do I want my audience to become? What do I want my audience to do?

The title is the last thing that I write on the preliminary page before moving to my outline. The title is hard work for me. I am not naturally creative or clever; therefore, I have to work very diligently on my titles. One method I have found effective is strolling through the aisles of bookstores and perusing titles in the stacks. I find their wordings helpful when I wrestle with titling a text.

One caution to observe when crafting sermons and titles is to try not to select a title before writing the sermon. The idea is not the title, and if it is, remember to let the text feed the idea rather than a story, quote, or situation. This may be difficult when an idea comes to you. While you may possess the cognitive ability to tie titles to text, I have difficulty functioning that way. On the other hand, if you are a topical preacher, it may suit you just fine to determine the title first, then the text.

Sample Preliminary Page

Text:	Hosea 14:1–9
CIT:	God commanded Israel to repent and promised his forgiveness and renewal.
MOT:	Consecrative
Thesis:	Going home to God and being home with him require returning and receiving the forgiveness God offers us.
MOS:	We may be at home with God. Sin estranges us from God, but if we repent and accept the forgiveness of God, we may reestablish our relationship with him. This is what God desires for us.
Title:	"Going Home to God"
Outline:	1. Going home to God is returning to him for our redemption (vv. 1–3). 2. Going home to God is receiving from him our spiritual renewal (vv. 4–7). 3. Going home to God is removing anything that obstructs our reconciliation to him (vv. 8–9).

WEAVING THE WEFT

In weaving, the *warp*, the taut vertical threads, are interwoven with the *weft*, the horizontal threads, to form fabric. I can see the fabric of my sermon beginning to take shape. I am now ready to script my outline. I construct it from movements in the text. Regardless of their number—whether one, two, or five—I want to determine the movements by the text. The text must shape my sermon because Scripture is my authority. Whatever may be the issue, need, or subject I am addressing, its authority is rooted in the ancient text. The "Supremacy of God" in preaching is my passion and aim in proclamation; thus, the Bible is my authority.

THREADING THE NEEDLE

Our culture is characterized as philosophically relativistic, essentially rejecting all moral, ethical, and spiritual absolutes. Herein lies the necessity for a truth that is absolute—the Bible becomes that truth: "All Scripture is God-breathed and is useful for teaching, rebuking, correcting and training in righteousness" (2 Tim. 3:16, NIV). Christian preaching, then, should contain two elements: (1) the centrality of Christ in the proclamation, and (2) biblical content.

Once I have established the central idea of the text, determined the main objective of the text, written the thesis sentence, settled the main objective of the sermon, and written the outline, I move to the next level. Having entered the text and walked around in it, I find that it is time to exit and allow the text to get into me. It is now time to ask the question God posed to Ezekiel, "Can these bones live?" and to respond as Ezekiel did, "O Lord GOD, You know" (Ezek. 37:1–3, NKJV).

How do I approach compiling all of this information into a sermon? I work with a schedule. This helps me to plan and utilize my time more effectively. My aim is to complete the work on Monday evening. I am a nocturnal creature whose assignment in life is to help the Creator keep watch of the night world. So, I work late into the night. Nevertheless, I usually miss my self-imposed Monday night deadline, completing my sermon on Thursday night instead.

Sermon Preparation Schedule

Monday	Complete Preliminary Page (CIT, MOT, Thesis, MOS, determine movements)
Tuesday	Write sermon synopsis
Wednesday	Write draft of sermon
Thursday	Complete sermon; prepare final manuscript; pray

BEATING THE FABRIC

As fabric forms from the weaving of the warp and the weft, the weaver "beats" it to maintain its tautness. The preacher must ensure that his or her sermon is taut, giving attention to each detail. The beating process starts with my introduction. The introduction is significant. From listening to the evening news, I discover the power of opening words. The television presents a talking head giving fast-paced, attention-grabbing highlights of news reports in the first few seconds of the program, with promises that details will follow after a short commercial break. A few moments later the talking head returns, making good on the promises.

If at the outset the anchorperson announces "Three men held up a bank today, details in a moment," one can expect that he or she will return talking not about the stock market or the latest weather update, but about the three men who held up the bank. So it is with my sermon introductions. If my introduction is not an attention-getter, I risk losing my audience before I get off the ground. I write it so that it will not be boring, insulting, or incomprehensible.

The amount of time I have to get the attention of my hearers is limited, so I want my introduction to be focused and timed adequately. Some of my opening words are a statement, or a quote, even a story, but I know my audience—I have one or two minutes to draw them into the message or I will lose them.

As I continue to weave the threads of the message, the pattern takes shape. At this point, the literary genre of the passage becomes important. Genre dictates how I approach the sermon's development. If the genre is narrative, I weave the thread as a story, allowing the listeners to hear and sense the movements. However, if I am working with prose or poetry, I handle it differently. For example, the proverb "Train up a child in the way he should go, and when he is old he will not depart from it" (Prov. 22:6, NKJV) is not to be understood hermeneutically as a moral absolute. The principle this text teaches is that if a child is reared in the way of God, he or she will not stray from the path; rather, the possibility of departure is lessened because of the way of the Lord.

I derive the points of my sermon directly from the biblical text. I remember that I am preaching the Word of God. This is where my knowledge of biblical languages is indispensable. I locate those points and or movements by block-diagramming the passage. In his book *Toward an Exegetical Theology*, Walter Kaiser provides some good illustrations of this practice. I use it to identify the dominant and subordinate clauses of the text. A question I am often asked concerns the number of points a sermon should have. The answer is, at least one, or as many as the text under development presents. I no longer identify my points as first, second, third, and so on, mainly because I enjoy the conversational method of speaking.

Rarely if ever in a conversation do you say to someone, "Let me say three things to you" and enumerate them as you speak. Normally, you initiate a conversation, and simply say what you want to say; for example, "Oh, I'm on my way to Alabama." "Which city?" "Birmingham." "I know something about Birmingham." "I know that the summers are sweltering." "Yes, but the people are nice." "I agree. Have you visited the civil rights museum?" "Have you visited the one in Memphis? Now, there's a city for you. The food and the music are to die for." This is what I mean by the term *movements*.

A sermon may have many movements in feeding the idea. I simply allow the text to flow—it is what governs the direction of the conversation. Initially, this method was uncomfortable to me. Now I am not as impressed with my outline as I am intrigued by the development of the idea.

This may appear at first to restrict creativity. I assure you that it does not. There are times when I may focus on the subordinate and develop a sermon from it without obscuring the dominant. Remember, for a sermon to be a biblical sermon the biblical text must shape, move, and feed it.

The points of my message serve to inform, explain, and illustrate the thesis of my message. Every movement defends the message on one hand and explains it on the other. Herein lies the importance of illustrations. My illustrations clarify my points by illuminating something that may not be clear. I am often asked where I get my illustrations. The answer is, from everywhere. Part of my reading includes biography. I read about interesting people from the past as well as fascinating contemporary persons. My reading list is not limited to religious contributors but to the nonreligious as well, even scandalous people.

I love real-life illustrations. My children have been the source of many wonderful bright lights. Now that they are older I am careful to ask their permission. At other times I may use a quote, a poem, a hymn, or a story. However, I never want to lose focus on the purpose of my illustration, that is, to clarify the point I am making. I caution against excessive illustrating. You can become so engrossed with your cleverness that you might clutter the message rather than bring light to it.

It is my unswerving conviction that the Bible is relevant in today's world and that this ancient text speaks to every need of people living in the twenty-first century. I am always mindful that my challenge is to close the hermeneutical gap for my listeners—to help them understand what the text meant when it was written thousands of years ago and what it means today. My purpose transcends the mere impartation of knowledge—I want them to hear from God and to respond to him in obedience and faith. To this end, I seriously consider the application.

The application has been called the "slice of life." In its formulation I repeat the questions I posed at the outset: What are the hearers to do with this message? What do I want listeners to learn or to become? If the cloth has no practical use—that is, a blanket, rug, or basket—then the weaver's efforts are wasted. The sermon must be something the people can use or they will ask, "So what?" If I don't show my congregation how to apply the message, I have reduced it to a mere report. However, it is critical that the message mean something to the people who hear it.

For example, if I am preaching on prayer, I want the people to know what prayer is and how it works. I want them to become conscious of God and to spend time with him. In short, I want my people to obey the message and grow from it.

In approaching the application, I try to determine (1) how the author intended the text to apply when he wrote it; (2) how his application(s) may apply today; (3) the principles that the text teaches; and (4) how to relate these principles to real-life situations. I extract some of the data for these real-life situations from (1) church-related individual and corporate matters; (2) religious, political, and social concerns; (3) cultural concerns; and (4) local, state, national, and international events.

DRAWING THE STRINGS

Sermons should have well-prepared conclusions. The preacher must draw the string so that the people will say they got the message. Otherwise, the fabric of the sermon is left there to unravel. Final impressions are important. The conclusion helps to establish these impressions. Having said this, I admit that this is a challenging task for me. I have to think hard about how I want to end my sermon. I tend to get lazy and to rely on the inspiration of the moment. I want to draw every significant fiber and bring all of them to a close. One strategy for concluding my messages is to summarize my main points. Actually, this "summary" is simply the sequential reiteration of the main points. This serves to keep the message unified and reinforces it in the minds of the people.

Another approach to closure that works quite well for me is an illustration, primarily telling a story. This helps me to stay focused. Like the weaver "beats the warp" to pack the cloth tightly, so my story packs my sermon. In this way, I avoid prolonging the closing, thereby causing it to lose its effect. I also avoid straying from the original thesis. This closing illustration clarifies the message as a whole. This illustration is different from the ones I mentioned earlier that serve to clarify my major points. If related well, the closing illustration makes an impact; the people "get it." I strive to ensure that it is meaningful. No matter how brilliant my closing may be to me, if the people do not get the message, I have failed in my purpose.

THE FINISHED PRODUCT

Having designed and fashioned a product that will be admired and appreciated, the weaver stands back and considers his or her handiwork. All the thought and time that was invested in its production was well worth it. If the quality is good, the product is ready for market. Having crafted his sermon, the preacher must now give thought to delivering it. Robert Smith of Beeson Divinity School lists several processes in sermon delivery: investigation, familiarization, memorization, internalization, and picturization.

The last thing I do when my sermon is complete is to "turn in." I want to live the message now. It becomes my sermon. I employ Smith's processes as strategies to help me "get into" my sermon. I love to see how the data obtained from my investigation develops, taking a shape and a form. I familiarize myself with every aspect of my sermon. Familiarization, in turn, leads to memorization. When I memorize the message, I can preach it with freedom. Though I write a manuscript for each sermon, I do not use it when preaching. I carefully internalize the message; it becomes part of me.

In picturization I work to make it colorful. I see pictures, hear sounds, and feel emotions. All my senses are involved. I hear the crash of the waves against the breakers as Moses lifts the rod over the sea. I see the majestic mountains capped with the whiteness of snow as the Creator speaks the world into existence. I experience the lonely, desolate barrenness of the desert where Jesus fasts and is tempted. Finally, I pray. I thank the Lord for allowing me to grow through this process. I ask him to bless his people through this message and to be glorified in it.

Sermon: Declare These Things
Titus 1:11–15

RALPH WEST

They must be silenced, because they are ruining whole households by teaching things they ought not to teach—and that for the sake of dishonest gain. Even one of their own prophets has said, "Cretans are always liars, evil brutes, lazy gluttons." This testimony is true. Therefore, rebuke them sharply, so that they will be sound in the faith and will pay no attention to Jewish myths or to the commands of those who reject the truth. To the pure, all things are pure, but to those who are corrupted and do not believe, nothing is pure. In fact, both their minds and consciences are corrupted. (NIV)

Letting go is difficult—especially when letting go involves a person you love. Yet, in order for that person to reach his or her potential, letting go is necessary.

This summer, my wife Sheretta and I felt the gravity of this when we took our son, Ralph, to Atlanta to attend Morehouse College. It was probably the most difficult thing that Ree and I have experienced, leaving our firstborn in a different city with people we did not know to educate, yea, even cultivate him. Not knowing what to expect, we asked ourselves: Did we make the right choice in schools? How will he adjust? Will he and his roommate mesh? And, of course, the silent questions that remained housed in our hearts.

After Ralph was settled in his dormitory and our day of departure arrived, I felt that I needed to give my son one lasting gift. Pulling Ralph to the side, I laid my hand on his shoulder and told him how proud I was of him. I reinforced that I loved him and that there was nothing that he could do to make me love him more than I did at that moment. I confessed to him that I had made many mistakes as a father. I told Ralph that I did my best in rearing him. Since I had not been a father before, I asked him to forgive me for the many times that I had neglected the important details in his development and allowed ministry to interfere.

Finally, I reminded Ralph of a few things that have governed my life for more than twenty-six years. He has heard me speak of these things publicly. I gave them to him as a compass to navigate through the most treacherous and tranquil waters of his life: "Always remember God. Love God with all your heart, mind, soul, and strength. Read the Bible. Hide the Word in your heart that you might not sin against God. Remember to pray without ceasing. Finally, son, go to church. Don't neglect church attendance. The church is the fellowship of Christians." I ended by simply saying, "Remember these things."

Titus had been left in Crete, after Paul and he had evangelized the island, to set the Cretan church in order. He was to complete what Paul had initiated. The circumstances in Crete were difficult because the church lacked qualified spiritual leadership. Selecting and appointing godly leaders would be Pastor Titus's primary pastoral challenge. He would fulfill his twofold task of exhorting and encouraging the faithful and confronting the opponents of the gospel (vv. 9–10).

Titus (2:7–8) sets an example for them. Human beings are imitative by nature. We need models to give us direction, challenge, and inspiration. Paul did not hesitate to offer himself for the churches to imitate. "Follow my example," he wrote, "as I follow the example of Christ." Paul expected Timothy and Titus to provide a model—"types"—a prototype or pattern for the churches to follow. Old Testament characters are "types" for us to learn from. God has not provided us with dead models only (whether patriarchs in the Old Testament or apostles in the New); he wants us to have living models as well. Chief among these should be the presbyter-bishops of the local church.

Titus was, however, to influence the young men of Crete not only by example, but also by teaching. Teaching and example, the verbal and the visual, always form a powerful combination. His teaching was to embody three characteristics: integrity, seriousness, and soundness of speech that cannot be condemned. Perhaps the most important emphasis here is on seriousness in the preacher's manner and delivery. Richard Baxter says, "Whatever you do, let the people see that you are earnest. You cannot break men's hearts by jesting with them."

Paul gives the theological basis for Christian living. Although our subject passage reflects Paul's theology of salvation as a past-present-future reality, the structure reveals that Paul's chief concern is to tell God's people what salvation means.

Phillip Yancey asked, "What's so amazing about grace?" The question answers itself. Grace is amazing. This grace was brilliantly seen in the birth of Jesus, winsomely heard in his words, delightfully dramatized in his deeds, compassionately seen in his crucifixion, and resplendently realized in his resurrection and one day shall be shouted in his second coming. Epiphanies are the visible appearance of something or someone hitherto invisible; a coming into view of what has been previously concealed. God who is invisible became visible that we might see his grace. God's grace has appeared like a sunrise on the horizon.

Paul could write about grace because he was a recipient of that amazing grace. He was an opponent of the church, yet grace appeared to him, called him, commissioned him, and consigned him into the ministry of Jesus Christ. As Titus put the organizational structure of the church in place, he sought to show the Cretans the indiscriminate grace of Christ. His grace was transgenerational—Titus taught the old and the young. His grace was transgenderational—Titus taught the men and the women.

D. T. Niles has well summarized the ways in which Jesus showed equal concern for the good of all. He enlisted Simon the Zealot as a disciple, setting aside political distinction. He dined with Zacchaeus, setting aside class distinction. He conversed with the woman of Samaria, setting aside sex distinction. He responded to the appeal of the Syrophoenician woman, setting aside race distinction. He extolled the faith of the centurion, setting aside popular distinction. He allowed the woman who was a sinner to touch him, setting aside reputation distinction. He praised the poor widow who gave her mite, setting aside economic distinction. He washed his disciples' feet, setting aside the master-servant distinction. He rebuked his disciples for their intolerance toward that follower who was not of the twelve, setting aside denominational distinction. He enjoyed the company of children, setting aside age distinction.

BEYOND THE SOCIAL BARRIER

Paul personifies the grace of God. We must now ask what grace teaches us. First, grace teaches us to say "no" to ungodliness and worldly passions. Second, grace teaches us to live self-controlled, upright, and godly lives (v. 12). Thus grace teaches us to renounce our old life and to live a new life. To turn from ungodliness to godliness, to turn from self-centeredness to self-control, from the world's devious way to fair dealing with one another.

In the 1980s, Nancy Reagan's "Just say no" was heard around the world. That phrase has now become a mantra for everything that is protested. Paul, on the other hand, said to never say no to anything without presenting a better way of living. We are to denounce the culture and develop Christian character.

This present age is different from anything that we have seen before. Postmodernity aptly describes the culture. It is a good time to be alive. The possibilities to minister to this culture are challenging and constraining. The language has changed. Verbal and nonverbal speech challenges the minister and threatens our sacred cows. What are we to say to this generation? Let me suggest that you develop a postmodern hermeneutic. This is where we learn not merely how to interpret the biblical text, but we learn how to exegete the culture in which we live. This is what Paul does when he instructs Titus on how to pastor the Cretan congregation. Take a look at the people and their behavior, and start there in declaring the grace of God that brings salvation to all people.

H. Richard Niebuhr's *Christ and Culture* is indispensable at this point. This book helps us understand not only whether we as preachers begin with culture, but also how we deal with culture in doctrinal preaching.

The basic problem Niebuhr addresses is not a new one in Christian history. It is the problem of dual citizenship. How can the believer live in the kingdom of God and in the present-day culture at the same time? The answer depends on which of the five types presented by Niebuhr we adopt: Christ against, of, above, in paradox with culture, or Christ as transformer of culture. Transformation preaching shows how the gospel can change culture.

DECLARE THE GLORY OF GOD

He who appeared briefly in human history bringing salvation to the world and then exiting the stage will one day reappear. Our great God and Savior has appeared in grace but will one day appear in glory. This is our motivation to do good works.

One of the grand themes of the Bible is the glory of God. The glory of God is not to be mistaken for an attribute of God; it is the character of God. We see the glory of God early in the Old Testament writing where Moses desires to see his glory and in God's compassion; Moses is given a glimpse of his glory. Again, the glory of God is seen at the Tent of Meetings. God is so involved in his glory that he sent glory in Jesus and man tried to kill glory on the cross, man tried to bury glory in the grave, but the glory of God is stubborn and tenacious and got up in resurrection. Today, glory is in the church, but one day glory will return, split the heavens, and we shall behold him as he is.

The emphasis is on grace—God's lavish favor on undeserving sinners. Thus, we are enjoying direct continuity with the Old Testament people of God, for we are his redeemed people and he is our Passover, our exodus, and our Sinai.

Grace reforms us because God purifies us and makes us his own special possession. This process of purification is called *sanctification*; its goal is to make the believer more like Jesus Christ. Sanctification is not only separation from sin; it is also devotion to God. We are no longer the same since we have put on the Lord Jesus Christ.

DECLARE THESE THINGS

Christian ministers should keep these things in their preaching arsenal so that they may encourage the church and rebuke the wayward. And they must do this with all authority, which, of course, is theirs by relationship to Paul. You can preach and teach with that same authority because of your relationship with Jesus Christ.

Charles Wesley summarizes these things in his words:

> A charge to keep I have,
> A God to glorify,
> A never-dying soul to save,
> And fit it for the sky.
> To serve the present age,
> My calling to fulfill;
> O may it all my powers engage
> To do my Master's will.
> (Charles Wesley, "A Charge to Keep I Have")

CPSIA information can be obtained
at www.ICGtesting.com
Printed in the USA
LVHW09s2158231018
594605LV00012B/202/P